The Grand Permission

New Writings on Poetics and Motherhood

Edited by
Patricia Dienstfrey and Brenda Hillman

Wesleyan University Press
Middletown, Connecticut

Published by Wesleyan University Press, Middletown, CT 06459

© 2003 by Patricia Dienstfrey and Brenda Hillman

All rights reserved

Printed in the United States of America

Interior design, composition, and project management by Happenstance Type-O-Rama

Composed in Vendetta with display lines in Snell Roundhand

Cover and interior photograph courtesy of Quemadura

ISBN 0-8195-6643-8 cloth

ISBN 0-8195-6644-6 paper

5 4 3 2 1

The following publishers have generously given permission to use extended quotations from copyrighted works:
From *The Collected Books of Jack Spicer*, by Jack Spicer. Copyright 1975 by the Estate of Jack Spicer. Material reprinted with the permission of Black Sparrow Press. ■ From *Collected Works*, by Lorine Niedecker, edited by Jenny Penberthy, 2002/The Regents of University of California. ■ From *The Collected Works of Velimir Khlebnikov, Volume I, Letters and Theoretical Writings*, translated by Paul Schmidt, edited by Charlotte Douglass, Harvard University Press, Cambridge, 1987. Reprinted with permission of Harvard University Press. ■ From *Lift Every Voice*, ed. Mary Potter Engle and Susan Brooks Thistlethwaite. Copyright 1990 by Harper & Row Publishers, Inc. ■ From "Motherhood and Poetics," by Maxine Kumin, in *Always Beginning: Essays on a Life in Poetry*. Copyright 2000 by Maxine Kumin. Reprinted with the permission of Copper Canyon Press, P.O. Box 271, Port Townsend, WA 98368-0271. All rights reserved. ■ From "Narratives from the Crib," by Jean Day, *The Literal World*, Atelos, 1998. Copyright 1998 by Jean Day. Reprinted with permission of Jean Day. ■ From "Shared Custody," by Brenda Hillman, in *Cascadia*, Wesleyan University Press, Middletown, Connecticut. Copyright 2001 by Brenda Hillman. Reprinted with permission of Brenda Hillman. ■ From "To book as in to foal. To son.," by Kathleen Fraser, in *Translating the Unspeakable, Poetry and the Innovative Necessity*, University of Alabama Press. Copyright 2000 by Kathleen Fraser. Reprinted with permission of publisher and Kathleen Fraser. ■ From "Unpicturing (Fair) Realism: Notes on Barbara Guest's Poetics of (Defensive) Rapture," by Ann Lauterbach, in *American Letters & Commentary*. Copyright 1995 by Ann Lauterbach. Reprinted by permission of Ann Lauterbach.

"Eighty-Five Notes" by Mei-mei Berssenbrugge, excerpts previously published in *Five Fingers Review*, issue 19, 2001. ■ "Emergence" by Carolyn Forché, previously published, with changes, in *Salmagundi*, no. 123, Summer, 1999. ■ "Language and the Gaze at the Other—A Poetics of Birth" by Gillian Conoley, previously published, with changes, in *Five Fingers Review*, issue 17, 1998. ■ "Parallel/Play" by Carla Harryman, draft previously published in *HOW2*, vol. I, no. 5, Spring 2001. ■ "Untitled (M)," by Norma Cole, previously published by ruth now, with changes, in *hemorrhagingimaging*, issue 6. ■ "Writing *Natural Birth*" by Toi Derricotte, from the "Introduction" in *Natural Childbirth*, Firebrand Books, Milford, Connecticut. Copyright 2000 by Toi Derricotte. Reprinted with permission of Toi Derricotte.

All essays except Toi Derricotte's "Writing *Natural Birth*" were originally written for this anthology.

Contents

Part One

Piecing Commotion: Social and Historical Contexts

Part Two

Ob (lit) eration: Genre and Representation

Part Three

Signals Given: Language Paradigms

Part Four

A Third Space: Temporal and Other Crossings

Foreword

BY RACHEL BLAU DuPLESSIS

In 1971 in "One Out of Twelve: Women Who Are Writers in Our Century," Tillie Olsen helped to jumpstart the field of feminist criticism—investigations of gender and creativity, female authorship, the literary career for women, the passionate analysis of institutions that support and thwart artistic work. Among her reflections, suggestions, and analyses of material and ideological "circumstance," Olsen provided a stunning list of women writers (mainly writers of fiction) who had not been mothers. "Until very recently (she said) almost all distinguished achievement has come from childless women."[1] This seemed to be a condition of employment for women writers—was it a chosen fact? an unspoken tax? a biographical accident? Was it a happy fact? a poignant one? an unhappy one? Could there be any generalization here? Did these women mother other people besides children? Does the maternal impulse demand children for its fulfillment? In fact, Olsen was using this criterion as a baseline to measure women's progress to full human citizenship (and human citizenship to be as naturally female as male).

And the "childless" list is exceedingly impressive: Woolf, for example, Stein, Richardson, Barnes, Nin, Hurston, Wharton, Mansfield, O'Connor. Surveying modern poets, for every one example of a modernist woman who combined the two "careers"—H.D. (whose child was often raised by Bryher anyway) or Loy (who had four children and lost two to death, and left her children with servants for extended periods of time), there were many others—Moore, Dickinson, Lowell, Bishop, Niedecker—who didn't have children at all. In pointing out that motherhood and writing did not historically seem to go together, Olsen wasn't approving of this—although she was exploring great feelings of woundedness that welled up, as if this fact allegorically indicated grief for the losses of human fulfillment over generations. Olsen was reporting "childlessness" as a fact of the conditions of "employment" for many women writers.

Then, in an Olsen footnote in *Silences*, as we come closer and closer to the present—with Paley, Kumin, Rich (who herself wrote major works about the female career and motherhood), Howard, Walker, Le Guin, Guest, and further still, another claim begins to be made. Combinations of motherhood and the literary career are possible, plausible, emergent. Olsen's first list, rhetorically palpable, and the footnote, rhetorically secondary, made for some startled considerations, especially if you were both hoping to be a writer and hoping to be a mother. It seemed to be nervy, nervous territory. Was it possible? What made it difficult? Would one choice cancel out the other? On what forces did it depend? Would one passionate commitment sap the other—or transform it? Who would help you out here? On what institutional arrangements could you depend? Reading Olsen's mix of apocalyptic defiance and ever re-emergent grief for blockage, a person might wonder how her hands might be tied by gender and how she might rip off the bonds of ideology and practices, of nay-saying institutions and advice-mongers, of the force of circumstances. Facing motherhood and writing, facing forms of professional life and family life as desirous but perhaps untested people, there emerged for women in this period a curious frayed, suspicious, fearful, and hopeful set of emotions.

It's now about thirty years later, and we have a new century. A tremendous social, intellectual, material, and ideological change has occurred in the past thirty years, a change that is also not enough—not yet fair, not yet for all, not yet complete. (In the largest sense, this change *is* feminism, even if unacknowledged or entering one's life in diffuse and dispersed fashions.) However, this major shift of consciousness and institutions, case by case, movement by movement, choice by choice not only makes motherhood and writing possible to do in the same life but proposes motherhood as a source of deep and enriching meditations on the nature of poetry and the writing vocation. This anthology documents this change and is its fruit.

A second aspect of Olsen's analytic grief is the question of "lost knowledges"—materials, ideas, emotions unexpressed, structures of feeling not stated within the unwritten literature whose lack she mourns. Why does it matter if writers have no children? Olsen responds: "Might there not have been other marvels as well [besides the books the women did write], or other dimensions to these marvels? Might there not have been present profound aspects and understandings of human life as yet largely absent in literature?"[2] Carla Harryman states this in a way that differs interestingly in pluralism but retains the probe of lost knowledges: "Then we might be able to examine forms of knowledge or habits of mind that might not have received the attention they deserve. I don't mean to gender this as much as it might sound. There are after all 'male mothers' ... Lack of articulation about significant daily experience [with children] undermines consciousness, creates a condition for repression, doubt, insecurity. Then social norms that may not serve the best interest of 'the mother' or 'the child' can take hold."[3] Alice Notley similarly links the politics and ethics of the almost-missing knowledge to a sustaining, attentive defiance that she calls "the poetics of disobedience": "how it seemed one had to disobey the past and the practices of literary males in order to talk about what was going on most literally around one, the pregnant body, and babies for example. There were no babies in poetry then. How could that have been? What are we leaving out now?"[4] Telling your truth, opening your knowledge is a form of resistance against cultural repression, against bland ideological implants, against commercial concoctions of womanhood that come in a well-marketed box.

This book marks a beginning in all those knowledges, for these essays shed new light on the nature of language and genre, the practical life of mothering, and the writing vocation. This book selects some women poets who write with originality and commitment about the startling, intense, and dynamic connections between motherhood and creative achievement. These contributors—from the jaunty to the mystical—have had a variety of responses to motherhood, and they work to achieve the subtle understanding of feeling and form that brings these feelings into articulation. These essays meditate on some aspect of motherhood, its responsibilities, and its vast storehouse of emotions, intersecting with creative achievement in poetry. Motherhood leads to, demands, provokes, and excites innovations in poetry and inventions in poetics. This is an implicit thesis, and it makes *The Grand Permission* a book of fascination and of sweet power. Because the anthology takes hold of motherhood as "permission," it responds to amazing changes in material and ideological possibility.

What does "motherhood and poetics" entail? Essays about the phenomenology of birthing and sense of connectedness in infancy. Essays about motherhood and literary convention or cultural reconfiguration. Essays on motherhood and struggles actually to get one's work done. Essays on how one's kids inspire one. Essays about social struggles in relationship to motherhood. In short, motherhood is incredibly tangled, a space in which one is learning and changing all the time, understanding process in a new way. Thus motherhood leads to knowledge, to thinking, to literary thinking, and to poetics. These essays focus on exactly what motherhood has given to and taken from these women's writing, in scrupulous detail and with an imaginative pulse in the writing. The book is able to combine a confessional honesty, intimacy of tone, and serious personal issues with a varied and inventive sense of form, genre, and language.

For this is also a "poet's book" with a rich and diverse sense of form and language. The book continues the unfolding tradition of innovative, essayistic writing by contemporary women, whether this occurs via French feminism in the essays of Cixous, Kristeva, and Irigaray, or in writing on poetics by Kathleen Fraser in *Translating the Unspeakable: Poetry and the Innovative Necessity* (University of Alabama Press, 2000), Susan Howe in *My Emily Dickinson* (North Atlantic, 1985), Lyn Hejinian in *The Language of Inquiry* (University of California Press, 2000), or my book *The Pink Guitar: Writing as Feminist Practice* (Routledge, 1990). There is something very generative in the combination of intimate writing and formal innovation in these essays, a rich site for investigation in genre and gender (in general) that also emerges the work of such more recent writers as Juliana Spahr, Caroline Bergvall, Harryette Mullen, and Lisa Robertson.

This is not to say that everything is included—though it is always hard to generalize about anthologies. There is a fascinating absence of partners (other parents, family configuration, husbands) in most of the essays, and some discretion about material conditions and social class (the work-life of these mothers, the economic impact of life situations such as divorce). Were contributors parenting in relatively traditional ways or untraditional ways? What impact was there of family configuration on the material conditions of mothering that leads to artworks? One might also notice other things that are (generally) missing: the middle-aged child—I mean the kid from about 8–13—is somewhat sparse, and there are even fewer essays when the child is in the throes of adolescence. The anthology still registers a strongly "dyadic" ideology about children, and thus stands in some relationship with the theorizing about motherhood, merging, separation, and individuation from psychoanalytic theorists as different as Nancy Chodorow, Luce Irigaray, and Julia Kristeva. These are essays in general about "good enough" motherhood (to pun on Winnecott) and not really about motherhood that, for one reason or another, blows up in your face.

The categories chosen to organize this material are fructifying—there are essays about material, social, and ideological contexts for motherhood and poetry and essays about genre, suggestions of new genres, critiques of genre, elaborations of genre issues, and sometimes enactments of new genres of writing. As befits the center in poetics, other essays concern language, poetry's sound, voice, formal embodiments of one's "voice" or child voice, and how motherhood may move a person into a different use of language. A final section concerns a "third space"—the theorizing of an intersubjective ethical and aesthetic space. It's kind of a category of between—in between mother and child. A reconfigured terrain that comes from motherhood as a psychological and intellectual state. A metaphysics of motherhood. It's also true and clear that a lot of the essays are about a lot of the categories at once—that is interesting, and it says how compelling these materials are, and how necessarily interlinked these topics are.

Readers should find something provocative and heartening in the diversity of attitudes and issues taken up. This book gives a set of serious, inspiring models for meditations on motherhood, and a propulsive permission for facing the challenges of motherhood and creative work.

NOTES

1. Tillie Olsen, *Silences*. New York: Bantam Doubleday Dell, 1989 (reprint), p. 31.

2. Olsen, *Silences*, p. 32.

3. Carla Harryman interview, *Contemporary Literature* 37, issue 4, Winter 1996, pp. 523–524.

4. Alice Notley, "The Poetics of Disobedience," conference on Contemporary American and English Poetics, King's College, London, Centre for American Studies, 1998. Available at http://epc.buffalo.edu/authors/notley/disob.html.

Introduction

Yet I was a poetess only last year,
And good at my art, for a woman, men said;
But this woman, this, who is agonized here,
The east sea and west sea rhyme on in her head
Forever instead.[1]

I.

We introduce *The Grand Permission* with a stanza from a poem by Elizabeth Barrett Browning called "Mother and Poet," written in the persona of a nineteenth-century Italian poet, Laura Savio, who lost two sons in the struggles over the unification of Italy in the 1860s. The poem as a meditation about the difficulties of being a woman, a writer, and a mother in a time of war has historical significance for this book. After reflecting on the difficulties of writing, Browning goes on to consider how the responsibilities of motherhood and civic duty pull at opposing loyalties in ways that seem both irreconcilable and experientially true.

Similar reflections on the multiple facets of a woman's life—cast among different concerns, of course—inspire the present volume. This is an inclusive collection of thirty-two essays by contemporary American women[2] who have written and published poetry and raised children. The essayists bring these two parts of life together, often exploring artistic choices made in light of their circumstances as mothers. While some have written *about* motherhood in their poems, others have not; many are considering the topic here for the first time and are challenged by the newness of the subject.

◊

We edited this anthology with an understanding that a book on writing and mothering as dual vocations might be of great interest at this point in history when women are struggling to balance conflicting demands on their time and emotional resources. But the assembled collection is not another self-help or how-to book on this important subject. Nor is it a work of academic research—though there is scholarship to be found here. We take pleasure in the book's variety of voices, even in its inconsistencies, and invite the reader to go into the collection as an explorer. We hope that, because of its hybridity, it will be both of practical use and of aesthetic interest to a range of readers—not just poets, women, or mothers.

Since we started the project, we have heard many people express eagerness for its publication—and we are not surprised; it is a book that is long overdue. This is perhaps the first time in history such a volume could have been assembled. As has been frequently noted, the woman who was both a mother and a published poet was far less common. Many women have been writers and mothers before this time, and in the nineteenth century there was a burgeoning of publications run by and for women. While these venues established new areas of authority for women and provided important platforms for change, even the most popular magazines limited the audience of women poets and their subject matter. Most of our own great literary "mothers" of recent history were childless. Because of these historical circumstances, the critical mass of women's writing necessary for an anthology such as this was reached only during the women's movement of the seventies.

In the sixties, two inspiring poets who were also mothers, Sylvia Plath and Anne Sexton, significantly influenced several generations of writers, in part because they broke down barriers that kept women from confronting psychological and domestic issues in poetry, and in part because, despite their great skill, the brevity of their lives was determined by their situations. A shadow was cast over the lives of women poets by their suicides, and these two became haunting muses. Several decades later, even though we are at a point where the well-known poet who is also a mother is not the central figure in a cautionary tale, women setting out to become both poets and mothers still fear being isolated in domestic space and wrestle with themselves for perspective as they balance home life and work.

Of the numerous writings that laid the groundwork for change in the sixties and seventies, for us, the works of Adrienne Rich and Simone de Beauvoir stand out. Rich's *Diving into the Wreck* and *Of Woman Born*[3] profoundly challenged traditional views of women's powers of self-determination and creation. And after the publication of de Beauvoir's *The Second Sex*,[4] women's issues surrounding creativity and domestic responsibility suddenly mattered. In addition, the French theorists Luce Irigaray, Julia Kristeva, and Hélène Cixous made it possible to reexamine philosophical concepts such as identity and collectivity and to open up possible new forms of linguistic expression in poetry as well as prose. The title we chose, *The Grand Permission*, reflects this opening; it is adapted from Henri Michaux's remark, cited by Eavan Boland in her essay, that although, as a young writer, he didn't consider himself to be a surrealist, surrealism had given him "le grand permission."

It was also significant to the development of women's poetry—to the "opening of the field" (to quote Robert Duncan)[5]—that the very nature of poetry itself was undergoing a shift in the seventies and eighties. Lyric poetry increasingly accommodated experiments in form, genre, and voice. In part, this could be characterized as a movement from the idea of poetry as talismanic object to a concept of writing that could include process as part of the poem. It also introduced a renaissance of the meditative traditions associated with John Donne and Wallace Stevens. Literary theory and philosophical shifts in the notions of the self played a large role in these changes, as did abstract expressionist New York School writing, Language poetry, and the founding of a number of small literary presses, including Alice James Books, Kelsey St. Press and *How(ever)* magazine. There was also a widening range of practices in the autobiographical narrative poetry, sometimes called "confessional," in which apparently personal subjects were freely explored by such writers as Sharon Olds and Lucille Clifton. Just as the free-standing isolated models of selfhood were being questioned in literary theory, so was the sanctity of the individual poem. By the end of the eighties, things had changed significantly for poetry in general and for women's poetry in particular. Many subjects had opened, including motherhood and women's identity issues, and the available poetic forms had changed drastically. All these developments yielded to a need for new historical markers, of which this anthology is one.

◊

The specific impetus for this project grew out of a series of San Francisco Bay Area conferences on mothers and artists held in the nineties. The most recent of these, which we organized with artist Amy Trachtenberg in the spring of 1996, was entitled "Art and Motherhood: Work, Identity, and Creation," held at New College in San Francisco. The conference generated personal responses from men as well as women. It was a gathering of different ages and backgrounds—teenagers, single parents, women with and without children and in a variety of partnerships—all wondering how to balance options, or sometimes simply how to get through a day with an intact sense of self. Having had these conversations, we were passionately engaged with the ideas they generated and a perceived opportunity to add to them.

In approaching this project, we could have asked writers to consider how motherhood serves as subject matter for their writing, thus carrying on a conversation that began three decades ago. But because of our own interests in the writing process and because of the richness of the materials on this subject that came out of the conference, we chose instead to ask authors to reflect on the relationship between the life of mothering and the development of poetic form, inviting them to examine the cross-influences of these two subjects that are so difficult to limit and contain. At the same time, we invited the writers to approach the traditional essay form in exploratory ways, as they do their poetry. We expected an array of voices and ideas, with many renegade outcroppings. And, in fact, that is what we received: a wide range of women's experiences—some writing in their third, or fifth, or seventh decade—about how their poems have been shaped in tandem with, or parallel to, their lives as mothers.

In the course of working with the essays, we reflected on some of the book's unspoken assumptions. Here we do not make an essential or causal connection between the experiences of creative acts and motherhood, but we think that there are important ways in which they might influence each other. The evidence presented by the collection is that for many women who write and publish poetry, the life choice to become a mother has had an impact on the writing. A second assumption implied or stated in many of the essays is that there is something different about the mother/child caretaking bond that could affect artistic life, either because of cultural expectation or because of biological necessity. Is the bond more "special" than the father/child bond? This is a terribly loaded question, and one a number of writers in the book address. Surely a child can be nurtured responsibly and lovingly equally by men or women. And yet for all the efforts on the part of men and women to approach parity, most of the childcare still falls to women. The dearth of fathers depicted as responsible adults involved in childcare in advertisements (and not just as "one of the kids") testifies to this, as does the fact that children's products are near the women's hygiene section in supermarkets and that diaper-changing stations are most commonly found in women's restrooms.

The word "form" appears frequently in these pages. As we use it here, we refer to the features of style and structure in a piece of writing, and to an ineffable quality of mental life that shapes a work of art. Some of these shaping aspects might be technical: the measure of lines and stanzas, the choice of whether or not to use conventional sentences or asyntactical disjunctions, blips, lurchings, fragments. Form in a poem alludes to nearly everything that makes the poem unique: sound, space, meter, stress, choice of genre, diction, and revisionary punctuation. It might include aspects of lineation and imagery.

The question of form also becomes evident in the style of the essays themselves, not just in the poetry they discuss. We have mentioned the hybrid experimental writing that developed in the seventies and eighties; some of that work is reflected in the essay styles. A reader might grapple with the more elliptical writings—their mixtures of prose and poetry, fragmented sentence structure, and disjunctive imagery—and ask, "Why not just say it in plain English?" One brief answer is that such discontinuous forms of prose get at the discontinuity of human experience in a very necessary way, just as an abstract painting may call up impressions associatively and make completely different kinds of demands on the viewer from those made by realistic representations, bringing up new ways of seeing and thinking.

One other point to note is more subtle: the intimate tone that threads through the volume. It is an intimacy that is beyond the "confessional," in the usual sense of the word, and is representative of private materials and taboo subjects. The presence of deeply felt experience lends a tensile strength to these linked accounts. It taps into a source of power in women's poetry at one of its most vulnerable points, an emotionality that, when it appears, has evoked dismissal, a critical censure that has deterred women from writing, not only as mothers, but as women presuming to write at all.

II.

Given the revisionary mind at work in these essays, we faced a challenge in grouping them in clearly articulated categories. Their tendencies run counter to categorization in favor of inclusive models, particular cases, approximations, and indeterminacies. But the desire, on the whole, is not to do away with categories; as Kimiko Hahn points out, her "life of mother, wife, teacher, ... writer" *is* compartmentalized, and it must be if she is to live it as fully as possible. Having decided that divisions would be both appropriate to the collection and useful to readers, we probed the book's double gravities—motherhood and writing—and devised four sections we consider to be accurate to the book's content.

Part I foregrounds the social and historical contexts of the topic of motherhood, Part II addresses considerations of genre and form, Part III examines language paradigms as they reflect motherhood and child-rearing, and Part IV explores a "third space," a charged territory of "betweens."

Part One Piecing Commotion: Social and Historical Contexts

Several women in this opening section came to writing in the postwar years of the fifties and early sixties. At that time, the orthodoxy of the mother at home with her children was powerful, marginalizing the working mother, the single mother, the divorcee. At the same time, the image of the poet was associated with a bohemian life style that attracted middle class disapproval as well as curiosity. As for ideas about gender and related arrangements, Maxine Kumin writes: "I grew up understanding that a man's world was in every way superior to a woman's." In the more elastic world from the seventies to the present, women are freer to travel, to change partners, to choose same sex partners, to pursue careers. In fact, the norm in essays here written by young women in the nineties is that urban middle class mothers are expected to work. Finally, the bright currency of social norms and political events join with the more shadowy interiorities of domestic experience to create new arenas for thinking and living, as well as new, or recontextualized, questions, anxieties, and possibilities.

Kumin's retrospective essay recalls her encounters with the Harvard literary establishment in the fifties and the celebrated poets who taught the university's writing programs. There she encounters a "sexist condescension" toward domestic subject matter as poetic content and a complete dismissal of the genre of juvenile literature that she enjoys. She doesn't go up against conventions alone but in the company of another poet and mother, Anne Sexton, a close personal friend and formidable ally. A decade later, Maureen Owen takes pleasure in her time as a young wife, mother, and poet in Japan, a society she experiences as having a keen interest in poetry and a special appreciation of children. During this period, her young son's questions bring to her poetry a Zen "startled awake" point of view. Back in the States, she "must face the economic and political realities of motherhood" and stretch the clock to find time to work full time, write, and raise her children as a single mother.

Erica Hunt's life as a mother and writer is configured as a performance in which "several minds must occupy the same space (stage) at once." Inverting this compression, she ties her multiple life roles to a "myth of infinite capacity," which she finds sweetly seductive and links to Devi, Hindu goddess of the manifold and tirelessly creative. She develops a persona of a mediated self who writes to know what she thinks and who she is and to "practice knowledge" as revolutionary. Within a different framework of the manifold and tireless, Stephanie Brown's essay evokes Wallace Stevens's "pressure of reality,"[6] which is paired with an image of the "Mom-chic, perfect mom: *the ideal.*" She writes in the nineties, and norms are perpetuated by merchandizing and corporate strategies. Still, Brown's version of doing-it-all calls down the hubris of classical Greek drama, suffering that leads to profound revisions in her expectations for herself and her children.

The traditional heterosexual family is background for Camille Roy's account of her motherhood as part of a lesbian/gay extended family. She wonders how the feelings she has—as a parent who is "closer to the role of father than the biological father, not in father-gender but as in father-not-mom"—might correspond to a woman's whose situation is closer to the norm. Out of a shifting motherhood comes a writing that is vitalized by disturbance and more complicated views of the baby as a pleasure-loving individual. Quite different questions binding individual and community values are engaged in Claudia Keelan's poetics. Comparing texts by John Keats, Simone Weil, and Martin Luther King, she finds a commonality in their "Utopian idealities, keyed to a reciprocity between self and others." In Keelan's community not of the status quo but of the "living spirit of the world," home is a home*land,* and her very young son is "a world becoming."

In Toi Derricotte's essay, "Natural Childbirth," "natural" stands as a comment on normative views of motherhood that surrounded her pregnancy with her son. In 1962, she writes, it was "a terrible thing, especially for a black middle-class girl, to come up pregnant." The stigma attached to unwed motherhood becomes a deeply internalized censor and critic of this subject matter and of herself. It is a self-silencing that, after many years, Derricotte is able to transform into a book-length poem. Carolyn Forché, on the other hand, finds her pregnancy an unexpected asset while she travels with an international human rights organization in South Africa, as it lends her an invisibility that allows her to slip through strictly guarded borders. Like a number of other writers in this collection, she is deeply influenced by her childhood's spiritual life, lessons learned from the nuns who taught her catechism as well as from college professors and admired writers. After the birth of her son, her poems pass through a "sieve of revisionary practice" into a new writing space in which poetic form is not a container but a force.

Part Two Ob (lit) eration: Genre and Representation

As poetic form is one of the book's dual focuses, the place of formal considerations in these essays is one of a slight shift to the foreground. The writers here offer critiques of traditional forms and genres in writings that often reflect on and incorporate other writers' works. A number interweave personal and scholarly research and employ variations on the essay form to model the possibility of conceptual and social change. Different formal combinations appear, such as prose-poetry and dramatic sketches, that resonate with interrupted, fragmented, and collaged writings in other sections of the book.

Eavan Boland writes that in three late poems Sylvia Plath changes the instruction set for the nature poem that emerged from the nineteenth-century English romantic tradition. Boland's thesis is that Plath redirects the "historical energy" of the nature poem by writing as a mother who is no longer instructed by nature but who "*is* nature … able to command the natural world because she herself is generative of it." In these poems, Boland also finds the seeds for a reconfiguration of the Plath legend of the "self-destructive sibyl." While Plath is seen to reconfigure an important western poetic form, Kimiko Hahn finds a usable tradition in the Japanese *zuihitsu*, which gathers together brief writings on random topics. Developed during the Heian Period in the work of several notable women writers, the form provides Hahn with a model for setting down the disparate bits of thought, sense impression, and event that occur in the course of a day. But her writing is, she goes on to note, also shaped by an influence prior to literature: her own generative female body. And it is here, in the woman's pregnant body, that Susan Griffin reconfigures the early literary form of the epic, juxtaposing changes from conception through birth with the warrior hero on a quest. In her revision, a young girl becoming a mother must permit her armor "to be pierced." It is at this moment of allowance and opening that the basis of a new epic form is born, when "everywhere connection becomes more evident to her" in a larger story of generations.

This idea of connection is examined in another way as Mary Margaret Sloan considers iconographic images of the mother and child in Renaissance paintings. While the development of perspective opened up space for more naturalistic depiction of human figures, Sloan writes, the interior universe of this painterly relationship idealized the pair, erasing its true bondedness. Recalling her own experience of early mothering, she demonstrates other ways of reading this active bond between mother and newborn, calling it a "psychophysiological expanse of mutual ignorance" in a space of sensuous intelligence. In another kind of space/time characterized as "an acausal orderedness," Patricia Dienstfrey finds a story form that is universal. Its visible sign is a radiance, seen as the halos in sacred paintings and in children's early drawings, the ovals that resemble images of the basic human cell. She connects this radiance to her children's imaginative play and representations of love that shape works by writers such as Walter Benjamin and Jean Genet.

In Laura Moriarty's postmodern family, "the writer doesn't have to be a mother to be a mother." Her epigrammatic essay tracks the splits, refractions, mirrorings in which reading shapes experience and experience enters texts. She quotes liberally from Jean Day's book of prose and poetry, *The Literal World,* which, itself, intercuts Day's writings on her experience as a mother with studies of early language acquisition in Katherine Nelson's *Narratives from the Crib,* which is, in turn, a multidisciplinary work. Carla Harryman also intercuts texts, writings by Jacques Lacan and Nathalie Sarraute, and her own narrations of being a mother, writer, and citizen, setting her compositions in columns on facing pages. As she assembles the pieces, her interest lies "in the competing claims of the erotic life, knowledge, and imagination," in motherhood and writing as "interventions" in complexity, and in literary and cultural models in which acts have consequences that cannot be anticipated.

Part Three Signals Given: Language Paradigms

Language here encompasses a wide range of styles and usages—conversation, songs, games, nursery rhymes. A number of essays incorporate baby talk, that deeply private, quasi-verbal language elicited by babies that can embarrass an outsider overhearing it. They shed light on several problematics surrounding the mother/infant dyad—its intimacy, deep emotionality, and exclusiveness. In many of the essays, the importance of speech to writing—the words sung by mothers, stories told by fathers, and the phonemes and tropes of children learning to speak—is valorized over linguistic structures. For a number of these writers, a delight in language shared with their children leads to literary collaborations, with young children and with grown children who become (or remain) poets as adults.

Giving birth, Alice Notley writes, is about doubling, as are marriage, poetry, and being "a self." The figure is extended to an unusual pairing of home life and the poetry scene that crowds into the New York City apartment she shares with her poet husband. During these gatherings, her young sons join in a variety of OuLiPian[7] writing practices and appear as cowriters in her published work. Kathleen Fraser presents cowriting of another kind. Opening with a series of oddly juxtaposed infinitives—"To book as in to foal. To son"—she suspends clear separations between speaker and writer. In this way, she opens a field for writing-with-a-difference, which she locates directly in her experience of writing-as-a-mother. If odd sonorities and slant meanings emerge, they can be explained, she observes, but only if there is someone willing to listen.

In her essay entitled "Listen," Alicia Ostriker's private journal entry is almost certain to stir up strong feelings in the twenty-first century as it would have had it been published when it was written in 1985. Language, Ostriker writes, is female—emotional, intimate, unmannered. The language that suppresses this language's truths in published poetry is male. Her poetics manifesto is one she must live up to as she searches for truth-telling words in which to address a poem to an adult daughter about the pain caused by her rejection—to articulate the perhaps unacceptable, humiliating feelings that this time will be published. In the midst of the confusing messages of her own internal reflections and sometimes self-critical reviews, Pam Rehm catches glimpses of a simple truth that resides in "a pace in time." But in daily life, she observes, it's "hardly that simple." Nor is it easy for her to be certain what it means to be a woman or how to define "Love, God, and World." Born into a family in which men were the storytellers and the spoken word was a male domain, she uses "words, on the page" to speak for herself until, after her son is born she discovers her "out loud voice."

Voice and sound also figure in as Frances Phillips traces the linguistic features of a mother/infant relationship in lullabies and nonsense verse improvised while walking, soothing, feeding her infant daughter. In this dailiness of nearly unbroken intimacy she locates a habit of rhyme. Language is linked to the smells of milk, its bonding power in a world that is "damp, physical." Then language and poems change as the household accommodates a schoolgirl who wants nothing of baby talk. Like Phillips, Jill Bialosky addresses stigmas of intimate feeling and sentimentality that surround conventional depictions of motherhood. Following the deaths of two of her children, afraid that she will not be able to give "appropriate voice to the power of those experiences," she researches poems written by women on the subjects of love and death, finding a usable tradition in the great childless poets a number of whom have been previously mentioned. But she also uncovers a flowering of this tradition in poems directly about motherhood, loss of children, and fear of their loss written by late-twentieth-century poets whose work she cites.

"My ideas about what is beautiful, what is a poem," Carol Muske-Dukes observes, "remain pretty much inseparable from my earliest sense of language." Her poetics and sense of prosody derive from her Czech mother, the sound of her voice as she intersperses Slavic words with English, creating a "syntactical anarchy." This matrilineal prosodic line, unpredictable and destabilizing, is changed by the birth of Muske-Dukes's daughter. A new generation introduces a revised mimetic balance and fresh sense of familial and poetic "likeness." To the piecings and collagings that characterize many of these essays, C.D. Wright adds a driving pace introduced by the exigencies of childcare, marriage, and work. She reflects that as time is crucial to both mothering and writing, it may be that they are in a "practical sense exclusive." Yet she finds in poetry and mothering a symbiotic relationship, observing that as a writer she has benefited from both the distraction and the attachment her son provides.

Part Four   A Third Space: Temporal and Other Crossings

The essays in this section position their observations in a context of overlapping and contingent realities. They explore a field of extensions, permissions, and restraints charted by a wide variety of practitioners—philosophers, psychologists, mystics, poets, naturalists—and by the Bible, myths, and fairytales. For a number of these writers, to be an implicated observer in the activities of birth, childcare, and death is to find forms and meanings in a numinous life on the borders of the physical world. Writings here suggest that in a "third space reality" ideas about the great poetic themes of love, "being," and beauty might be borrowed from uncertainty and engage unknowns and paradoxical states as territory.

In the energetically charged space of "the gaze" between the mother and the infant, Gillian Conoley locates a collective "third world" that predates language. Here, in an engagement in which clearly bounded identity matters less, she finds "a time of great enchantment and joy" and a powerful source of poetry. She draws on her reading, particularly of Julia Kristeva and Hélène Cixous, to delineate a site formed of "two biologies ... two souls," which opens into a psychic deepening. Mei-mei Berssenbrugge's "Eighty-Five Notes" address changes in her world view after her daughter's birth, opening with a filigree of abstract specificity: "I think about the ideal, my relationship to it, and the relationship of change to the ideal." That speech resonates the unsaid is not a new idea in contemporary linguistic theory, but Berssenbrugge configures this idea another way. With a child, she writes, so much is unsaid that speech becomes simple and meaning can be experienced with no "mediation of perception and interpretation."

Presented as a procession of careful inhalations and exhalations, the couplets of Susan Gevirtz's opening poem render a swift elision between birth and death. A life force in an oceanic sense of time is summoned by linked events: her daughter's birth and the death of her grandmother within the span of a month. Here, to vocabularies of pace and measure in these essays—walking, rushing, standing, stopping, forging ahead, dodging— she adds the movements of a swimmer on her way into the future on a path of a return. In a montage-poem-essay, Norma Cole maps another terra incognita, one of questions and forgetfulness, a field of "no final analysis." Here, children extend the field of signs, evincing their human beginnings and mythic immortality. Using quotations from Simone Weil and H.D., Cole fashions a diaphanous, netlike form to capture the feeling and impression of the poet/mother in her essay "Untitled (M)."

Dale Going's neologism, "Poetma," links motherhood and *step*motherhood, defining a relationship to her daughter that is not physical, but "of the imagination." In a family constellation of "close distances," language offers its syntactic orders as emotional and mental furniture that can shape poems and family life. From models drawn from readings of feminist mother/artists, she concludes that a poetics that has an aura of authority may not be writing that, for her, is real—or art. Passion, the depth and power of feeling itself, is the basis of Barbara Einzig's poetics. It arises at the marriage of appearance and the ephemeral as the site of identity of a human being and a text. In her view, both motherhood and poetry require, as conditions of their realization, a pre-realization in "the whole world of human beings." Her writing proceeds as a series of iterations of the present as time passing: in a garden, in gestures, in the relationship of a mother and child, in the state of the State, and in memory.

In Brenda Hillman's poetics of custody, metaphor, in its transitive powers, is the ground of a radical metaphysics and of a reconfiguration of her poetic style through a reframing of relationship itself. Her experience of divorce and shifting family constellations becomes a practice of a writing in which "closure becomes unlikely." Like a child traveling back and forth between houses, poetic language is seen as a reverberation between modes of creation. In another kind of crossing, Elizabeth Robinson proposes a series of unities: a bio-aesthetic experience of synesthesia, the Christian gospel of the Word made flesh, and pregnancy. Robinson's unifying figures suggest views different from Alice Notley's doublings; but within their contexts, they are not exactly opposed. Both writers observe a continuum of bonds and unions, and it seems likely that Notley would agree with Robinson's view that to separate motherhood and writing would make a "false distinction."

Finally, Fanny Howe's essay addresses two of the collection's underlying issues: the unique sense of urgency that radiates from the life of a child and the ambiguities that surround the figure of the mother as a creative force in Western culture. Motherhood and poetry, she points out, are bound together in stories from their beginnings, noting their linked appearances in creation myths, gnostic texts, and the ambiguous mother/child world of fairy tales. Raising children and writing poetry share the border states between a good and a bad mother and between a storybook child, like Pinocchio, and a real child. Howe makes a moral template of the shared elements of disquieting tales that penetrate to the heart of questions of children's innocence and of the darkest and most luminous figures of motherhood. These early tales of human imperfection bring to contemporary life not only the permission to fail and to strive, but the pressures of necessity that can become one's truest and most useful guides.

◊

Even as so many of these authors configure a writing life that is bound to a variety of spatial, temporal, social, literary, and environmental networks, there is a way in which each one sits alone at her desk and in a room apart. Yet in whatever space she writes, the contemporary woman is no longer isolated in domestic space but is instead accompanied by a rich set of poetic traditions not available to women writing just half a century ago. Though the contemporary poet's work is individual, she writes in orbits of radiating influence. Browning's tragic nineteenth-century heroine, torn between loyalties and seeking means of reconciliation, is reconfigured here as an actor with a wide range of models and choices. And as the array of possibilities has opened up, so has the need to recognize opportunities for discipline, as C.D. Wright observes: motherhood, in its distractions and attachments, has given her the most complete set of circumstances possible for her to be the writer that she has needed to be. In this collection, daily acts of improvisation, exploration, and acceptance address the ways in which women in the twenty-first century live with expanded possibilities while observing numerous unavoidable constraints. The remarkable resilience that is manifest in this book is accompanied by a particularly modern desire to create a responsible life that is simply enough.

NOTES

1. Elizabeth Barrett Browning, "Mother and Poet" in *The Norton Anthology of English Literature*, Vol. 2, Fifth Edition. New York: W.W. Norton & Company, 1986, p. 1091.

2. The writers in the collection are all American, with the exception of Eavan Boland, who is Irish and teaches at Stanford University.

3. Adrienne Rich, *Diving into the Wreck*. New York: W.W. Norton & Company, 1973. Adrienne Rich, *Of Woman Born: Motherhood as Experience and Institution*. New York: W.W. Norton & Company, 1999.

4. Simone de Beauvoir, *The Second Sex*, trans. H.M. Parshley. New York: Knopf, 1952; reprinted by Vintage, 1989.

5. Robert Edward Duncan, *The Opening of the Field*. New York: W.W. Norton & Company, 1973, p. 39.

6. Wallace Stevens, *The Necessary Angel*. New York: Random House, 1965, p. 13.

7. *OuLiPo* is a compound French word meaning "workshop of potential literature."

Part One

Piecing Commotion:
Social and Historical Contexts

Motherhood and Poetics

Maxine Kumin

I came to motherhood in 1948 at the age of 24. Somewhat blithely, given our limited finances, we managed to have three children clustered together under the age of five. I came to poetry in desperation during that third pregnancy, through the back door.

Although I was an ardent adolescent poet, a trait I shared with virtually all the poets I know, I was shocked into abandoning creative writing my freshman year in college. My instructor, the late Wallace Stegner, who I now realize was only a few years older and wiser than I, had told me to "say it with flowers, but for God's sake don't write poems about it." An unworldly 17-year-old, I had been exempted from taking the standard freshman English composition class and thrust into an upper-level course in which I was the quivering naïf. Stegner was right: my poems were sentimental and morbid, but "when lonely on an August night I lie/wide-eyed beneath the mysteries of space,"[1] they were cries from the heart. After his scrawled comment I put them aside for several years.

1953 was the winter of my discontent. Pregnant for the third time, restless, unhappy with my closet poems that seemed fixated on death and loss, I was overwhelmed with guilt that I was not happy. Didn't I have everything any modern woman could want? What was this nagging unease, and where would it lead?

In 1946, the summer that I graduated from college and married, I had been offered a fellowship to attend the University of Grenoble, repository of Stendhal's manuscripts. I declined easily, thoughtlessly, without regret. The war was over; we were recklessly in love and plunged headlong into our new lives. Marry in haste, goes the aphorism. It wasn't that I was repenting at leisure. But I was looking back hard at the road not taken.

A passage in Sonya Tolstoy's diary, written while Lev was absent on one of his many excursions, speaks to this situation. She had totally dedicated her life to caring for him and the many children they had together, "all of which," she said, "is happiness of a kind, but why do I feel so woeful all the time?"[2] I had arrived at that place.

I couldn't admit that I was depressed. I began to write light verse, a genre I had always admired. I would have preferred to write librettos for Broadway musicals, but filler verse was at least within my grasp. A small poem is infinitely portable. The strictures of rhyme and meter could be sorted through in my head while doing the daily chores.

For $3.95 I bought a text by Richard Armour, *Writing Light Verse*, and slavishly followed his prescriptions. My card file was a little cedar box labeled Recipes. On 3 X 5 cards I kept track of every poem I submitted and vowed a private vow that if I were still unpublished by the time this third baby arrived, I would abandon the entire enterprise.

In March, the *Christian Science Monitor* printed a four-liner I still remember:

> There never blows so red the rose
> so sound the round tomato
> as March's catalogs disclose
> and yearly I fall prey to.[3]

Our son Danny was born in June. By the end of the year I was publishing four- to eight-liners in journals as disparate as the *Saturday Evening Post*, *Baby Talk*, and the *New York Herald Tribune*. Heartened by my acceptances, I scribbled away at odd hours. The older two children were in nursery school; the new baby took lovely long naps. I adopted the slovenly practice of going directly to my desk whenever silence reigned and picked away at my bone pile of ideas while dishes and laundry, unmade beds and unvacuumed rooms yawned. I learned early that one can do housework and tend to minors at the same time, chauffeur an underage cellist to a lesson and occupy that quiet hour in the car with a worksheet. To this day, much of my best writing time takes place in what I think of as the interstices. The anonymity of a bustling airport between connections is one of my favorite workplaces.

In 1957, with three children under the age of ten, I screwed my courage to the sticking point and signed up for a poetry workshop conducted by poet and Tufts University professor John Holmes at the Boston Center for Adult Education. Anne Sexton and I met in that class.

I still carry Anne around with me, a vivid presence, a reminder of how humbly we began, first in John Holmes's workshop, then as members of the New England Poetry Club, which at that time was for the most part composed of Boston Brahmins of a certain age.

Enter two outlanders, two young mothers from the suburbs, Anne in high heels, pan-cake makeup, and with flowers in her hair, I dressed as Anne has characterized me, "the frump of frumps." Because Holmes, the club's president, had proposed us, we were admit-ted to the inner sanctum, but only, we were cautioned, on a provisional basis. Within six months we had each had a poem accepted by the *New Yorker* and another by *Harper's*, magazines the older members aspired to but rarely reached. Our provisional status was hastily dropped.

Our kids' ages overlapped only slightly. Anne's older daughter, Linda, and my youngest, Danny, were pretty much the same age, but Anne became a golden sort of godmother to my daughters. They looked up to her as someone far more worldly and stylish than their own mother. And when Linda began to write poetry of her own in high school, I became her mentor and mother figure.

Anne performed the same function for my daughter Judy, who went on to win the Untermeyer Award at Harvard in her junior year. When Anne formed her chamber rock group, "Anne Sexton and Her Kind," Danny composed the musical background to her recitation of "The Little Peasant" (from *Transformations*). It has been singled out for its wit and jauntiness.

Back in the late fifties, leaving our little children in the care of husbands or babysitters, Anne and I trudged off together to poetry readings all over greater Boston. Some were electrifying—Robert Frost playacting the part of lovable old curmudgeon, unforgettable John Crowe Ransom, a pink, bald kewpie doll of a man rocking onto his toes while recit-ing "Then up rose Captain Carpenter" in a cadence that echoes still in my head. We observed, rather than heard, Marianne Moore's reading at Wellesley—she was all but inaudible.

We were inching our way into the inner sanctum by way of publications and readings. We were striking out like Conrad's secret sharer, stroking into the deep waters of an ocean that had until then virtually excluded women from the swim. The fact that we had young children at home was rarely alluded to. Children were an encumbrance, domestic duties held a woman back. We both knew this.

Getting published at all was a triumph. Everyone knew that men wrote the really inter-esting poems about war, politics, hunting—in short, poems about the world. Women only wrote about relationships, emotions, domestic arcana. Poetry by women was soupy and romantic. It was immature. No wonder women poets frequently hid behind their first-name initials. We wrote in dread of being labeled little three-name Letitia ladies.

For two aspiring female poets, a leap of the Grand Canyon was no more formidable than daring to establish a profoundly secure friendship. It was a bond I had initially resisted, having only the year before lost a good friend to suicide during, again, a postpartum depression—Anne's first hospitalization, after the birth of her second child, had been for a postpartum depression. Doesn't this say something about the culture, the medical establishment, women's roles in the United States of the fifties? Our bond gradually tightened until I understood I had finally found the one best friend and confidante my teenage years had never provided.

Over the last thirty years I have acquired several true-blue women friends and confidantes, poets and writers in other genres, but it seems I had to traverse some rocky terrain before I could reach out to others of my sex. Part of this resistance was cultural. I grew up understanding that a man's world was in every way superior to a woman's. At cocktail and dinner parties, on one side of the room men conducted in-depth conversations about politics, religion, baseball. On the other, women talked about sterilizing infant formulas, how to prepare carrot sticks, where to find replacements for broken china patterns. Intelligent, well-educated women demeaned themselves in this way.

The change was gradual, but the truth is that the women's movement, which sanctioned assertiveness and creativity, changed my life and the lives of my contemporaries. For some of us the change was subtle, a filtering down of new beliefs. For others it meant royal warfare, divorces, new destiny. Certainly knowing and loving Anne helped me to know and love women, appreciate my own gender, see ever more clearly the struggle in which we were engaged to make our own way, to legitimize our own goals and ideals.

After our successful foray into the Boston Center's poetry workshop, five of us— Holmes, George Starbuck, Sam Albert, Sexton, and I—developed a workshop of our own. For more than two years we met every other week in one another's houses and wrangled long into the night over poems in process. My children, seeing me set out glasses and plates, would ask, "Company? Who's coming?" "No," I'd say, "it's just the workshop." They would set up a collective groan. "Oh, not the poets again! Can we go sleep in the room over the garage?"

I don't know how Anne and I managed not to intrude on each other's voice. We listened, sympathized, made suggestions. But we were operating under very different influences. And from the very beginning of exploring each other's worksheets we both knew intuitively that it was essential to preserve our individuality. The mutual influence led of course to some cross-fertilization. I was able to become more personal, more daring in my poems. Anne perhaps took from me the advice that constraints of meter and form are paradoxically freeing agents.

Of course we had no women mentors. Although between us we knew a dozen of Millay's sonnets by heart, although we admired Marianne Moore from afar and were hugely in awe of Elizabeth Bishop, our poet models were all male. Sexton drew heavily on Snodgrass and Lowell; I frankly studied and imitated Auden and Karl Shapiro.

At the tail end of the fifties, armed with a Radcliffe M.A. in comparative literature acquired just before the birth of our first child and thanks to Holmes's intercession on my behalf, I began to teach at Tufts University. Admittedly, it was only as an adjunct. As a part-time female, I was deemed eligible to teach freshman composition only to the phys ed majors and the dental technicians. My husband, Victor, was genuinely pleased for me; even this low-paying job was a coup for a woman. We both understood the value of extra money coming in. Now that our third child was in kindergarten, I was able to arrange with a kind neighbor to pick him up and deliver him to the local grammar school three times a week when I commuted to Medford to meet my freshman comp classes.

Some of my neighbors were appalled that I would abandon my children in this wanton fashion. Others were not surprised, for by then they had stumbled upon my light verse in the *Ladies Home Journal* and *Good Housekeeping*, magazines they treasured. But it was clear to all that I was not sufficiently focused on my homemaker duties. These devoted mothers were hand-decorating birthday cakes, hand-sewing Halloween costumes, polishing their silver flatware, tending their backyard flower gardens, finding wholesome domestic outlets for their creative abilities.

Looking back, it is hard to believe how judgmental and corrosive these criticisms were to me. A little guilt makes the world go round, but I was almost convinced that I was short-changing my children, a bad mother daring to nibble around the edges of an actual career.

In 1961, Sexton and I were both selected for charter membership in the Radcliffe Institute for Independent Study, later renamed the Bunting Institute. We were lionized, interviewed by the press and scrutinized by the local community. The Institute conferred legitimacy on our activities. I especially remember Anne saying that she had not previously been able to cut short a telephone conversation by saying that she was writing a poem; she would dissemble and announce that she was in the middle of making gravy or had a cake in the oven. (Gorgeous lies. A cook she was not.)

Election to the Institute meant social intercourse with gifted women in other fields. Sculptors, painters, historians, scientists all came together for the weekly seminars. Among us we counted at least two dozen small children. We were sharing the same space and the same struggle, and we talked about it freely. A lot of flatware went blessedly unpolished.

Coincidentally in 1961 I published my first children's book, a story in rhyme called *Sebastian and the Dragon*. Inspired by my children who were enthusiastic listeners, I wrote and published twenty juveniles. Initially, I viewed my success in this genre as an embarrassment. Kiddie lit was not something a serious self-respecting poet ought to undertake. It simply reinforced the domestic-poet stereotype. It was a given that the distinctly female voice, as well as the voice directed to children, represented inferior art. But several well-known male poets—William Jay Smith, Ted Hughes, Randall Jarrell, John Ciardi—were also invading the genre, conferring aesthetic validation upon it.

During the sixties, Sexton and I wrote four children's books together. I confess that our approach was downright giddy. We took turns at the typewriter and at dictating the story line. Whoever was typing at the moment had veto power. On at least one occasion we took turns floating around in Anne's swimming pool and worked with the typewriter precariously balanced on the lip. For years after, we argued over who had come up with the critical line that provides the fulcrum to *Joey and the Birthday Present*: "And they both agreed a birthday present cannot run away."[4]

Now we were heroes to our kids. We were writing books they could be proud of, take to school, read aloud to youngsters in classes below theirs. And what a good time we'd had!

I've since written, but have not been able to publish, three children's stories that were inspired by my grandchildren. I see an extra jaunty note creeping into my poetry, too. But looking back I understand my reticence about the juvenile books and the light verse. Although several very successful light versifiers were male—Shel Silverstein, Ogden

Nash—light verse bore the taint of domesticity. Who today reads Phyllis McGinley, a superb poet? I have many of her poems by heart, particularly "Ballade of Lost Objects," which is chiseled on my brain pan. Think of finding four good rhymes for her refrain line, "Where in the world did the children vanish?" McGinley makes it look easy. Here are her daughters

> rending the air with
> Gossip and terrible radios.
> Neither my friends nor quite my foes,
> Alien, beautiful, stern, and clannish,
> Here they dwell, while the wonder grows:
> Where in the world did the children vanish?[5]

Anyone with daughters will resonate with those lines.

There is still a bountiful supply of sexist condescension that regards poems about domestic relationships as possibly charming and appealing but unworthy of serious critique. Poems about women's bodies and women's bodily functions still arouse a degree of terror and antipathy in certain quarters, but when I look back forty years to the seminal poems of Sexton, Kizer, Plath, and other innovators, I am heartened.

I have shamelessly drawn on the lives of my children as a sourcebook for my work. The intimate familial relationships, particularly mother-daughter ones, fed my poetry. The serious artistic voice has no gender, in my opinion, but it may assuredly take a stance. From the earliest observations of separation ("Nightmare" and "Poem for my Son" from *Halfway*) to the anguish as grown offspring leave home ("Address to the Angels," "Making the Jam without You," "The Journey," "For My Son on the Highways of His Mind," "Sunbathing on a Rooftop in Berkeley," and "Seeing the Bones" from *Selected Poems 1960–1990*) to somewhat more distanced and nuanced poems like "The Bangkok Gong" (*Selected Poems*) and "After the Cleansing of Bosnia" (*Connecting the Dots*), my poems have been inextricably enmeshed in my role as mother.[6]

This role has informed almost every poem I have written. Indeed, even as I have turned more of my attention to the natural world of farm and forest, especially to the nonverbal communication that takes place between humans and other creatures, I would have to acknowledge that the animals, my confederates, constitute our second family. With children grown and gone, we continue to raise and care for horses, dogs, cats, and in summer, a friend's visiting ewes.

Even with these commitments, I am not able, it seems, to eschew writing about grand-children: *vide* "A Game of Monopoly in Chavannes" and "We Stood There Singing" (*Looking for Luck*),[7] and "The Height of the Season," "Beans Beans Beans," and "The Riddle of Noah" (*Connecting the Dots*). Yet I do edit and self-censor my work to keep from cross-ing certain boundaries of privacy and decorum. I am fond of saying to fearful students who turn in poems about family members, "Now that you have made art of it, it belongs to the ages." But of course there are matters of taste and tact. Sometimes just putting a searing poem away for a few days, months, or years will solve the problem. Sometimes, as you "await the birth-hour of a new clarity," as Rilke advised Mr. Kappus, a path around the emotional obstacle will appear.[8] And eventually, truly, it will belong to the ages.

NOTES

1. My own quote, unpublished, this fragment from memory.

2. O. A. Golinenko, ed., *The Diaries of Sophia Tolstoi*, trans. Cathy Porter. New York: Random House, 1985, p. 8.

3. Quatrain from the *Christian Science Monitor*, March 1953.

4. Maxine Kumin and Anne Sexton, *Joey and the Birthday Present*. New York: McGraw-Hill Book Company, 1971.

5. Phyllis McGinley, "Ballade of Lost Objects" in *The Love Letters of Phyllis McGinley*. New York: Viking Press, 1954, p. 17.

6. Maxine Kumin, *Halfway*, New York: Holt, Rinehart and Winston, 1961; *Selected Poems 1960–1990*, New York: W.W. Norton & Company, 1997; *Connecting the Dots*, New York: W.W. Norton & Company, 1996.

7. Maxine Kumin, *Looking for Luck*. New York: W.W. Norton & Company, 1992.

8. Rainer Maria Rilke, *Letters to a Young Poet*. New York: W.W. Norton & Company, 1954, p. 30.

◊

MAXINE KUMIN has been married for 55 years to Victor Kumin; their offspring are Jane, Judith, and Daniel, born in 1948, 1950, and 1953. Their grandchildren, Yann and Noah, were born in 1982 and 1990. Kumin won the Pulitzer Prize in 1973; she has subsequently been awarded the Aiken Taylor Prize, the Poets' Prize, the Harvard Graduate School of Arts and Sciences Centennial Award, and the Ruth E. Lilly Prize, among others. In 1980–81, she served as Consultant in Poetry to the Library of Congress before that post was renamed Poet Laureate of the United States. She and her husband live on a farm in New Hampshire.

When as a Girl on the Plains of Minnesota

Maureen Owen | March 10, 1997

Almost as soon as I knew I wanted to be a poet, I envisioned that I would be a poet who led a full life. In my eleven-year-old mind that meant that I would not sit back and be an observer, writing about what I saw, but that I would do all those things that people do, myself, so I could observe them from the inside out. I would not be, I thought, an "ivory tower poet." I would be involved.

This early decision for a life style of a kind of freedom and determination has not made for an easy time, and it has cost me dearly in some aspects: alienation from my own mother during Civil Rights demonstrations; alienation from my soldier brother during peace demonstrations against the Vietnam war; confusion and hurt for the ones who loved me and couldn't understand "where I got those ideas." But the decision to have children, to become a mother, as part of my plan to experience it all, has been the one that surprised me most.

I have three sons, Ulysses, Patrick, and Kyran. My two eldest boys, Ulysses and Patrick, were born while I was traveling in Japan with their father in the late 1960s. We were much on the road in those times, staying for brief spells in small villages and at the hospitality of local Japanese English teachers. I kept a series of notebooks that I jotted down ideas for poems in whenever I could. We taught English at various local schools and I often carried one of my babies on my back as I stood in the front of the classroom teaching. I was in Japan and with a person who felt that even though it was necessary for me to work during the day, the responsibility of taking care of the babies during those hours would be mine. So it was an exhausting time. But I think that having no choice but to almost make myself "one" with my children, to integrate them into every aspect of my day and night, to include them in the moments when I pulled out my notebooks and wrote, gave me occasion to make them part of my poems in a way that might never have happened to us otherwise. They were completely in my life, in my day. When I read or listened to the wonderful, spontaneous recitations of haiku around the Japanese hosts' dinner table, they were a part of my experience. So in this way, early on, my children entered into my poems. Sometimes by name (I am not one to protect the innocent), sometimes as that image of "baby," sometimes with their bolt out of the blue, instant Zen questions and observations. As in this poem written after we had returned to the States and lived for a time in Branson, Missouri, on my sons' grandfather's place on the edge of that town which was then a speck in the middle of nowhere.

THERE ARE TOO MANY OF ME
lying on the bluff
naked in the local sun

it's so perfect here

no radio
          no mail
  no papers delivered

groggy

      drifting out
      an amorphous mind
      over the hardly moving river
I feel like a thick   steamy   morning fog

my body rising up

a thousand microscopic beads of water.

Ulysses bobbing along the top of the stone wall
so full of questions
tiny bare feet at my elbow asking:
      "Does the government go poo poo?"[1]

Having my first two children in Japan, a country where children seem truly loved and tolerated and where poetry is a part of daily life, had a profound influence on my work. I believe it was during this time that I went from writing objectively to writing from that place that I had pledged to be in when I was an eleven-year-old on the wild Minnesota prairie. Nothing I had done before the birth of my children, including intense political involvements, made me as *vulnerable* as I suddenly and quite unexpectedly found myself with my babies. Suddenly I wasn't one person, but three. The world around me and everything in it took on a new perspective and a new danger. The *danger* that would evolve through the years as accidents, cars, sirens in the night, the draft, knives, bullets, and bombs created in me a kind of raw edge like nothing that had come before. I have lived, in that barely disguised terror, as probably all parents before and after me have managed. But it took my work into a dark, subterranean urgency and cast an anxious glow about my poems. It was a change instant and final. A nervousness I would never be able to shake. The new perspective entered my work as the opposite, a balance to the inconsolable vulnerability of the knowledge that a part of me would be in the world outside of me and yet every cell in my body would cry out to be with that part and protect it. Children are you and not you. They are themselves with their separate lives that belong to them alone. The new perspective they gave to me, to myself as a poet, was like being shaken awake after dozing off. How had I fallen asleep while on watch? I thought I had taken such care to keep an open heart to the space around me. Yet time after time the children would say something that cut like a knife through water. Then they would just stand there or be off somewhere else, and I would find myself tossed into the sky, or bursting up through depths into sharp stinging air gasping in astonishment.

They forced me to become vulnerable to information, to sounds, to situations in ways that I must have been once, but had forgotten. The boys taught me so much! They marched into my poems and demanded the moment be the thing. No Roshi at a Zen temple, no instant of enlightenment could have brought me into the Now as they did. I relearned dailiness.

> Sometimes I think I've learned   everything I know
> Kyran explained at breakfast   how if you have a diaper on   you
> don't need to wear underwear[2]

Through their constant needs and breathtaking impatience, they brought me nose to nose with my visceral inheritance. I began to see lyric not only in the classic and grandiose sense, but in the absolute plainness of common motions.

> The baby bangs his forehead into the spoon.
>   Usually I am speechless   struck dumb   encased
> in silence.[3]

The news they brought sometimes seemed so full of irrational joy as to be from another world:

> O Uncomplicated One!
>   littlest fat face amid the sheets   a commotion
> of arms flapping   palest rouge of flippers crazily rowing
> When I simply say   "Good Morning."[4]

I sat them down in my poems, to crawl, to run, to smash a dozen eggs. I opened the page to them. They were my reality and my reality check. And in that I gave myself license to let off the steam that constant motherhood stores up. Those afternoons I'd try to sneak in a few lines with my typewriter and the mere sound of it brought them running. My attention was somewhere else! Those nights the house was such a mess it was impossible to write in it. (I am someone who needs to first impose order before I can work.) Those brief interludes where I just wanted for no good reason to be in the bathroom *by myself*!

Perhaps to the detriment of my image as mom, I have exploded in my poems:

> ...Some mornings it is cleansing
> to lean from bed   lift the window   and scream   I HATE CHILDREN
> into the lovely green yard.[5]

In fact, it may be that to write down such needs and then be over them, as I did, and not actually scream into the yard, startling children and neighbors, is a fine way to put your writing to work for you.

When I came back to the States, I began working at a day job full time, continued being a mom, and was writing my poems, editing a small press magazine (*Telephone*), and running a small press (Telephone Books Press). Along the way I had learned to face the economic and political realities of motherhood. The community of poets I had joined at the St. Mark's Poetry Project in New York and other poets I met in other parts of the country were a community in the best sense of including children. But the truth was that to get to a poetry reading I often had to find a sitter for my children. After the reading, when everyone else went out for beers, I had to get home. I couldn't go and discuss for hours the work I had just heard read and entertain other opinions and brilliant asides, glean inside knowledge, collect names of books to read or other poets I should be discovering. I couldn't get involved with extra events that would have been wonderful to me and that I felt then would have enhanced my development as a poet. I couldn't just hang out with people who were on my same wavelength and trade stories. I had economic and care responsibilities that my childless contemporaries did not. In many ways, having children kept me in a separate space. But something else was happening. In that separate, desperate space I was getting a lot of writing done. When I went straight home from a reading, I wasn't fried from talking for hours and having drinks. I was fired up from the poetry itself, and after reading to the boys and putting them to bed, I went to my typewriter. I would take all the energy I had from the reading and put it into my poetry. Of course, I would be tired from working and being a mom all day, so it cuts both ways, but I do think that having the children to pull me home grounded me and reminded me of my sense of purpose: to write.

By the time my youngest son, Kyran, was born, my economic straits and the New York City public school system—as well as my concern for the general welfare of Ulysses and Patrick, now in elementary classes—caused me to leave the city and move to Connecticut. My day job at that time was still in the city, so I was quite stretched in terms of being there for the boys, working to bring home the broccoli, and trying to keep up with my writing. Working in the city with the boys at home in Connecticut made me feel wildly far away from them and when I caught that last train home I was driven with a frenzy of need to spend as much time as possible with them. This and the long commute pressed my writing time to even more desperate hours. My late nights gradually started to become later and later. During this period I began to experiment with my own exhaustion. I would keep typing even in a half-asleep state. A sort of somnambulant verse evolved. Often in the morning I would rush into my study to see what I had written the night before, since I did not have any clear recollection of it. It was like exploring a nether realm inside my own brain. As though a strange language spoke to me out of the dark and the air and my own kind of crazed, zombie state.

Even when I was home all evening I would seldom get into my study until ten or eleven o'clock. After the boys were tucked in I would attempt putting a sense of order back into our rooms: pick up or sweep all the toys to one side; put school bags in order; make lunches; plan our next meal. Then I would go to my typewriter and begin to work. This became the pattern I have kept for years (and am so in the habit that I continue it even now, though my youngest son has just gone off as a freshman to college). Starting to write around ten and working until one or two in the morning, I was somehow still able to get up at 6:30 and begin the next day in fairly reasonable condition. Sometimes I would fall asleep while reading to the boys. I'm sure they have memories of waking me up to finish the story or book. Sometimes I would be so exhausted while writing that I would doze over the typewriter keys and just catch myself up. (My great fear for years was that I would fall asleep and topple headfirst into the keys and break my nose or teeth.) I definitely suffered from sleep deprivation.

But I stuck to this schedule past all messages my body was shouting out to me, "Get some sleep!" Because without it I would have had no time to write at all. Those long nights were my only hope. I had my children and my writing. They were interwoven. The boys were part of my poems, they surfaced and resurfaced in them. And my poetry made it possible for me to be the kind of mother I wanted to be. One grounded the other. And both exhausted. When Edna St. Vincent Millay wrote:

> My candle burns at both ends;
> It will not last the night;
> But ah, my foes, and oh, my friends—
> It gives a lovely light![6]

she was not describing a night of wild debauchery—she was unknowingly envisioning motherhood.

NOTES

1. Maureen Owen, "THERE ARE TOO MANY OF ME" in *Hearts in Space*. New York: Kulchur Press, 1980, p. 61.

2. Maureen Owen, "Tuesday   the first letter" in *Zombie Notes*. New York: Sun Press, 1985, p. 43.

3. Owen, "For Fanny" in *Hearts in Space*, p. 21.

4. Owen "All That Glitters…" in *Hearts in Space*, p. 22.

5. Owen, "for Bill Kushner" in *Zombie Notes*, p. 9.

6. Edna St. Vincent Millay, "First Fig," *A Few Figs from Thistles*. New York: Harper and Bros., 1922, p. 38.

◊

MAUREEN OWEN, an Irish American from Minnesota, now of Connecticut and New York, edited at Telephone Books Press and *Telephone* magazine working on over thirty titles of the press and nineteen issues of the magazine to date. She is the author of nine books of poetry, some of which include *Hearts in Space* (Kulchur Press, 1980), *Zombie Notes* (Sun Press, 1985), *Amelia Earhart* (Vortex Editions, 1984), *Imaginary Income* (Hanging Loose Press, 1992), and *American Rush: Selected Poems* (Talisman House, 1998). Recent anthologies her work has appeared in include *Moving Borders: Three Decades of Innovative Writing by Women* (Talisman House, 1998), *The United States of Poetry* (Abrams, 1996), and *Ladies, Start Your Engines* (Faber and Faber, 1996). *Talisman: A Journal of Contemporary Poetry and Poetics* has an issue dedicated to her work. She is mother to Ulysses, Patrick, and Kyran, born in 1965, 1967, and 1977.

The World Is Not Precisely Round:
Piecing Commotion (on writing and motherhood)

Erica Hunt

Having exchanged
My night for day
My occupations came
Sunlit, optical
Visible to the eye
Not as is said in a
Close to extinct
Literature, visible
To the heart.

I

Displacement. Or, in so many words, several minds must occupy the same space (stage) at once. The theater trope comes to mind because so often in the beginning I would improvise the roles of writer and mother, two roles on roll call, performances on demand. Rational, practical, imaginative, investigative, empathetic, affirmative, forbidding, alluring, demonstrative, demonstrative, *and* observant, these roles began as situational and wind up constitutive.

Displacement. Each mind or role (mother, wife, Black woman, social justice worker, artist, lazy bones) starts as a relation, a position to be claimed until the position claims me back, to form finally, a rough equivalence to the self that I woke up with today.

Displacement. Each role is entered, in any case, with a sense of maximum possibility, promising to exceed expectations, rewrite the gridded lines of socialization. Throughout my thirties, the superwoman routine was reflexive, instantaneous, externally generated, psychologically formative and absorptive, the muscles of enactment created a hyper-real maternal body and mind.

If the script calls for tenderness, I can be tenderness embodied, evincing compassion that is new even to myself. If my daughter asks a question that cuts to the core of the world (as children will, oblivious of the prompts and cautions), I can be honest, even wise, without shading or draining the world of its complexity. I don't know how I do it, this trick of deciphering. Often I will not even have noticed that here was a code waiting to be opened. I am astonished that I can break into the vault of human behavior and from there into the sometimes more tightly locked box of my own knowledge. I can only say that love drives me to it, and there is no gainsaying love as an epistemological force.

But neither writing nor motherhood is mere attitude. Each performance is a hard-won process, an action selected freeze-framed from a sequence of failed attempts to match an aesthetic or emotional ideal. Each act of writing or mothering stuns by the immensity of its hidden archaeology of failure, riddled origins, hidden clauses, minute pleasures achieved through tactical approximations. Poetry and mothering have this in common with other human activities that manage to be part of the real, and in doing so they can transform our sense of the real, even as they are incomplete, imperfect, or impartial.

Is this the paraphrase: *Some poetries are the assertion of incomplete propositions of the real— erratic rhythm of ache and satisfaction, like an unfolding map of unexpected destination.*

In poetry, then, displacement is part of the method, transferred into the material circumstances of the composition, the text, and the reader.

II

There is something sweetly seductive about the myth of infinite capacity; in every woman there is an ancient Devi, goddess of the Hindu manifold, multi-armed, tirelessly creative in all aspects of her modern, amortized life, ready to sign on yet another dotted line, because it is all endlessly possible.

Not surprisingly, I have become ferocious about moments without interruption. There has never been a time that I haven't had a room of my own, albeit with semi-permeable doors...but with a door—and soundproof.

The passion for uninterrupted privacy extends to the dream books and journals that are a part of every writer's life, supple encyclopedia of primary sources. These journals log points of departure, skeleton keys to layers of subterranean parables of menace and joy under guard, hidden seams and splits in architecture of language, freedom in the verb, connecting tunnel between emphases, and so on. I am out of the way in these journals and the thinking is untied from the tyranny of my always-good intentions.

Nevertheless, there is a strain in seeing life as so many roles to be juggled. The roles pile up, collisions between expectation and promise lead to tangled wrecks, self-blame. And even when the traffic's moving "normally," I yearn for single-mindedness. A blue intensity I imagine exists for others, where the performance of language into text is sovereign.

> *Dear A*
> *I can almost see you in the morning, mist-shrouded Pacific Northwest, wreathed by wind slanted cypress and towering pines. You smoke and chew gum simultaneously, a tribute to your enormous productivity. A neat pile of manuscript, 25 inches high piles up beside you. The voices of your characters steadily hum,* without interruption, *and animate your dreams, waking and sleeping. You know them and are fearless in your knowledge.*

This fantasy is gripping, even in the face of contrary evidence that few writers are possessed of the orderly private lives that I imagine as essential to the satisfactory practice of the craft. We live in the spin cycle of avarice, violence, panic, and moral indifference celebrated by cowboy capitalists as human nature.

We all know writers who write in the same room as their MTV-watching children, who write on their jobs as security guards, who write behind bars. We know writers who suffer from mysterious undiagnosed ailments, having outlived the unquestioned good health of their youth without benefit of major medical. We know writers who write under the influence of pharmaceutical mood editors, lifted, lowered, or compressed. We all know writers who handle their wits like whips, who walk on the backs of rickety chairs, their eyes closed in metempsychotic trance dances. They lift the curtain on marvelous tricks of language and then exit the stage to retire to an obscurity that seems mismatched, never to be heard of again.

Some of those described above are female, some are mothers, and others are not. These examples form part of the refutation to reductive formulas writers who sometimes take too limited a view, as if writing were an either/or proposition, writing and motherhood two rigid poles diametrically apart, that when by choosing one the other is abandoned, instead of points connected and traveling the loop.

I can never stand apart from the loop; it is like trying to catch yourself blinking in the mirror. But for seconds at a time, I can see the two parts of my life are interpenetrated, they inform one another, even when the door to my room is closed.

At every seam I ask, "Is this true?" Do I believe in this loop of contained possibilities— that *instead of linear achievements, the sense that writing and mothering form a continuum where a reflective life is a constant value and that tensions can be turned into productive, dialectical sources of paradox and creativity.*

III

I have written that I write to know what I think. I might as well have written that I write to know who I am. This mediated self, the practicing self is the only way in and frequently the only way out into the practice of knowledge as revolutionary, as fearless, dynamic, and critical as what "I" project (with the hubris of one who believes she possesses and is not possessed by her words).

The field of practice expands. The practicing self improvises a thousand sound positions, fielding questions, turning statements into queries, reading, writing, and listening.

I was born awake
There was no choice
But to write it down
With eyes open.
Intending to mend my ways
By letting the
Roar of the house fall
Around the contents of
A book
Looking
Square in the eye.

Literature is the sum of the reflective practices of readers and writers, producing meanings, values, and experiences from the store of their experience, the contexts and history of book and spoken arts.

If we have more experiences of bravery, then that bravery lets us experience more freedom, details included. That's the practice.

The falling away, which reminds that we are groundless, that it is all still highly arbitrary, that we might spell our names in Pashtun or Uzbek, Hutu or Tutsi, Serb or Croatian, means we must, and as we perch on some fragile excuse of meaning and orderliness, we must conjure the nets strong enough to halt the fall. That's the theory.

Theory seems particularly out of place in a time when people are readily stroked into forgetting what they know, what their interests are, and how each of us is more complex than our identity cards suggest, that we are contradictory and we have the power to be the agents of our own history and reality. I am interested in poetry and poetic practice that illumines the barely apprehended limits of conventional forms, the limitlessness of the past and future that we protect against and the bravery we wear in the face of it all. Poetry might be the demonstration of what occurs in the word in this life we're given, produce and create amidst the unexpressed potentials of every social encounter.

Poetry as the saturated or cooled brimming racket applied to phoneme, morpheme, grapheme, syntax, situation, revelation, context, genre, torqued provocatively to demonstrate the usually noiseless mechanics of text and meaning.

IV

I am drawn to writing as a form of address. Letters from dream time to day time or from the possible to the present. Or from the reader to the writer of a text, this text. I am drawn also to the cycle of writerly production and readerly co-creation in the languages of more conventional address, speech, sermon, monologue, dialogue, correspondence, journal, call and response, the invited and the peeping tom, the paying customer and the voyeur, nestled in the same body, the social body with barely acknowledged sinews.

Even this essay has taken shape under the sign of interrogation.

Some of the strongest forms of interrogation are film texts: the films of Abigail Child, Trinh T. Minh-ha, Yvonne Rainier, Isaac Julien, Chantal Ackerman propose formally distinct visual symphonies where looking is a labor of love, and examples of cinematic poetry completing its mission in reception.

Not just address, then, but composition.

Address creates a circle along which authority may pass from writer to reader and to the person at next remove, moving by degrees, further from the immediate circles of familiarity to wider social realms. The text, as they say, has a life of its own, and its form of address *pieces together* an audience larger than the "author" banished from the room in the first place.

Listen: up until the last ten years, I never felt permission to address anything larger than an immediate circle, and certainly never with any material that could be construed as personal. The larger circle invited too many risks—judgments in Black and white, type-casting, rewards for singularity or obedience, at least eight kinds of silencing, a few so well disguised to appear to be social opprobrium.

> *We walk on thin air*
> *Each day we draw breath.*

In the last years, the nature of address changed as I came to understand the nuances of poetic register, the suppler forms of circle, the variety of connections between public and private. Poetic register scores location, places us that each might find coordinates of the specific instance of the poem.

There are those who know me as a poet, can talk to me only as poet. They know only part. There are others who know me as a mother, and make the small and large talk of parenthood; they know only part. The people able to comprehend my life as composed in several registers offer me most as a writer.

My children share my register, stand in the range of my address, and then simultaneously stand apart. Where I try to suggest a world, composed not only of what is already out there but a world ready to be made, they derive hopefully a North Star, not a sky full of stars.

> *Were I to call the night brother*
> *I would call him the brother of her*
>
> *Raisin blue night pot*
> *Like the bottom of indigo*
>
> *Tipped to fill a promise*
> *Faith full*
>
> *Love transparent*
> *Never ready made*
> *Off the shelf.*

These acts of address suggest an edge and syntactical clarity where I would not ordinarily go. They rise from the margins of my inattention I can't imagine dwelling on brought to sudden and complete focus on the minute waverings in the present tense. I am compelled to slow down to hear about the shuttling of 11-year-olds in parallel works or the breakdown of language and loss among the 3's at the point of burning need. No one could possibly keep a cheat sheet, a counterfeit connection would be immediately detected.

V

We do not live the circumscribed lives of our great-grandmothers, grandmothers, or even our mothers. Social change has come at breathtaking speed in the last half century, especially when compared to the century before. Consider, if you are part of the post-war baby boom generation, your mother's life. If you are younger, born in 1965 or later, consider your parents and then their parents.

I know that I have more choices than my mother, a jazz composer and pianist who with great difficulty and despite a World War, left home before she was married. Her life in art was a struggle to break into a jazz scene fundamentally antithetical to her upbringing as a "good" girl. A contemporary of Duke Ellington, she came from a family of self-employed Black people, craftspeople literate in scripture and classics, without much material privilege but using a similar moral and social compass. The will to frequent speakeasies, the brothels, and segregated clubs that featured so much of American jazz, eluded her. And though she had her music played by Count Basie, W.C. Handy, and others, and her compositions could be heard on the radio, she could only play in the "decent" places. She played in every church in Harlem, at the Y, the social clubs and lodges, but in no place where you could build a career in jazz.

I can recall, when I was a child, my mother sending out songs to the music agencies of a Tin Pan Alley already in decline. I remember her making a demo, sending out the scores of holiday songs on Christmas cards. At 83, she still has not surrendered, recently completing a suite of sacred music metrically based on the seven days of creation, asking for my help to secure information about composers' grants. But permission and possibility occurred slowly for her, in part due to her temperament, circumstance (she lost her sight early in her life), and the "forces" of history ("patriarchy"). There are only so many barriers any Black woman born in 1918 can bear to smash and expect to survive, so no cost went unmeasured. She gauged as best she could.

And so while the rate of change between the first part of the century and now was swift, it has slowed. There is less difference between my daughter's range of choices and my own. And yet we are a long way from emancipation.

VI

Before and after.

What is enough?

When I began this essay, I went to my journals, spanning 30 years. I divided them into two piles, before the birth of Madeleine, my daughter and oldest child, and then after. My intention was to read through what I had written on the topic of writing and motherhood since her birth and up until the birth of Julian, my son. The "after" pile covering a period of 15 years was larger, better written, more detailed, less about the work of others, and more about experience than what lay in the "before" pile. The "after" spans the rest of my life, that's enough.

◊

ERICA HUNT's publications include the chapbook *Piece Logic* (Carolina Wren Press, 2002), *Arcade* (Kelsey St. Press, 1996), and *Local History* (Roof Books, 1994). Her essays have been published in many places, most recently, "Roots of the Black Avant Garde" appeared in *Tripwire* (2001), and "Poetry and Politics" appeared in a website of the Poetry Society of America. Hunt was the recipient of the Poetry award from the Foundation for Contemporary Performance Art in 2001. Hunt currently lives in New York with her partner Marty Ehrlich and her two children Madeleine, born in 1987, and Julian, born in 1995.

Not a Perfect Mother

Stephanie Brown

It's the hardest job you'll ever love...It's a challenge, but it's worth it...There is nothing more reward-ing... Sorry, no platitudes spoken here. At Super Kmart on a Sunday afternoon a car pulls into the parking space next to my car; the personalized license plate says something like LV2BMOM. This is one among many of the cars I see every day: 4MYKIDS, 4MY6BOYZ, NO1MOM, etc., along with the bumper sticker I see all the time: MOTHERHOOD IS A PROUD PROFESSION. Mom-chic, perfect mom: *the ideal.*

The real: Inside Super Kmart I see a mother frantically trying to calm down her young baby. The sharp tone in her voice startles me as she says to her older child, "Push the cart! Help me out!" So sharp that I turn around and look. The mother walks by, carrying the screaming, red-cheeked toddler out of the store. The mother turns to look at me as she walks by, smiles and shakes her head; I nod back in understanding. *Been there.* A couple of aisles later I see another mother angrily yelling at her daughter, "Sit down before you fall out and hurt yourself!" Her daughter is standing up in the shopping cart. Her son won't stop nagging at her—literally pulling at her shirt—for something. The mother is yelling at him now, her face is angry, she is lost in her anger, unaware of the world around her, a step away from a violent act. I turn my gaze away from the pillow bins we've both been looking in, close my eyes and say a quick prayer for her. Maybe she doesn't want it or need it (maybe there is no God), but I'll do it anyway.

Been there. Been a screaming maniac. Been really tense, angry, hopeless with frustration, without shame in public. I no longer make any assumptions about the qualifications of other mothers, fathers, or marriages. I've failed by my own standards many times. As soon as I passed judgment on someone's late, remedial potty training, I was karmically given this same problem. Cleaning up shit—is there anything more humbling—better yet, *numbing*? Actually, three months of colic with my first child were more numbing. Deadening, soul-killing. It was hard to nurture a red-faced screaming new little life (day after night after day after day): nothing could pacify or soothe, except time, his growing out of it. If you've been there, you know. If you haven't been, please don't tell me your theory of why babies have colic.

There's been a trend for several years now for women to want to stay at home with their kids, and I believe it is currently a status symbol—to be able to stay at home means you have enough money to do so. It is as much a status symbol as the kind of car you drive. Before I had kids, to be a "stay-at-home mom" seemed revolutionary to me. Before I had kids I knew that I wanted to spend most of my time raising them myself. (I felt like I was being daring and different, but then I found out a whole generation of people felt the same way.) Once it became the norm for women to work, to *not* put career first was to have élan, to be the economic top-dog, as it had been chic and smart to juggle career and motherhood in the 1970s and 1980s. I used to select books for purchase when I worked in a library. In the early 1990s I noticed a then-new trend in publishing: titles about how to drop out, stay at home, and later, to simplify. With magazines like *Working Mother* being well-established staples on our shelves, this was definitely a departure. However, in my heart, I was not really old-fashioned or trend-setting as other stay-at-home moms that I knew: when someone said, "My husband and kids come first, nothing is more important to me," I'd nod, agree—but secretly I'd think, no, my writing comes first, my writing is most important to me.

I've had to be honest with myself: I'm not really a stay-at-home mother. For the first few years my kids were little, I worked part time. When at home, I'm looking for time to write. Additionally, the new status-symbol life style of participating in school and volunteer events doesn't thrill me all that much. It's a full-time career for many women to devote themselves entirely to volunteering for their schools, churches, and clubs. I try to stay involved, but I have no desire to become a part of the power nexus of the classroom. I am helpful and friendly, I don't complain about donating the ten bucks here and there, the few hours here and there, I'm not a gossip or a negative person. But I'm no star mother, I'm not the room mom, the soccer coach, the great birthday party giver, the mom who has all the kids over to play. At one time I thought I would be this person: I thought it was something I could apply myself to, like graduate school or some other goal, but I found that I was not cut out for it. I want *the time that I have* for myself. I want *the time that I have* for my writing. In the past, I felt competitive with other women, and felt pretty darn okay about myself. I never would admit that my life was less than perfect. I would never admit to any feelings of doubt, insecurity, anger, disappointment: to myself or to a confidant. I wanted it all to look effortless. If the opportunity ever presented itself where I could be real and let down my guard, I could not do it. But I've found out a lot about my limitations since I had children. Now, when I have the opportunity to be honest, I am forthcoming to the appropriate level for the relationship. I don't pretend to be more than I am.

When our first son, Nathaniel, was born, my husband began a three-and-a-half-year MBA program while he worked full time in a corporation. One surprising thing I enjoyed about being married was the way my husband and I worked together on goals. This satisfied me more than romance. We planned and we made our plans happen. We set goals for each year, for three, five, ten years. We saved, invested, never went into debt. We did what we wanted, and we did not listen to naysayers. I enjoyed this kind of energy and focus being in my life. I was able to accomplish a lot. I published a lot more work after I had a baby than I ever had before that. I had pursued a career (librarian) that would support me and my writing. I liked doing research—essentially the librarian's job—and I liked the job I had in a busy public library. I did well at my job, maxed out my pay sooner than most, and fully expected to get promotions and work full-time as soon as my son was older. There was a well-defined career path to follow in the field of librarianship, and I intended to follow it. I had a flexible part-time schedule. We hired a babysitter and made use of grandparents. My husband and I joked about having five sons—but we were almost serious about it.

I suppose hubris snares everyone at some point in life. We were high on our competence at family life when I got pregnant with our second child. I found that working and pregnancy and caring for another child was a lot harder the second time around. I was older, I was more tired, my older son was entering his needy "terrible twos." But I kept at it, for three years after the birth of my second child, Thomas. With each succeeding year I felt the energy and enthusiasm drain from me a little more. I had our lives carefully scheduled and planned. When either of us would have to change our work hours, I could be thrown into an abyss of frustration and anger. If we didn't have a babysitter, it could pitch the day, the week, into the wastebasket. We went out a lot as a couple, but I don't remember really enjoying our time together. I was in a constant battle against fatigue. I started visibly to age and it depressed me. There were two consecutive years where we spent the months from September to March fighting one virus and infection after another: surely this was hell on earth. I started to burn out on work; I opened my eyes to the fact that part-timers were not taken seriously as promotion candidates, even if this was not a corporate job. With two toddlers, I realized it would be a long time before I could really focus on my career. My only reward was the occasional comment from someone like, "I don't know how you do it!" or "You have it all together!" or, to us as a couple, "I'm impressed!" with how we had juggled my husband's graduate school, two jobs, kids. I liked those comments; they were my only remaining reward for what I was doing. I also couldn't help noticing how I no longer heard compliments I liked and had come to expect: "You look great!" or "That's a cute outfit!" Now people said to me—complete strangers as well as people I knew—"You look *tired*" and smiled with pity or, I sometimes suspected, *schadenfreude*. I decided that hearing that phrase again and again ("You look *tired*") was the very worst thing about becoming a mother.

When I finally got a promotion that I thought I wanted, my eyes opened to a truth that I had not noticed before. Library headquarters, where I worked, was where we aspired to be: management, the highest paying jobs, the most power. I looked around and noticed that all the women who worked full time in these positions of power had no children. The only one who did had adopted a baby in her late forties. Truly, it was not that they had grown children and had taken up their careers at a later age: they had never had children. They were the most successful at climbing the bureaucratic ladder. I started to think about the library managers who were a step below these women: most of them, too, had no children. If they did, they had one child only, and this was likely the reason they were not yet in upper management. I started to think of other women I knew in other walks of life: if they had been able to climb the ladders of their professions or creative fields, they had no children, or one at the most. I had paid attention to the notable exceptions: those dynamos with three or four kids, a full-time career and maybe a side business, an active volunteer, civic, or public life—I knew a few and was impressed with their capabilities. I always thought I was one of them. But now I realized: *they are notable exceptions. I am not one of them.* Not only that: *most* people are not one of them. Most people have made a choice or a compromise. And I knew I would choose my poetry over this job, my kids over promotions. If I had been younger and less tired, I probably would have kept at what I was doing just to prove that I could!

I also didn't want to admit to myself the biggest reason why I wanted to keep working: I really didn't want to have to stay home with my kids all the time. My boys were extremely active. They required so much effort. They were constant motion, noise, energy. I was physically exhausted at the end of each day. Around this time I read *Of Woman Born* by Adrienne Rich. The story of Joanne Michulski, the mother of eight who goes crazy and kills two of her children—there but for the grace of God go I?[1] My own mother, the other mothers of her generation with six, eight, eleven kids—people we knew—had seemed barely to survive it. I was constantly yelling at my kids. They drove me crazy. I really did not like to be around them. I wanted to get them into school and away from me. I resented their needs and intrusions. At home I felt like a robot when I did not feel like a janitor, cleaning up the *prima materia*: shit, not to mention pee, snot, food glop, mud, spilled pink antibiotic liquid, puddles of puked M & M's all over the car seat.

Around the same time, it became blatantly obvious to me that my older son demanded a lot more time and attention from me than I wanted to give him. He needed work with every single seemingly easy thing: sitting down in a chair for a whole meal, walking down the street without bumping into people, putting on clothes, drawing a circle. I had to accept this basic fact about him and get over my disappointment that he was so difficult. He was very emotional: he was full of delight, enthusiasm, and joy, but he also cried a lot—a cry that shook me down to my backbone with irritation. He was easily frustrated, but extremely sure of himself so it was hard to teach anything to him. I *didn't like this*. I wanted this to go AWAY. In my efforts to teach and to civilize my son, I felt like Annie Sullivan with Helen Keller, I told my husband. ("That's so mean!" he replied.) I daydreamed about how soon my son would be in school full time so that I could get a promotion to library manager. Sometimes at church I would pray about what to do to help him, and I would hear the answer: *be with him*. I ignored it; I really didn't want to. As time went on and he neared the time to enter kindergarten, it became obvious that he would not be able to start full-time kindergarten right away; he had a fall birthday, he was immature; there was no way he would be ready for school. I panicked at this.

Soon his private school pre-kindergarten class proved to be too difficult for him. I felt like a failure, as *my* kid should be the smartest, the most talented. However, my husband didn't see it as any kind of failure, he saw it as an opportunity, and eventually his contrary view of the situation turned out to be right. I quit my job, and we withdrew him from the school. My son and I spent the day together every day for seven months. Teaching him was not easy, but it could be done. My husband worked with him every night on printing his letters. I found that the more I was around him, the more I liked him, and therefore the easier it was to be around him, therefore I was less frustrated, therefore it was easier to be around him, therefore...I became, I think, a kinder person and more compassionate toward others and their limitations, having faced my own. Eventually my son was able to go to school, but he didn't love school. I had forgotten: I really hated elementary school too.

My kids want me around: they want me to run races, to "catch me if you can!" They want to roller skate, run, climb, skateboard. They wrestle each other and literally bounce off the walls. They balance-walk along high garden walls. They jump from the highest places to the ground, shouting, giggling. They get really dirty. They dig and dig and dig in the dirt. They want me to go to the beach every day. They want to go to the park. They want me to play too. ("Come *on*, Mom!") They are not happy if I want to sit on the sand or the grass behind my sunglasses and read. They like me to do goofy faces and silly voices. They want to laugh! So now I play with them. Now I run and play and read with them and I pay attention. It's been the antidote for my impatience.

Recently, the psychologist I've been talking to asked me, "What do you do for yourself, to take care of yourself?" "Um..." I stammered, "I exercise a lot." I spend a lot of time at my gym, yes. It occurred to me a month later that my answer is that I have a whole life separate from my life as a mother and my life as a wife. These parts of my life so rarely intersect that it never even occurred to me to tell her that I am a writer. I've always "hid in plain sight." Being a poet: how many people understand this? I've always been highly intuitive and empathic: the borders between me and the world are permeable. These qualities have mostly felt like a burden to me though they were the sources for the feelings and sensations I used when I wrote poetry. I had the ability to place myself in a spiral kind of time; to make use of daydream and reverie, to open myself to poems working through me rather than I working on them. Where am I today? Running a household. These tasks have drawn upon another side of me—one that was always there and kept me grounded: the manager who looks for the cost-effective solution, takes inventory of the household goods, looks for bargains, makes lists, keeps records, resolves conflict. The part of me that sought to be a librarian because I would have a steady paycheck in order to support my writing. The part of me that married a businessman and not a poet. Nowadays there is little time for reverie. I don't live in timelessness. My kids do, and I have to be the one to say, "Come on, put your shoes on, let's go!" because on the way to get their shoes, they might be suddenly pulled into a toy's imaginative possibilities, and start flying rockets or pretending to be a tiger. I have to be the one who brings them back to the real: *socks and shoes. Now.* I have to answer their imaginative questions with unimaginative, logical, down-to-earth answers: "Where does the sun go at night?" "Why does an airplane go faster than a car?" "Why does a fish live in the ocean?"

"Let's go!" I say this to myself too. With my writing and revising, now I'm expedient: I don't revise as much as I used to. I try to get to the real point of what I'm writing about sooner, and I try to put it down right the first time. I sometimes talk into a tape recorder or write on post-it notes by the phone. Then I'm out the door. I try to hang onto lines in my head that come to me while driving or standing in line someplace by repeating them so that I can write them down later. Occasionally I have dropped everything I'm doing (polishing the furniture, sweeping the floor) and run to my computer to write a full-blown poem. The practice of yoga has helped me to focus my mind, which, with active children, has become unfocused and distracted. I have found that when I do it on a regular basis, I will often finish my session with a whole written poem in my head that needs little revision. I am a lighthearted, objective, and forthright critic of my work these days: "this is dumb," "cut this," "lame," "this is great": I don't dwell on it. If I have maybe only an hour to work on my writing today, my revisions must be more bold: no time for dilly-dallying. I move on to the next thing. Expediency. It's hard to write and to have kids. Don't let anyone tell you that it's not. You cannot get lost in the easy wind and downy flake of motherhood and then turn around, focus, and produce work. You have to be cunning, practical, and selfish. You have to steal time. Time is your enemy, your gift, your wanton desire, and you will never have enough of it.

But other than this change in the way I write and the way I revise, I can see no connection between poetry and motherhood. To say otherwise would be a lie. There is no connection via language, no oracle at Delphi or Masonic ritual that changes one into a hybrid of *motherpoet*. And if there were, I wouldn't want to know about it. It's hard enough to be a writer and be a woman too. Does anyone ask this question of fathers? Of course not. And who cares, anyway? Men writing on fatherhood would be as self-indulgent as men writing on golf. Any change in my self or my poetry has been a result of aging and maturing, and motherhood has significantly contributed to both my aging and maturing. However, I would write if I were single, incarcerated, or insane. I wrote when I was a girl, when I was a teenage pothead chasing cute surfer boys, when I was a college student, a graduate student, when I drank, when I was sober, when I didn't have a husband and wanted one, when I had him and didn't want him, when I had kids and when I did not have kids.

Life is going by. The shorter it seems to me, the larger my ambitions for my writing grow. I've learned that my kids wither under the relentless kind of goal-setting personality that I have. If I am to put my steamroller self into anything, it's not going to be my kids' careers as professional skateboarders or ivy league grads. I have to be my kids' teacher, nurse, advocate, and provider, and so there are lots of things I can't find the time to do anymore.

My plans to start playing tennis regularly, which I had when I was a girl, have not materialized. Major life decisions used to revolve around having the perfect thing to wear, but the clotheshorse side of me has just sort of...left me.

Ambition. Really, women are not supposed to have that much of it. To talk about it is like talking about personal debt—a secret, an embarrassment. Modesty: perfect mothers do not have big ambitions for themselves. It's more acceptable to be a stage mother or a sports mother than to have one's own designs on trophies and awards. Are poets supposed to be ambitious? Not on your life! (But of course they are.) A teacher I had in graduate school likened being a poet to being a monk—a contemplative, renouncing the world. *Baloney,* I thought then, and think now. As if poets need to retreat from the world any more than they are likely to!

Sometimes—standing in Super Kmart—I feel like one of the many women in Margaret Atwood's *The Handmaid's Tale,* hypnotized, albeit more subtly, with our slogans and our puttingkidsfirst and our family values—our real selves, our feelings and our minds kept under cover of our Mother-uniforms. Looking at some towels, I hear a song come on the Kmart sound system that I like: "Diamonds and Rust" sung by Judy Collins. I like it—but wait—here comes the part I hate; her lover's opinion: "My poetry was *lousy,* you said...." Of course he did! Suddenly I'm filled with rage about...somnambulist women wandering around shopping as an über-voice (and a woman's, yet) sings about love entwined with criticism. Hey, these things do not automatically go together! But would anyone here in Super Kmart care if I told them what I'm thinking about? No. I find some great sale items, buy them, and go home.

Notes

1. Adrienne Rich, *Of Woman Born: Motherhood as Experience and Institution, Tenth Anniversary Edition.* New York: W.W. Norton & Company, 1986, pp. 256–280.

◊

STEPHANIE BROWN, a "late in life" baby born to the parents of six children, was raised on the beaches of Southern California, where she still lives today. Since 1988, her work has appeared numerous times in *American Poetry Review* and has been selected for three volumes of the annual *The Best American Poetry* anthology (Scribner). The University of Georgia Press published her first volume of poetry, *Allegory of the Supermarket,* in 1998. In 1994 she won *American Poetry Review*'s Jessica Nobel Maxwell poetry prize and was awarded a National Endowment for the Arts Fellowship in poetry in 2001. She has been married since 1991 to Derek Christiansen and has two children, Nathaniel, born in 1992, and Thomas, born in 1994.

My Motherhood

CAMILLE ROY

My son is three. I am forty-one, a writer and a dyke, a co-mother with my partner of eighteen years, and a close friend of the father and his partner, and we are all engaged in this project of "lesbian/gay extended family raising a child." While I had fears when I entered this situation, I had nothing much in the way of agenda or expectations. Idealism expressed toward family life holds no interest for me. The first surprise, then, is that nothing is as I expected. The persistent odd fluidity of our situation undoes the qualities that I brought to it. The astonishment and rapid changes of early childhood combine with the surprises inherent in my own family structure. I find myself hustling to keep up, with a family whose terms I don't even understand.

I am the adoptive mother. My partner is the birth mother. I wonder how my experience corresponds to that of birth mothers in other kinds of families. I suspect I feel a special fragility in my connection to my son. (The Republican judge who reluctantly approved the adoption told us it wasn't worth the paper it was printed on.) The day-to-day rituals and work of family life ground our connection, while also sheltering it from societal disrespect. My fear of being inauthentic as a parent is persistently countered by his sturdy needs, his weakness and love.

How curious it is to find myself in some respects closer to the role of father than the biological father. Not as in father-gender, but as in father-not-mom. I am closest adult outside the dyad of birth mother and child, and thus I have been the first representative of outside, of separation and mobility. This morning my son said to me, "Minka goes everywhere, where is Minka going?"

Family is an organizer of psychic life. I think of it as a location of viruses, from which each member leaves as a carrier, prepared to transmit to others. Women, it seems to me, are understood to be the carriers of the virus of human bonds, persons who are absorbed and lost in their connections, whereas men carry the virus of separation, distance, and repression. These are only symbolic expressions. They have no inherent truth value, but nonetheless these polarities are present everywhere.

So I am in a family in which the basic equations are mutated. I am in the position of primary other, but not male. Therefore, otherness will not be male. Organization of emotional life, self and other, will not be organized around the polarities of biological sex. Or maybe it will be. Who knows what will happen, because the structure of family in my family has undergone a deformation.

> My son will never remember his first breath.
> He won't remember his body arriving, either.

Body is strange. In early childhood I would say that there is no sexuality because eroticism has not been distinguished from the physical. It's not distinct. As a parent raising a young child, I feel this as waiting for the injury. The relation of baby to body will be ripped apart and then organized by shame, so that my son will grow into the deep disturbance that affects all of us. Perhaps it is this waiting period that inspires silence in parents. It is difficult to speak of that haze of physical joy and exploration in which he seems to live, which is so contrary to my weariness, though it also refreshes me.

I'm reminded of my archeologist father. One hot day, when he was hauling rocks and dripping with sweat, he matter-of-factly told me, "You have to choose between the body and the mind." What was he talking about? Meanwhile my son swarms, emotionally, physically, in language—an entering that goes on and on. His growth absorbs whatever is around him. In the light of his gaze, I become solid, claimed as "parent."

His entering language pulls me back, splits my consciousness to challenge me to remember what came before—gender, for example. I guess you imitate the form, and the meaning comes later. Is it violating his future understanding of himself to describe to you how he loves his one and only dress? How he wanted my partner to buy him one, and then wore it for forty-eight hours straight? He's the only one in the family who loves dresses. Being the single dyke family in the neighborhood, and with a son in a dress to boot, I watch him with some misgivings. He'll take a fall—everyone does. Waiting for it soaks me with dread and tenderness.

He's gentle and arrived folded, against the grain of my understanding, which is accumulating and dark. He waits, hungry, leaning against my leg, while I'm at the butcher block, knife to the bread. Slice it, butter it. Pray for compassion, soiled and turning over.

Then there's his language, growing in all directions like flesh sprouting among twigs. Unlikely, foreign. Why is it there, what is it—his grammar brain. It seems prepared yet mysterious, dark spot, only quiet for a moment, then expanding into the emptiness that is our speech. "Goodnight, sweetheart," I say, and he murmurs that back to me as I turn out the light.

◊

Now my son is five and in kindergarten—that makes things different. School is a barrage of systems plus experiences. The outside pours in, in a big way: teachers, friends, teasing, traumas, and excitement. It all arrives with a whoosh. Socialization coming down the chimney, like Santa. Even queer families can't escape that.

When I look at what I wrote when he was three, it seems oddly innocent. Excuse me if I detect at moments in my own writing the radiance of early childhood. It must be infectious. I love the way young children seem to be opening toward unknown questions—to which the answer, adulthood, sometimes seems like little more than a rude slap.

Kindergarten arrived like a tanker. Right now it seems to carry everything that is real. Maybe kindergarten should be renamed "The Law," as in, "I took my child to the first day of The Law." The gender police start operating with a vengeance. My son sadly told me how his friends at school say he should make ugly pictures, because he's a boy. He'd rather make beautiful ones of fairies, mermaids, and princesses.

I no longer feel like a lesbian father. Probably that is because my son doesn't need one. We spend afternoons stringing beads at the dining room table, in colors that match his ruby slippers. He tells me that the two of us are the jewelry queens of the household.

In other words, gender has arrived, as well as all the landmarks of language: lies, stories, jokes, and complaints. My son's (at this point) unconventional sense of his gender and its meaning came with the package. It popped out of him with the first joke. I don't believe our unconventional family had anything to do with it.

Living with all of this is a bit like living inside a Book of Transformations. What does it have to do with my writing practice? Is there any commonality? Should there be? Well, there's this: time passes through both of them. My texts are performative regardless of form; in my imagination they are always enacted in time, even when they are not specifically pieces for performance. I am a playwright, yet I write poems and stories as well, and in all of these forms, every event has a before and after; crisis is like a heat wave, moving through and distorting a moment. I've been consistently interested in these time-based effects in my work (although they are sometimes excruciatingly difficult to achieve), but I've never been able to frame their appearance in my life. Being a mother has made this easier, in writing as well as living, perhaps because change is explicit and constant in my son's life. I'm more used to it.

Motherhood is a lot emptier than I thought. I expected it to be stuffed to the point of suffocation, static and irritating. I'm not sure how I expected to deal with that. But I find that it is more like a practice, being something that repeats, but is otherwise empty. It is about arrival and profound change, and only emptiness can make room for that. It's possible that being a mother has made me more comfortable with a combination of waiting and constant change. Acceptance, in other words. I don't particularly want to be an "accepting" writer, but I do want to have a writing practice that accepts whatever comes. That seems more possible now.

◊

CAMILLE ROY is a writer and performer of plays, poetry, and fiction. Some of her books include *SWARM* (San Francisco's Black Star Series, 1998), *The Rosy Medallions* (Kelsey St. Press, 1995), and *Cold Haven* (O Books, 1993). Her plays include *Cheap Speech*, which was produced at St. Mark's Poetry Project in New York City and winner of the Bay Area Award in 1995, *Lucky*, *Bye Bye Brunhilde*, *Southside*, and *Numb and Dumber*. In 1998 she was the recipient of a Lannan Writers At Work Residency at Just Buffalo Literary Center. She is the founding editor of the online journal *Narrativity* (www.sfsu.edu/~newlit/narrativity). She has been with her partner Angela Romagnoli since 1978, and their son, Reese, was born in 1993. The writer Robert Glück is the father.

Erasing Names, Multiplying Alliances

Claudia Keelan

> *We must take the feeling of being at home into exile;*
> *we must be rooted in the absence of place.*
> —Simone Weil, *Gravity and Grace*[1]

The growing body of Benjamin, the one I call "my" child, has clarified the ethics of my writing. Committed by nature and historical circumstance to indeterminacy, I've found solidarity in the work of John Keats, Simone Weil, and Martin Luther King, Jr., whose definitions of self and community decentralized the inherent power of either concept. Though the Romantic poet, French philosopher, and American civil rights leader share little, either in terms of historicity or individual disciplines, their writings all propose Utopian idealities, keyed to a reciprocity between self and other.

Keats's concept of negative capability necessitated a negation of self, a Nobody in service of a stance that contained Everybody:

> a poet is the most unpoetical thing of any thing in existence; because he has no Identity—his is continually in for—and filling in some other body...it is a wretched thing to confess; but it is a very fact that not one word I ever utter can be taken for granted...when I am in a room with people...the identity of everyone in the room begins to press upon me that, I am in a very little time annihilated...[2]

Keats's definition suggests that the poet, perhaps freely, perhaps by virtue of her will to powerlessness, relinquish notions of identity further to free the vehicle of her perception. Interestingly, his urge to "annihilation" is not a metaphysical or metaphorical urge. Rather, it prefigures concepts of annihilation evolved by particle physics, concepts that posit a thermodynamic dialectic between elementary particles and antiparticles. Keats's figure of the poet engages such.

Simone Weil raises similar questions regarding self and community, proposing a similar model of powerlessness:

> We possess nothing in the world...except the power to say "I." That is what we have to give to God, in other words, to destroy.[3]

Though a philosopher, Weil more closely resembles a mystic saint, modeling a *via nega-tiva*, or "negative way," in which redemption depends upon principles of negation. She understood, of course, that dependence upon accepted versions of community loses sight of those who live outside that community. She struggled for years in the Communist Party, where much of the debate over the worker's fate disintegrated into factionalism, the visionary idea of autonomy Marx envisioned falling down around dependence upon proper nouns, i.e., the Party, the Trotskyites, etc. George Steiner, among others, has called Weil an anti-Semite, because in her refusal to accept the word as she found it, she refused the designation Jew. Her late work, still clearly invested in society, takes its imperative from natural law, and the ways in which it suggests moral law.

Martin Luther King's dream of the beloved community that would ascend from the body of the civil rights movement also debunked conventional ideas of self and community. The power the nonviolent demonstrator achieved through passive resistance was simi-larly a negative power, instilling in its proponent a generative ethic regarding her role in obtaining civil rights:

> A second basic fact that characterizes nonviolence is that it does not seek to defeat or humiliate the opponent, but to win his friendship and understanding...If he is opposing racial injustice, the nonviolent resister has the vision to see that the basic tension between white people and Negro people is not between races...the tension is, at bottom, between justice and injustice, between the forces of light and the forces of darkness...[4]

In the face of violence, choose nonviolence; in the reality of racial injustice, see the com-prehensive injustice. King's "beloved community" is ever evolving and by necessity, never achieved, as each new participant willingly relinquishes self-interest. Keats would prob-ably abhor the canonization of his work, since his letters (the only surviving statements regarding his faith, or, if you will, his poetics) clearly demand poetic exile. Historically, both Weil and King chose diaspora so they might better work toward the more inclusive homeland.

The exile I have imagined as the authentic stance follows me everywhere, even into this room in which I write, fifteen miles west into the desert from Las Vegas, the city where I teach. It defines my life as a moving toward, a becoming; places are seen, loved, grow old, and die very quickly in me. Exile is the paradigm that ensures my poetry's restless individuation, its refusal of community. In the moments after Benjamin was born, after he'd crawled the short distance from some other where to my face, my husband took him to the nursery for his first bath. I followed, a nurse pushing me in a wheelchair, and at the first sight of a baby boy in a tub of water, I said, "He's so beautiful…" The nurse said, "That's not your son, he's right there, with your husband." I said, "He's beautiful too." I'd heard that a new mother cannot recognize the face of her own child among a group of babies, but only later did my lack of recognition sting me with its necessity. Increasingly since his birth I see how necessary it is for me to be a writer, a mother, a woman, who is still aspiring to be Nobody, the miraculous fact of his existence reinforcing my desire for an ever-emerging homeland. The ambitions of his voice and eyes, of his growing legs, is a cosmos of an other who began in me. Benjamin's growth and continual evolution proves that no thing is about any other thing but is of and in itself a world becoming. "I also am other than what I imagine myself to be," intones Weil.[5] Born into a world where the script is over determined by documented, revisionist, and projective claims, Benjamin will need a special mirror. In it, I hope he sees me, his first image: Nobody with her hand in his.

◊

The search for equilibrium is bad because it is imaginary. Even if in fact we kill or torture our enemy it is, in a sense, imaginary.[6]

Two pressures doing what they do make a new pressure. The poet is one pressure, the subject is another, and the poem is the thing they are together when they are together. Wind is another example. It is two currents, two pressures *in relation* to each other that create erasure. Weil's preoccupation with physical law after her religious conversion prompted her to see the world in its terms: "Two forces rule the universe: light and gravity."[7] Her understanding of gravity and the spiritual utility she forged from that understanding enacted models for correct action that were based on function, not ideology—for example, the world won't change because it should; the world will change because it must. Wind is another example. It is only years later when the caravan reaches a great absence and names it *valley* that *valley* signifies in the conventional sense.

◊

This is imperative, like gravity. How can one gain deliverance?
How gain deliverance from a force which is like gravity?[8]

The infant life of my child has necessitated a drawing in of self. In the drowse of his first two years, I listened often to the sound of my heart in my ears, listened to it and counted our breaths, in light and dark, waiting for the number when sleep would arrive and I might sneak away. The annihilation that Keats spoke of as essential to the poet exists for me in the body of Benjamin. Urged by the pressure of his immediate and future needs, we moved to Memphis where I was writer-in-residence at Rhodes College. A city known for its two tragic Kings, Memphis is nicknamed Bluff City because it sits on a bluff overlooking the Mississippi River. We lived in an apartment with bars on the window, and as I taught only two hours a week and winter made it hard to be outside, we spent most of our time behind those bars. What happened outside was something I could piece together only from the inside out. As I am internal by nature, my experience of the world has always been mediated by language, words of necessity coming prior to understanding. Now, my sense of self subsumed inside the nonverbal life of my son and my physical existence prescribed by what I could only glimpse between the bars of my apartment, my writing process was made literal. Martin Luther King had been the figure outside the family that I had loved first. His assassination at the Lorraine Motel had done something indelible to the eight-year-old girl I had been. In homage of him, I began a poem called "Bluff City" that year, negotiating the physical and ontological boundaries of inside and out. Within the demands of my child, I heard the demands of the child that I had been asking me to account for her brokenness. Nobody and her son inside a city where the heart—the king who asked all to consider all—was dead, watched the ravaged bodies of his dream steal car after car in their neighborhood that year.

◊

> First, it must be emphasized that nonviolent resistance is not a method for cowards; it does resist...for while the nonviolent resister is passive in the sense that he is not physically aggressive towards his opponent, his mind and emotions are always active, constantly seeking to persuade his opponent that he is wrong...[9]

Just as saintliness is unnatural in the willing mortification of the flesh, and passive resistance is unnatural in its acceptance of pain and death for the betterment of the whole, so I've found there is, in the violation of language's conventions, a wholly unnatural inclusiveness to be accomplished. Weil's life and work are instructive here. At first an ardent communist, she ended her life dismantling language and thus the "empirical self" political movements depend upon. "The effort of expression..." she writes in a letter to Gustav Thibon, "has a bearing not only on the form but on the thought and on the whole inner being..."[10] The essays in what we now know as *Gravity and Grace* emerge via fragments, the fitting "expression" for one intent on delineating a reality invested in self's erasure for the sake of the Whole. Likewise, King's dedication to passive resistance required a nation's replacing the text called Self with the one called Other, still being written. To that end, I tried in "Bluff City" to write toward a constantly emerging center, the poem's insistence on a simultaneity of action from differing points of view, my experiment in passive resistance beginning with the pronoun.

During the year that Benjamin and I lived in Memphis, many of the people who lived in my neighborhood had their houses robbed, their cars stolen. As Christmas approached, the thefts became more daring, occurring in day as well as night until one day a woman coming home from work early, surprised one of the thieves who broke her nose with a pistol and fled with her purse and car. She was white; he was black. It is often a strange and oppressive solidarity that makes a group out of people, and the neighborhood watch group that formed in response to this woman's victimization was no exception. The indeterminate, shifting point of view in "Bluff City" came from Nobody's recognition that the car owners and the car thieves were the two sides of King's failed dream for social autonomy:

No dream possible,

he's back (we're
back), or a version of us
"looking into your window with a knife," or
further
down the street   "back from the army and looking for a
friend..."

Something misnamed,
halted in the weightlifter's   STOP THERE OR I'LL SHOOT
(I'm not kidding)
in the neighborhood's WATCH GROUP
the names, the numbers we exchange.[11]

In Tennessee, it is legal to carry a gun. One night in their fear, the neighborhood watch group held a young black man at gun point; he was stuttering as he tried to explain he was on leave from the army and only trying to visit his friend in the apartment adjoining mine. In the dialogue I overheard that evening, King's idea of the "beloved community" was again failing to become. The passive resistance method vital to the spirit of the civil rights movement, a method "physically passive, but strongly active spiritually,"[12] meant refusing to see the community as either the center or the goal, focusing instead on resistance to those ideas as the vehicle to a new inclusiveness. The neighborhood's watch group failed simply because it gave autonomy to the word *neighborhood*, thereby limiting its possibilities. Method in "Bluff City" is predicated on a commitment to a passive body (i.e., the text which refuses a center, i.e., my self, refusing to be named) in order to keep a promise to the child I'd been and to the child I held in my arms on the floor in an apartment in Memphis. A poetry of social wholeness, in the terms of "Bluff City"

            (meant staying inside)   (a child)
    (inside)   (a nation)[13]

In grammar, parentheses contain that part of the subject that is considered additional, supplementary, and indeed not truly necessary to the sentence. In algebra, parentheses standing side by side multiply reciprocally, all the factors inside them. In trying to find a way to write the interior, which in some crucial way still belonged to the child I'd been, I'd been forced to retrieve her from that part of my mind that had been relegated to the margin. Conversely, in trying to find a way to reach the utopian outside King had proposed, I discovered the charity of proliferation which allowed me both to merge pronouns and to place clusters of words side by side.

In the process of writing "Bluff City" I pored through civil rights documents and found an account of Elizabeth Eckford, one of the "Little Rock Nine," black children who had sought to enter that city's all-white Central High School in 1957. Her action paved the way to the Supreme Court's ruling that made segregation in schools illegal. "She Walked Alone" describes Elizabeth's walk through a screaming white crowd, which included the National Guard, and the two white citizens whose assistance saved her from being hanged.[14] In "Bluff City" Elizabeth works as an extension of the unnamed child who takes various forms in the poem. In depicting her experience, I attempted to grammatically multiply both the military action of the guards and the charitable action of the two good citizens so that the reader is compelled, simply by reading the poem, to witness both forms of action:

    She walked alone.
                    (at the corner)(I tried to pass)
    (through)   (the guards the crowd)   (was quiet)
                    (I tried to squeeze)   (past him)
    (they raised his) (bayonet)   (and they raised their)
                    (bayonets)   (somebody yelling lynch
    and lynch her)   (Drag her to the etc.)
                    (the branch seemed safe to me) (a white lady)
    (very nice)   (put me on the bus)   (a white man)
    (patted my)   (raised my)   (said don't let them
                    see you cry).[15]

Are these impossible claims to stake for language? Perhaps. I believe not. Yet, if they are, the place where I want Benjamin to live lives there. The endeavor acted on the surface of "Bluff City" is ultimately a spiritual endeavor, an *activity* that the reader reading shares:

> I had not begun not believing
>
> > in a center, a self's
>
> or this city's but thinking
>
> > to make one or to find
>
> one or only to find
>
> > one in the making...[16]

◊

The world, all that exists exterior to individual perception, is for a poet such as I, the place I try daily to find. Benjamin's presence demands my renewed commitment to that process. I knew the world was far less than perfect; but before he was born, I tried my best to ignore mere outside reality, thinking, I suppose, that this was the best way to find access to Nobody and the sainthood she promised. Most of the versions of community I see in my life—suburbs, universities, conferences, shopping malls, gardens, museums—fail the truest meaning of that word because they are predicated on a *status quo* which is anathema to the living spirit of the world. The versions of truth and beauty they embody are contained by income brackets, libraries, profession, seasonal changes in style, a fear of the wild, commitment to "Culture." To be honest, I am probably, like Groucho Marx, too self-loathing to be in a club that would want me as a member. I knew I felt this way, and yet I brought Benjamin here. I keep believing that if I continue to experiment with language, I will eventually find the architecture of community I find lacking here.

The structure of the Vietnam Memorial has pointed me toward this version of community, confounding as it does the boundaries of memorial in its architecture *and* emphasis on the memorial seeker—you there, with your walking shoes and tracing paper, searching out a name along a black wall. The Civil Rights Museum is also true to the world in its shape. Constructed in the motel where Martin Luther King, Jr., was killed, the museum begins on the balcony where he was shot, begins at the end of Martin's life, the effect of which immediately calls into question traditional narrative function. In time, we are always in the middle of the story, and being in the middle of the story, we participate with the present and the past simultaneously. The experience of walking in the Civil Rights Museum conflates that sense of time. Its circuitous passageways and walls completely filled with documents of civil crimes create a sense of infinite culpability in American history. Here, the patron must sit in Rosa Parks's seat and hear what the bus driver said to her. There, he must sit next to a plastic model of a young black man in a café, while watching footage of that man having coffee poured over his head in 1961. All the while, recorded voices are reading the debates of civil rights through American history, the cacophony through which I found, on my last day in Memphis, the beloved "outside" at last:

> I hadn't known it would be a motel
> on the edge of Memphis, turning away until he said, no

there,
a wreath over the number,
we were forced by the architecture
to start on the outside,
to start at the end
of Martin's life, the well photographed
balcony leading

> se
> quence of
> a a meta
> morphosis of the
> vis oral cul
> ture and religious
> tradition
> to insure the retaining of an
> a legacy

in nerve, in language on to Rosa's bus
and the inside of his room,
artificial coffee memorialized in black plastic
If there is no struggle there is no
  progress
Am I not a sister[17]

Ø

Creation is composed of the descending movement of gravity, the ascending movement of grace...Moral gravity makes us fall towards the heights...[18]

Music rises from a musical bear while he slowly shrinks in size. It's picnic time for the teddy bears, and all the teddy bears are having a wonderful time today. The barnyard animals are all losing their voices, goodbye moo, goodbye neigh, goodbye cockadoodle doo, goodbye, goodbye. In the pig's pink fur, the single socks, the one-year-old clothes, the missing and continually diminishing pieces of alphabet, what we are to each other, Benjamin, exists in ever-changing increase and breakdown. I arrange the pieces together in your room each night. I will you to see the piecing as whole.

NOTES

1. Simone Weil, *Gravity and Grace*. New York: Putnam, 1952, p. 86.

2. John Keats, *Letters of John Keats*, ed. Robert Gittings. Oxford: Oxford University Press, 1970, p. 157.

3. Weil, *Gravity and Grace*, p. 71.

4. Joanne Grant, ed., *Black Protest: History, Documents and Analysis 1619 to the Present*. New York: Harper and Row, 1968, p. 282.

5. Weil, *Gravity and Grace*, p. 54.

6. Ibid., p. 51.

7. Ibid., p. 45.

8. Ibid., p. 49.

9. Grant, ed., *Black Protest*, p. 288.

10. Weil, *Gravity and Grace*, p. 8.

11. Claudia Keelan, *Utopic*. Farmington, Maine: Alice James Books, 2000, p. 25.

12. Grant, ed., *Black Protest*, p. 281.

13. Keelan, *Utopic*, p. 25.

14. Grant, ed., *Black Protest*, p. 272.

15. Keelan, *Utopic*, p. 27.

16. Ibid., p. 28.

17. Ibid., p. 26.

18. Weil, *Gravity and Grace*, p. 48.

◊

CLAUDIA KEELAN lives in Las Vegas with Donald Revell and Benjamin Brecht Revell, born in 1994. She's published three books, *Refinery* (Cleveland State University Poetry Center, 1994), *The Secularist* (University of Georgia Press, 1997), and *Utopic* (Alice James Books, 2000), which won the Beatrice Hawley Award from Alice James Books. She teaches at University of Nevada, Las Vegas, and edits *Interim*.

Writing *Natural Birth*

Toi Derricotte

I wrote *Natural Birth* when my son was sixteen years old. He was away on an Outward Bound expedition in the mountains of Washington State. It was the first time we had been separated for such an extended time, not even in phone reach, and it brought up some of those initial feelings of wrenching separation when he was born.

I had told no one of the story of my son's birth in a home for unwed mothers, not even my best friend, and especially not my son.

When I was growing up people often faked the date of marriage, moving it three or four months earlier, so that their children wouldn't know they were conceived before their parents were legally married. If there were only a couple of offending months, they said the baby was born prematurely. It was a terrible thing for a girl to "come up pregnant." In those days, 1962, abortions were usually life-threatening, back alley adventures. By the time I found out the name of a doctor, I was too far gone, beyond three months, and he wouldn't do it. It happened to lots of girls, he assured me. I would be all right.

But I had been president of my senior class at Girls' Catholic Central High School. President of the student council. The year before I got pregnant I had been accepted into the Sisters of the Immaculate Heart of Mary and was to be their first black nun. (Years later I learned that their founder was not only a woman of color—Theresa Maxis Duchemin, whose mother was Haitian—but also "illegitimate.") I didn't go, partly because my mother was so firmly against it, but mostly, I think, because I didn't want to give up the pleasures of sex, which I was beginning to enjoy, and the hope of a "soul mate." I was afraid to be alone. Instead of becoming a nun I decided I would be a doctor.

It was a terrible thing, especially, for a black middle-class girl to come up pregnant. Part of the lifelong work of our class and gender was to prove beyond doubt that black people were civilized, not beasts. The rationalization for the horrors inflicted on the bodies of black women during slavery was that they deserved it, wanted it, or were used to it. According to the Cult of True Womanhood in the latter half of the eighteenth century, a good woman was supposed to be modest, domestic, and pure. My mother had seen pictures of black people in cages in her history book in the 1920s in Louisiana. They were called savages. *Woman* meant *white woman*. Black women weren't considered human. How much more impossible was our task?

I married my son's father when I was five months pregnant. He was a painter, a student, barely able to pay his own rent and put food on his table. We lived over a garage for two months, me hiding out, mostly, and, when I did go out, wearing a huge black wool coat in the middle of July so people (I thought) wouldn't know I was pregnant. We were supposed to go away to California, where nobody knew us, and give the baby up for adoption. He was supposed to make enough money to pay the way by doing charcoal portraits on the street and at fairs. I'd wait for him until late at night, but sometimes there wasn't even enough money to buy tomato soup, which I craved, and cans of bonito for sandwiches. Finally, when I was six months, I realized I'd have to make a plan for myself.

I braved the half block to the phone booth on John R, a busy thoroughfare on which I was sure to be recognized, and sorted through the Yellow Pages. The first person I confessed my secret to was the operator at Catholic Charities. After an evaluation by a social worker I was placed on the waiting list of a home for unwed mothers in another city. I had to ask my parents for money—four hundred dollars for room and board, and delivery. I sat on the floor of my mother's living room like a child. My mother, who had done everything to ensure that I would be an independent woman, comfortable and safe, wept.

I went to Kalamazoo, Michigan, on a train at 6:00 A.M., like so many young girls who left to visit relatives for a few months and then came back, as if nothing had happened, to be cheerleaders in high school. Many of these girls were blindfolded during birth in order to prevent bonding with their babies. I went a hundred miles from home into a pocket of experience that I kept hidden inside me for sixteen years, in some protected space between consciousness and unconsciousness, repressing it, hating it, and yet defending it by remembering, preserving every detail. I understood, a little at a time, that there was something to be said on behalf of all women, that repression had done terrible things to us, disconnecting us from feeling, from normal pleasure and its outward manifestation from our own children.

What if my baby knew I was such an imperfect mother? That he wasn't wanted from the moment he was conceived, that he hadn't been planned for, that it was not like a Hallmark card? For much of my pregnancy I had felt nothing but shame, guilt, anger, and depression. At the birth I felt numb, disconnected. If my son knew, would he feel unloved, unworthy? Would he feel it was his fault?

Some women have said to me, "What's the big deal? You got married." To many it seemed all right if the father wanted you, as if the real shame was not being pregnant, but being alone. I never understood that thinking. For if you had done "it" before you were married, and if it became obvious because you got "caught," then what did it matter if you quickly put on a ring? You still had given in, been weak, or made a choice expressing will and desire, a course even more grievously wrong, a mortal sin. Perhaps pregnancy was evidence even in women who had been safely married for years, evidence of a secret life, emptiness, a hole that should be neatly covered up. The most perfect mother was the Virgin Mary. It wasn't that I wanted to get rid of the baby, but that I couldn't tell where my shame ended and his life began.

It was as if my body betrayed me, became evidence against me. The flesh and bones pressed out "showing" what I so wanted to hide, my sexuality, and, mostly, my own helplessness and vulnerability. I was the daughter of a man who taught me, *Never show your fear*, and, about dogs, *They can smell it*. When he'd beat me, he'd say, "Wipe that look off your face or I'll knock it off," meaning anger, and even pain. I had been apprenticed in not showing for nineteen years. What could be more disruptive of the self I had constructed in great peril? What could be more alarming than this "showing" I couldn't stop, couldn't "wipe off"?

Two things happened that finally pushed me to speak. First, as I said, my son was away on an Outward Bound trip, and I think this signaled his independence. I felt he would be strong enough to hear the truth and bear it. Second, I read an article in *Ms.* magazine by author Catherine Breslin about a nun who, not knowing she was pregnant, had committed infanticide at the birth of the child. She had put a stocking around the newborn's neck, choked him, and left his body in the wastebasket. The principal of a Montessori school, she was pregnant and no one had noticed. At her trial, she said:

> I know it matters if I'm convicted, but I've already imprisoned myself in my mind and heart. I'm imprisoned because I can't escape from my thoughts. I want to know if I harmed the child. I know I must have, because I was the only one there.

The compassion I felt for her allowed me to see my experience in a different context. It connected me to feelings of sadness and rage that I had been unable to access before.

I wrote a poem about the nun and sent it to Ms. Breslin. She sent me back transcripts of the trial. Reading them, I made an eerie discovery: some of the details I used to describe the birth scene in the poem were remarkably like the description of the actual birth in the nun's testimony. One afternoon, tears in my eyes, I began a letter to Ms. Breslin, a stranger so removed from my circle of friends that I could confess without fear. She was the one person I trusted to understand.

As I was writing the letter the words started to take on another shape, a life of their own. They poured down the page, and I began to move my lips, as if a wind was coming out of me, playing my teeth and tongue like an instrument. I found myself writing a poem, in joy, and wrote for hours the birth section of *Natural Birth,* twenty-three pages. It was as if the words had been there all the time, for sixteen years, stored in the jar of my head, waiting for the right moment, the "inspiration," to release them. Memory was there, and feeling, reawakened. These demanded language. I knew then that the story of my son's birth would be written.

The long, difficult labor by which the book was "delivered"—not only the remembering of the experience, but the "transition," the shaping of it into art, which took years and hadn't, then, even begun yet—was the other natural birth that the book was named for. I meant it as irony, for so often the word *natural* implies a simple and uncomplicated state. For example, there were those who called Louis Armstrong a natural musician, implying, pejoratively, that he played in an instinctual, unlearned, or unsophisticated manner. Women read books about birth that made natural and painless synonymous, so that many went into labor believing (or hoping?) that if they just breathed as they had been taught, they wouldn't have pain. They were presented with images of women who, awake and free of drugs, had powerful "bonding" experiences at birth—a sudden rush of unequivocal love for their child. Having this feeling of love at the birth of your child was also presented as natural. Natural not only defined the way things were, but the way things should be—as I say in the book, what was "beautiful and right and good."

Ironically, the very options that were supposed to liberate women by encouraging them to take control of their bodies and not depend on doctors and drugs ended up dictating another kind of unrealistic ideal. Afterwards, many whose labors and deliveries hadn't matched the experiences of the women they had read about felt that they had done something wrong or, perhaps, something was wrong with them—that they or their feelings weren't natural. Shame and guilt silenced them.

By showing one woman's experience, which so diverged from the ideal, and yet which, in the end, I believe, does testify to the power of nature and love, I hoped to revise the revision of natural birth that had been attempted by those theories in the fifties and sixties. I wanted my natural birth to hold on to the mystery and power of that singular rite of passage, at the same time it stripped away the romantic and ideal. I wanted to imply that all creative acts, whether it is giving birth to a child, a work of art, or the self, are unique, arduous, and awe-full.

Aleksandro Solzhenitsyn, when he was in prison, had no paper or pen, so each day he took a match and put it to the side. Each match signified a page of his writing. When he was released, he wrote the five hundred pages of *The Gulag Archipelago* from these "notes." I always remembered this story, for it illustrated to me the mind's power to preserve significant experience until it can be told. Sometimes a story will be forgotten or buried for years, even for generations. Sometimes, in order to store and protect a story, the mind has to create a symbol, as Solzhenitsyn did with the matches. The meaning of the symbols may be forgotten, but they appear in our dreams, in our fears and obsessions. Eventually, when it is safe, the mind begins to unbury what it has hidden. Scientists have said that the most important purpose of human life is to pass it on, that we are no more than the carriers of genetic code. A writer could say that our most important purpose is to be carriers of memory.

Each day for a month, while my son was gone, I sat down and wrote a section of the book. The memories came backwards, so I started at the end of the book and worked forward, writing the first section last, moving from "Delivery" to "November." Some say women forget everything. I know it's not true, for I remembered every detail of feeling.

The manuscript spent several years in a drawer, buried by another kind of silence. When I wrote it, I couldn't figure out what it was, prose or poetry. I worked on it for months, both deleting the secrets I still didn't want my son to know, and trying to make it look "right." When I cut it, however, and made it look more like a "poem," I killed the life— maybe exactly the way we kill the things we love when we are made to feel ashamed and guilty. What I learned is that a poem is a living thing, and, like any living thing, we have to accept what we are given. Only then can we work with it and transform it into something beautiful. After this awareness came, I worked on the manuscript another two years before I sent it out.

I wasn't the only one in consternation about the shape of *Natural Birth*. Toni Morrison, then an editor at Random House, kept the manuscript for nine months (another pregnancy), hoping to publish it. Finally she wrote back: "It doesn't fit in our categories; we don't know where to put it."

I went to Womanbooks in New York, one of the first women's bookstores in the country, where I had heard that Adrienne Rich spent several months sitting on the floor between bookshelves, reading and studying while she wrote *Of Woman Born*. I looked through hundreds of books seeking a press and an editor who might be sympathetic to my book, who might understand (with its strange body) what *Natural Birth* was. Finally, I chose The Crossing Press, whose editor, Nancy Bereano, became a friend and supporter through these seventeen years since the book's publication and, at whose behest as publisher and editor of Firebrand Books, *Natural Birth* was republished.

My son is thirty-eight. It has been almost two decades since I wrote the book. Once, about five years ago, I read several sections to patients who are chronically ill and live at a residential hospital, Goldwater, in New York City. Through a program that poet Sharon Olds has established, poets come to teach, to do workshops and readings. One man couldn't speak. He had a kind of fixture on his head like a coal miner's lamp, and when he aimed it at symbols on a board, his words emerged in a strange mechanical voice. However, he could make guttural sounds, and, as I was reading *Natural Birth*, sounds came out of his throat, call and response, a kind of harmony both against and with my words. A running glissando.

Though I was saying the words, I was not "feeling" them. I had forgotten the feelings I had had when I wrote them, which were not exactly the feelings I had had at the birth itself. Rather, they were feelings that somehow compressed the birth feelings with the feelings of sorrow and compassion I had finally reached, enabling me to write the poem sixteen years later. I was saying the words, but I felt almost nothing. The sounds of the words must have reached the man's ears and given *him* a feeling, for he made sounds back. When the sounds he made reached my ears, they gave me a feeling. In fact, the same feelings I had had when I was writing the original text. Though there was a millisecond delay between my speaking and the instant when his sounds reached me—like an echo— I felt as if I was sitting at that table many years before, writing.

This was the very first time that I understood the power of a poem. That the poet constructs a container for words and sounds that then takes on its own life, having an energy completely independent of her. That that container, so perfectly fitted to hold her particular thoughts and feelings, has the ability to reach someone, a listener, and convey some aspect of the human experience the writer herself may have forgotten, or of which, at the moment, she is unaware. The writer, who has struggled so hard to be "seen," to make her deeply felt thoughts and feelings relevant, in some way becomes irrelevant.

And this is the paradoxical triumph: because the writing must convey without her and in spite of her. The better the writing is, the more irrelevant she becomes. Yet those same words reflect back to her, having the power to make her, too, as a listener, connect with what it is to be human. It amazes me that as separate and unique as our interior worlds are there are moments when—and this is what a poem can do—it seems we have company in our skins, that we are almost in the same space with another person, sharing our deepest realities, and that they understand.

Perhaps art can revisit the wounds of the past and, if not heal them, at least send us back with the reader as witness. In that moment at Goldwater, reading *Natural Birth*, I felt the loneliness of the woman in labor and the loneliness of the poet on her solitary journey to the poem, but I was not alone.

I hope this essay speaks to the complicated ways we love, bringing our own fears and wounds into the bargain. Perhaps our children choose us, ask for us before they are born in their desire to confront whatever we have not been able to move beyond, to take up our burden of love and move us one step closer. Perhaps we are the only ones who hold that possibility for them.

What was my son's reaction?

I gave him the manuscript when he was nineteen, the same age I was when I got pregnant. It had already been accepted for publication, and he knew nothing of the story of his birth. He took it up to his bedroom and read half of it, then came back down. "I can't read all of it in one sitting," he said. A few days later he finished. I was afraid my son's reaction would confirm my worst fears: the reason I had kept silent all those years was so that he wouldn't feel unlovable. Instead, he said, "Mom, I didn't know you had suffered so much."

Once, when I was cutting my son's very curly hair, I had apologized. "Oh, I'm sorry, Tony. I made a really bad cut." "That's okay, Mom, don't worry," he reassured me, "I have very pardoning hair."

Natural Birth was dedicated to my son, a wise and compassionate man whose labor of giving birth to himself is partly the labor of giving birth to his imperfect mother.

◊

TOI DERRICOTTE, born in Detroit, Michigan, has published four books of poetry and a memoir. Her latest book, *Tender* (University of Pittsburgh Press, 1997), received the Paterson Poetry Prize in 1998. Her memoir, *The Black Notebooks* (W.W. Norton & Company, 1997), was chosen by the *New York Times* to be a notable book of the year. Her second book, *Natural Birth*, was republished by Firebrand Press in February 2000. She is a professor in the English department at the University of Pittsburgh. She is cofounder of Cave Canem, the historic workshop retreat for African American poets. Derricotte lives alone in Pittsburgh, is the mother of Anthony, who was born in 1962, and has two grandchildren.

Emergence

Carolyn Forché | February 1999

> *Infancy is what is eternal, and the rest, all the rest*
> *is brevity, extreme brevity.*
> —Antonio Porchia[1]

> *Inspiration is not the granting of a secret or of words to*
> *someone already existing: it is the granting of existence to*
> *someone who does not yet exist.*
> —Maurice Blanchot[2]

I was five months pregnant with my first and only child when we arrived in Johannesburg for what was to have been two years. It was summer in the southern hemisphere, the sky poached by sun and fog, and my first impression was such that in letters home we would describe this place as a "California with slavery." We had come to document apartheid in photographs and text. Officially, my husband would work at the *Time* bureau, and I would accompany him as wife and expectant mother.

For a brief time, I was able to work with the Soweto parents of detained children, who wanted information about international human rights organizations. Without the necessary police permits which were impossible to obtain, we were nevertheless able to enter townships and homelands, led by churchworkers who knew how to avoid police roadblocks, and as my womb swelled, I also grew invisible, no longer attracting police who would not wish to involve themselves with so pregnant a white woman. My husband concealed his cameras, passing me the exposed film to keep under my maternity dress. The images produced from this film would not often appear in the press, however, as the media tacitly respected much of South Africa's ban on "visual documentation of unrest." Those who defied this ban found their employees deported, or unable to renew their visas, as would eventually happen to us. These were the last years of apartheid, as destiny would disclose, and South Africa was living under what was then called a "state of emergency."

"Emerge," I wrote, "emergence: to rise, to come into the light, to rise up out of a liquid in which the subject has been submerged."

My notebooks filled, as they had in other parts of the world: vignettes, aperçus, bits of utterance. There was world and paper, and each could cross the surface of the other, marking it lightly but indelibly. Writing was my way of knowing what was for me otherwise unknowable, and like Ryszard Kapuscinski whom I admired, I preferred to work "in the forest of things, on foot, in the world," which I hoped to participate in, rather than experience.

There was never a question of my giving birth in apartheid South Africa. The plan had been to drive overland to Zimbabwe when the time came. I'm not sure why I hadn't anticipated the arduousness of such a journey, nor recognized the risks incurred by a thirty-five-year-old "elderly *prima gravida*," electing to receive her prenatal care from obstetricians on three continents, but I had not yet experienced the sea-change of motherhood, holding rather to an image of life continuing much as it was, but with a sleeping baby tied to my back.

Suppressed perhaps were the labors of my childhood as the eldest daughter of seven, tri-folding clouds of diapers, running bed linens through the mangle, stirring Catholic school uniform shirts in pots of starch. Lost were the babies' cries, the slow-thickening puddings and white sauce, mounds of socks to be matched and toddlers watched never closely enough. Left behind me, Saturday mornings scrubbing foyer and bath tiles with Fels Naptha, taking pails of oil soap to the rows of wooden dining chairs. I made lunch for the "little ones" when I was six, and by seven baked my first loaf of bread. So standing evenings at the open window over foaming dishes I began subliminally to narrate a bearable selfhood. During endless hours of menial work, I spoke to God, who surrounded me, then to voices in books, and finally to fields and sky, where a presence was. Writing, I thought, formed itself elsewhere and passed through me, coming out of my hands. It was mysterious and foreign, but the experience of its making could not be compared to anything else. In the act of writing, there was heightened being, which could be remembered as ecstatic. There was, first, what could be said, and later, the way of saying, which was superior to the said.

My mother and I shared the arduous work of caring for the six children she bore in the ten years after my birth. She would bring the newborns home, wrapped in delicate "receiving" blankets, and I would steal into the darkness of my parents' room to gaze at a new one asleep in the straw bassinet, pale-haired and fragile, having made an arduous journey from God's world. My mother was almost a child herself when she began, or so it seems to me now. For reasons that can never be disclosed, she was perhaps ill-prepared for her brood: she had *wanted* many children, but had pictured us all as sleeping infants, wingless, perfect, and from heaven. She made ok novenas to the Mother of God, sang to us, wept, took to her bed and told us we would understand when we were grown. At night, while I read and wrote by flashlight under my blankets, I heard the clacking of her Royal manual typewriter, and eventually discovered the silvery Christmas box of her poems and stories, some clipped from newspapers, hidden in her mysterious closet among evening clothes no longer worn.

"Join the convent," she would advise me above the din during some shared task or another. So it was not as if I hadn't known.

◊

We left South Africa precipitously on March 17, 1986, a month to the day before my son was born because, among other reasons, we had broken unjust laws, and I was afraid to risk giving birth in jail. Specifically, we were accused of violating the restrictive "Group Areas Act" by having black houseguests, and it was suspected that we were also disseminating "images of unrest" to the outside world. Our arrest, fervently desired by our "Rhodesian" landlady, was considered by our lawyers unlikely but possible.

We left behind the tag-sale furniture we'd assembled into a serviceable household, including the straw cradle with its bridal mosquito net. In my hurry I left some of my notebooks, but these contained indecipherable drafts of poems and so would pose a problem for no one. I don't know if those lines will return to me in a patient hour, but the cradle appeared often for a time in my dreams.

I remember not feeling certain we were safe until the wheels were tucked into the belly of the plane. My son leapt and fluttered through the night. I wrote notes toward poems as we refueled in Madagascar, notes that had become, I thought, a substitute for what I had once considered "finished poems." We were en route to Paris, and as this was the last day of my pregnancy when I would be accepted as a passenger on a commercial carrier, my son would be born there. A French photographer, Gilles Peress, had offered us his place, as he would be returning to document "the Troubles" in Northern Ireland, and would not return to Paris again for some time.

So it was that we lived for a year at 11 rue Schoelcher, in an atelier identical to Simone de Beauvoir's, who lived beside us at 11 bis. until her death that April. The two-story windows opened on a luminous fresco of clouds, and from the little *loggia*, it was possible to gaze out over the graves in the cemetery of Montparnasse. In the armoire, there were books, and little paper soldiers fighting the Franco-Prussian war. At the farm-table, I translated the poet Robert Desnos, many afternoons alone with the windows open, conjugating the *future perfect*, ivy shivering on the cemetery walls, waiting for the infant to come, a Desnos line revealing itself, and I thought: *how is it possible that I am living here*, as if a childhood dream had found an empty theatre in which to mount a small production of its hopes?

By proclivity and circumstance, I had in recent years often been in countries shattered by suffering and war. Why? I might have asked, or well might have, anticipating the birth of a child. Men and women came into my life, offering to teach me things I could not otherwise learn, and I said *yes* out of curiosity, ignorance, a need to please, and a desire to obey God, for whom language had first come, in the form of spontaneous prayer-songs spoken when I thought no one listening.

During my childhood, the stars were more thickly clustered, and they whispered. I was not by myself often, but when I was, sometimes felt that my "self" opened and left, remaining nearby as the phrase would have us imagine. If I were in the house at those times, the furniture swelled toward me or diminished as if moving away, accompanied by a crescendo of air against glass, my own breath, some mysterious hum of world. This was a state my sister also experienced, and it terrified us both. I would later understand that objects remain where they are, and space dilates between them as time passes. If I were outside, however, in the woods or fields behind the house, this was not so disturbing, perhaps because one does not expect fixity in nature. God was there.

Despite the efforts of the Sisters of St. Dominic, Order of Preachers, to promote the idea of a carceral earth and a juridical cosmos, I imagined rather that the earth was a school, and that humans and other life forms were *already* burning, as light issued visibly from them, and the world, if saved at all, would be saved entire. If this were so, there was work to be done, and I hoped to comport myself well enough that God would give instructions in a form I could understand. Such was my spiritual pridefulness that I appended a request that this instruction not be given by an apparition, which would surely frighten me to death. After many years in the labyrinth of such expectations, it quite circuitously became clear to me that my instructions were to say *yes*.

Until now, until Paris, this *yes* had entailed what I *thought* had been an acceptance of mortality, a willingness to forego self-protection as circumstances required, and a faith in the luminous web of souls dedicated to what may have been simplistically conceived as a teleological endeavor. However, I was now an expectant mother, and what I imagined I was doing was about to change, utterly and for my ever, not in increments but as a whole, not by extension but in essence. This would also happen to my "work," a place-holding term for the labor of nurturing the self-propagation of language.

One writes inescapably out of one's obsessions—linguistic, philosophical, formal, cosmological. During my formative years as a poet (and in my educational milieu), "form" was regarded as a container rather than a force, examined for its features and flaws rather than the consequences of its use. The poem was, as Charles Simic once put it, "an antique pinball machine with metaphors instead of balls." It was to be read as expressive of the sensibility of the poet, whose "voice" it conjured, and as an unparaphrasable utterance of complex figural interplay and patterned sound. The reader installed herself in this poem, reading analytically or "closely," so as to discern the intricacies of its making, rather as a watchmaker approaches the works with spring-pin tool and dust-brush. Thus machined, the poem was regarded as a species of discourse, to be valued for itself and for its utility as communicator of feeling and thought.

My first two published poetry books were written during my teens and twenties, in the mode of the first-person, free-verse lyric, a writing which seemed to me very much to corroborate *le monde vécu*, the lived world. I thought of words as the crystalline precipitate of conscious attention: particular, precise, and resonant with as much "poetic" euphony as I could "hear." At first, mother's college English textbook provided models, and I wrote mostly rhymed quatrains in unvaried iambic pentameter. Later, the nuns assigned the writing of "paragraphs," and after a demonstration which persuaded them that I had not been plagiarizing from an unknown source, permitted me to dispense with the topic-sentence/body/conclusion format, whereupon I wrote elaborate descriptions of natural phenomena. In early adolescence, I was startled to read lined free verse for the first time, which I did not understand but tried to imitate with disappointing results. There were some years of this. When my first book, *Gathering the Tribes*, was chosen for the Yale Prize,

I received a letter from its judge, Stanley Kunitz, asking about my poetics, and as I was unaware of *having* a poetics, I wrote of my upbringing, and in response to questions regarding influences, named my mother and grandmother.

In my twenties, God's presence receded, and even the radiant and shivering poplars of my childhood achieved apparent visual stability. The world changed and changed again. I had been translating Salvadoran poet Claribel Alegría, because I was her daughter's friend, and because she was an older woman poet whose work had not yet appeared in English. So it was that when her nephew, Leonel Gomez Vides, appeared at my door for an unexpected three-day visit, I invited him in, whereupon he invited me to spend my Guggenheim year in El Salvador, then still at "peace," a euphemism for the silence of misery endured. I became what was later called a human rights worker, and this work partially informed my second book, *The Country Between Us*, written feverishly but without the remotest sense of its "political" character or utility. Critical reception in the United States was unexpectedly intense and mixed, but my focus was then on the collective work of building a network opposed to military intervention in Central America. Toward that end, I traveled through the United States for three years; later, human rights work would bring me to Northern Ireland, Israel, the West Bank, Lebanon, and South Africa. During that time, I didn't focus on poetics as such, but not for lack of interest.

The safe harbor of France was where my intellectual and poetical life resumed. We lived in that small, sparsely furnished atelier in a manner more conducive to work than I had ever previously known. Wind carried the scent of narcissus from the graves to our open casements. Mornings the knife-sharpener cried up from the street, and like the other women, I raced out to have the kitchen knives honed. Our supply of milk and cheese was kept for a time on the sill, to the amusement of our *quartier*, until we bought a small refrigerator. Daily I wheeled my basket to rue Daguerre market, where I bought unfamiliar species of fish, seasonal fruits and vegetables, aged cheese, young wines, and such things as I have never managed to replace: hard Normandy cider, fresh lavender from Grasse. My command of French was still provisional, however, and I once mistakenly tried to buy two and a half kilos of parsley, to the amusement of *le commerçant*.

Aside from domestic pursuits, I spent my days writing and reading (in those days Martin Buber, Emmanuel Lévinas, Jean-François Lyotard, Philippe Lacoue-Labarthes, Paul Celan, Francis Ponge, and Edmond Jabès), while translating Desnos, because I thought this effort would revive and improve my French. On the day before my delivery I completed the work, discovering on the final page some lines I had inscribed in a notebook during my first trip to Paris in 1977, and thus finding a poet for whom I had searched in the intervening years:

J'ai revé tellement fort de toi
J'ai tellement marché, tellement parlé
Tellement aimé ton ombre
Qu'il ne me reste plus rien de toi,
Il me reste d'etre l'ombre parmi les ombres
D'etre cent fois plus ombre que l'ombre
D'etre l'ombre qui viendra et reviendra
              dans ta vie ensoleillée

[I have dreamed so strongly of you
I have walked so much, talked so much
So much I have loved your shadow
That there now remains for me nothing more of you,
It remains with me to be a shadow among shadows
To be a hundred times darker than the darkness
To be the shadow that will come and come again
              into your sun-blessed life.][3]

The discovery seemed magical and auspicious, and the next morning my labor began, so lightly that I did not at first realize what it was, and regretted my life-long fear.

After twenty-six hours, my son was delivered by cesarean, something I had not anticipated, but that my husband and the doctor had known was likely for weeks. I chose to be awake. I remember surgical lights, instructions in French, the intelligence of the eyes above the masks, a pressure, a sense of being pulled apart without pain, and then a weakening, more oxygen, a rapid exchange among the physicians, then my son held above me, silent and white then suddenly rosy and crying. For a moment, they let me hold him, and when he heard my voice the crying stopped. "He knows who this is," my husband said. I told him that I was his mother, and that everything would be all right. A day later I was given an emergency transfusion of two liters of whole blood. For some reason still unknown to the hematologists, I had stopped making red cells after the birth. There were tense hours, waiting for my body to begin its necessary work again. My son was beside me in an incubator, quiet, alert. I was utterly there, and when I came back I was still there, in a small hospital in Paris with the windows open.

We called him Sean-Christophe, this little one, this Other, who now called me to responsibility, and whom I could neither evade, comprehend, nor possess as a *knowledge*. "The child lives," Martin Buber wrote, "between sleep and sleep…in the lightning and counter-lightning of encounter." With him I experienced a radiant interdependence of sensation and thought; he was of me but he was not "mine." He was as yet "unknown" to me, even though the egg that had contributed life to him had been with me since my own birth.

On paper in the following months, the "I" of my previous writing receded, having become an emptiness, replaced by a polyphonic and Schoenbergian symphony of cacophonous utterance. Absent this "I," whose selfhood the poems formerly served, words became material and translucent, no longer transparently communicative of the sensibility I no longer possessed. This movement did not entail a repudiation, but was marked by a radical sense of unfamiliarity. Each page began *mis en question*: white, open, each word in all its plenitude marked the site of a wound. Anxious at first, I returned to my notebooks filled with "notes toward poems," and discovered nascent versions of the same phenomenon. These were not notes but the work itself, begun during my pregnancy, and without my conscious collaboration.

This was a work happening *with* me that was not *about* me, having to do with attention rather than intention, a work that would eventually disclose itself as self-altering rather than self-expressive. Rather than writing discrete (individual) poems from beginning to end, and passing them through a sieve of revisionary practice, I found myself attending to the work's assemblage, aware that I was creating a reading space to be explored rather than received, but in the manner of one caught in a web of consequence. The historical density of the language seemed to limit its play of signification, as the cry of suffering remains a cry. This poetry did not have the function of recording or representing, but rather of attending to the making of its utterance.

The poems I had previously written now seemed the graveyard of possibilities. Tedium had taught me to narrate a self-in-the-world to relieve tedium. *Writing*, older than glass, younger than music, was no longer for me merely the guardian of the past, but a way into the open and the future. During the milk-hours of earliest morning, my son nursed beside the two-story windows filled with cloud islands of a forming world. He seemed to see something I did not see. The ancients thought that light traveled from the eye to the world and this seemed so with him. He was at the gates of language, where only the invisible is obvious. Or so it seems to me now.

NOTES

1. Antonio Porchia, *Voices: Aphorisms*, trans. W.S. Merwin. Chicago: Big Table Books, 1969, p. 11.

2. Maurice Blanchot, *The Space of Literature: A Translation of L'Espace Litteraire*, trans. Ann Smock. Lincoln: University of Nebraska Press, 1989, p. 227.

3. Robert Desnos, *The Selected Poems of Robert Desnos*, trans. Carolyn Forché and William Kulik. Hopewell, New Jersey: The Ecco Press, 1991, p. xii.

◊

CAROLYN FORCHÉ's most recent book is *Blue Hour* (HarperCollins, 2003). She has published three previous volumes, *Gathering the Tribes* (Yale University Press, 1976), winner of the Yale Younger Poets Award in 1976; *The Country Between Us* (HarperCollins, 1987), winner of the Lamont Prize of the Academy of American Poets in 1981; and *The Angel of History* (HarperCollins, 1994), winner of the Los Angeles Times Book Award in 1995. She has also edited *Against Forgetting: Twentieth Century Poetry of Witness* (W.W. Norton & Company, 1994). She received the Edita and Ira Morris Hiroshima Foundation Award for Peace and Culture from Stockholm, Sweden, in 1998. She lives with her husband, photographer Harry Mattison, and their son, Sean-Christophe, born in 1986, in Bethesda, Maryland, and teaches in the MFA program at George Mason University.

Part Two

Ob (lit) eration:
Genre and Representation

The Other Sylvia Plath

Eavan Boland

In 1952, Randall Jarrell published an essay called "The Other Robert Frost." In it, he put before the reader the dark and layered vision—"the bare sorrow"[1] as he called it—of Frost's best poems, thus helping to shift the perception that he was a facile, one-note lyricist. This essay is named for that one, in recognition of Jarrell's commitment to the deception and complication of a poet's achievement. And even more, in honor of Sylvia Plath's complex, radical poems of motherhood.

◊

In the decade following the English publication of *Ariel*, a critical response to Plath's work was formed in articles and essays. Most of it shared two characteristics that still haunt the transmission of her work. Her early critics refused to consider the poems separately from her suicide. And most of them glued the poems of the *Ariel* volume to the poet-image of Plath in the last three months of her life. These small critical detours led to an enormous navigational error.

But if the horizon had stretched back another twelve weeks, something else might have happened. That desperate woman in a London flat, exhausted by weather and hard-to-get child care, might have shimmered and dissolved into something else: into a poet and mother under the big stars of southwest England, in a beautiful October, almost able to hear her children breathing. A poet who, for all the shock and distress of her situation, was trying hopeful, daring things in language. "I am writing the best poems of my life, they will make my name," she wrote in a letter during this month.[2] A poet who, together with the poems of public rhetoric and gesture she wrote during these weeks—such as "Lady Lazarus" and "Daddy"—was also testing out a powerful language in poems like "Nick and the Candlestick," "The Night Dances," and "By Candlelight." And who, in these private and path-breaking poems of motherhood, changed the nature poem—its horizons and the location of its speaker and its inherited landscape. The writer of these October nature poems is not as convenient to myth-making as the distraught and self-destructive sibyl. Even now, Plath's legend refuses to allow the second version to complete the first. But this is the poet I have loved and admired. This is the other Plath.

◊

I was eighteen when Plath died. She was then twelve years older than I. I say *then* because I am now in my fifties, time has moved on, and yet she has remained that gifted, changeless, broken young woman of thirty.

That winter became notorious. She died at the bitter end of it, literally—in those first few days of February when snowdrops are already out and when the first crocuses are beginning to show their purples and orange-yellows at the roadsides. It was a freakish and unexpected season. I was in my first year of university in Dublin. By November a smoky frost was refusing to clear even by noon. At night the railings around Stephen's Green were like birthday party ice-trays—a tearing cold on the fingertips.

But October was beautiful and unusual. The customary humid pre-winter distances disappeared. The air was glittery and defined; it was clear and bitter. The rain held off.

October of 1962 was the last month Plath spent at Court Green, the house in Devon she and Ted Hughes had bought the previous year. Her son had been born there; her marriage had faltered there. Now she was packing, sheeting, and closing it to go to London. In the small village of North Tawton, five hours from London and an hour from the Atlantic coast of England, she began the poems that would become *Ariel*.

In some ways Court Green was a liability—big, unheated, and with no radiators. In the downstairs rooms, so her letters say, the temperature was thirty-eight degrees. The windows would have opened back into the fog of those orchards—"a thick, gray death-soup" as she called it in "Letter in November."[3]

But in that beautiful October there must also have been winning aspects. White fields in the morning. Windfalls gleaming through mist. Huge stars at night. The first winter of her baby boy Nick. "In a forest of frost, in a dawn of cornflowers," she wrote at the end of "Poppies in October."[4]

The extraordinary energies she tapped into in this month led her to write "By Candlelight" on October 24th, "Nick and the Candlestick" on the 28th, and just a few days into the next month, "Night Dances." Ten days at most separate these poems. They are as intense as any cluster of lyrics in *Ariel*. They have a common vocabulary and a shared strength. In her BBC broadcast in the following month she spoke with unusual directness of her strategy and purpose. "A mother nurses her baby son by candlelight," she said, "and finds in him a beauty which, while it may not ward off the world's ill, does redeem her share of it."[5]

As a reader, I often return there: to that creaking wintry house, to the estrangement of this young woman in a place that was not her own, looking for words that were. Here if anywhere it is appropriate to ask the question: What is it that changes when a woman poet becomes a mother? What is it that alters, shifts, turns the poem around? The answer must be—and Plath's poems are the model for this—that suddenly the nature poem opens to her: suddenly this poem defined by history, withheld by custom, is hers. All hers.

◊

The nature poem. So inscribed, so written, so set into the tradition of poetry that it can look like an arcane code. In fact, the nature poem is volatile, an accurate register of cultural and historic change. It may be too easy to say that before the Industrial Revolution it was a pastoral poem, and after it a pessimistic one, nevertheless it has always been right there, in the center of the action. Like so many other poetic conventions, it has its roots in deeply human things. Change those things, alter that angle of inscription, and the roots will give, will shift, will be ready to be put somewhere else.

I believe Plath—the other Plath—changed the nature poem. She shifted its course. She redirected its historic energy. *Ariel* may seem a slim text to argue this with. Then again, many of the shape-changing texts of nature poetry—whether "The Lyrical Ballads" or "North of Boston"—are modest and apparently unimposing single volumes: unimposing, that is, until you read them.

The tradition of nature poetry is baggy, vast, hard to collect in one place: no definition will put all of it in context. In its sober discussion, *The New Princeton Encyclopedia of Poetry and Poetics* registers the swerves and changes of nature poets as well as poems:

> They strongly feared—(this about the Romantic poets)—that men merely read meaning into a deterministic and meaningless world.[6]

Of Eliot and Crane:

> The typical nature of 20th century poetry is that of T.S. Eliot's "The Waste Land" and Hart Crane's "The Bridge" where the natural—and human—world is conceived as shattered, fragmentary, painful.[7]

These words offer a clue, if not a proof. Traditionally, most nature poems share a common feature: they are written by poets willing to be instructed by nature—whether in pessimism and dark apprehension like Frost, or ethical direction like Wordsworth. The nature poem—Lowell's "Skunk Hour" is an example—is therefore an account, not so much of nature, but of the instruction set.

Plath changed this. As the moon rises over a baby boy, as the stars plummet, as a blue light wanders to the window and then retreats, as colors blur and glitter, the landscape shifts and changes. The instruction set shifts as well. This is not a poet being instructed by nature. This is a poet instructing nature. How did this happen? Plath was a shrewd, gifted, and obdurate crafter of poems. But she was not theoretical and her aesthetic sense was instinctive. How did she come upon this radical, swift strategy that made these beautiful, shape-changing diagrams of the nature poem? *How?*

Years ago I interviewed John Ashbery for the *Irish Times*. He was reading in a small market town to the south of Dublin and it took me about an hour to drive down. It was a drizzling, shimmering spring afternoon. Many of his answers about his work and his aesthetic were eloquent. One in particular stuck with me for years. I asked him whether he was a surrealist, and he told me that he himself had asked the French poet Henri Michaux the very same question. No, Michaux replied, he was not a surrealist. But, for him, surrealism had been *le grand permission*.

Le grand permission. I believe this is exactly what Plath found in these poems that kept crowding into her last October. Her motherhood gave her a sense at last of her nature; her nature gave her a sense of active participation in the power and mystery of times, seasons, arrivals; her powerful, luminous sense of participation made her shift the speaker's historic location in the nature poem. No longer, in her version of the nature poem, was the poet instructed by nature. In these few lines, in these few poems, the speaker *is* nature.

◊

Plath wrote "By Candlelight" on October 24, 1962, the day before her birthday. The next day she would be thirty. It is the least compelling of the three poems: some of the cartoonish language of her early work is still in evidence. The internal rhymes are crude, the cadences are thrown-off and choppy, But there is an exhilarating freedom as well: if this is a cartoon, then it points toward a bigger, more somber work.

The scene is a nursery room at night—full of shadows and bells, with a candlestick near the cot. "The candlestick was a small brass image of Hercules," wrote Hughes in the notes to the *The Collected Poems*, "in his lion's pelt, kneeling under the candle. Behind his heels five brass balls completed the design."[8]

But if the language is occasionally uncertain, the stance of nature poet is anything but. This is a speaker with a new kind of control: able to command the natural world because she herself is generative of it. As a mother with her child—at the very center of that world—she can speak about seasons and times with a new freedom and invention. Here is a female Prospero, speaking from her shipwrecked island, never doubting that the elements will obey her. Where other nature poets have labored for accuracy, or imitation, or even awe, she will have none of it. This nature poem is an act of power, not deference:

> This is winter, this is night, small love—
> A sort of black horsehair,
> A rough, dumb country stuff
> Steeled with the sheen
> Of what green stars can make it to our gate.[9]

◊

If I could, I would reconstruct those last days of October 1962 in Devon. The house, with its cold rooms, must have seemed to be anticipating the change in weather. Plath had painted and scoured it. She had removed all clutter and made it spacious. In photographs, Court Green, under its giant wych elm, shows off its thatched roof, its unsparing stone exterior. In that part of England, at that time of the year, low cloud would have covered the fields long past dawn. But equally, when dark came, the skies must have been swept by early frosts. Here at the start of winter, in the upstairs room where her baby son slept and Plath revised her poems, the acoustics must have let in only the sound of freezing air and the squeak of starlight.

Sometime on the 29th of October, Plath finished revising "Nick and the Candlestick." It assembles the most disparate lyric elements imaginable: with a few bold strokes of language and music, a dark room and a sleeping baby are made over into a cave and its treasure. A big narrative unfolds, and a breathtakingly strange one.

> I am a miner. The light burns blue.
> Waxy stalactites
> Drip and thicken, tears
>
> The earthen womb
> Exudes from its dead boredom.[10]

Plath's statement in the BBC program bears repeating here:

> In this poem a mother nurses her baby son by candlelight and finds in him a beauty which, while it may not ward off the world's ill, does redeem her share of it.[11]

> Let the stars
> Plummet to their dark address,
>
> Let the mercuric
> Atoms that cripple drip
> Into the terrible well,
>
> You are the one
> Solid the spaces lean on, envious.[12]

So many conventions of the nineteenth century nature poem give, yield, slide away here. As if Plath had put her hand to a secret door, an entrance into a possibility that had remained hidden in poetry; unavailable until this moment. Do I think Plath's motherhood brought her there? Of course—but nothing is single or simple in poetry. There were other powerful agents in the shifting of voice and location within these poems. For instance, Plath may not have been a surrealist in the strict meaning of the term, nevertheless these poems show the signature intelligence of the committed surrealist: a sensibility hostile to the official measurements and surfaces of the world; a freedom in rearranging those surfaces; a determination to make the natural world dream with her. These are so evident in the third poem from this group, "The Night Dances," that it becomes impossible to ignore the powerful convergence between motherhood and modes of surrealism in Plath's final work.

◊

"The Night Dances" has a plain enough starting point: a baby boy gets up in his cot, swivels and gestures and turns as if he were dancing. "A revolving dance which her baby son performed at night in his crib," writes Hughes in his note.[13] But plain or not, this is Plath's great poem of motherhood. This is where all nature is summoned, invoked, sent away, and then recalled. At first it seems the dances are geometry rather than anything else:

> And how will your night dances
> Lose themselves. In mathematics?
>
> Such pure leaps and spirals—
> Surely they travel
>
> The world forever[14]

After this initial meditation, Plath opens the poem into an astonishing fission of suggestions, associations, fragments, and dream parts. The fragrance of the sleeping child is like lilies—but no, because lilies fold into coldness and egotism, and then the tiger's spots are violences, but also refer again to the flowers. This is a world of colors, shapes, natural references:

> Their flesh bears no relation.
> Cold folds of ego, the calla,
>
> And the tiger, embellishing itself—
> Spots, and a spread of hot petals.[15]

Then all at once, the earth leans back and looks up. The infant's gestures become cold planetary signs—figuring back into a mysterious space, where perhaps they came from. But once there, the spinning stops: geometry and nature are reunited.

> Why am I given
>
> These lamps, these planets
> Falling like blessings, like flakes
>
> Six sided, white
> On my eyes, my lips, my hair[16]

◊

Plath lived and died in a world that thought about poets in one way, although her poems pointed in another. Her posthumous reputation has suffered from a romantic expectation that her cooler, more rigorous adventures as a poet had no opportunity to change. Years have passed. The house in Devon is still there. The stars of southwest England look down. But now both its poet-owners are dead. At last a wider and more enquiring look at Plath's work can show that those months she spent there in October 1962— as young poet and high-wire surrealist—produced poems which open out the whole question of how a new possession of nature has made a new nature poem. This is a radical change. In this way, poetry is like progress: it can never turn back.

It stands to reason that a wonderful young mother, in an English pre-winter, with her baby boy and the early, clear-skied darks, had enough leverage to shift an ancient convention, should not be a surprise. This is the way radical change in poetry has always occurred. The only surprise should be that so little was made of it at the time. But the poems are there. The skies are still as dark and frost over that part of Devon. The little boy still swerves and turns in his cot. That marvelous young woman lives and speaks every time one of these poems is read. The words are changeless. It is only poetry that has been changed.

NOTES

1. Randall Jarrell, *Poetry and the Age*. New York: HarperCollins, 1953, p. 62.

2. Slyvia Plath, Letter of October 16, 1962 in *Letters Home: Correspondence 1950–1963*, ed. Aurelia S. Plath. New York: HarperCollins, 1975, p. 320.

3. Sylvia Plath, *Ariel*, ed. Robert Lowell. New York: HarperPerennial, 1999, p. 53.

4. Ibid., p. 20.

5. Peter Orr, "The Poet Speaks: A Reading and Interview with Sylvia Plath," recorded October 30, 1962 for the British Broadcasting Corporation.

6. Alex Preminger, T.V.F. Brogan, et al., ed., *The New Princeton Encyclopedia of Poetry and Poetics*. Princeton, New Jersey: Princeton University Press, 1993, p. 820.

7. Ibid., p. 822.

8. Sylvia Plath, *The Collected Poems*, ed. Ted Hughes. New York: HarperPerennial, 1996.

9. Plath, "By Candlelight" in *The Collected Poems*, p. 236.

10. Plath, "Nick and the Candlestick" in *Ariel*, p. 37.

11. Orr, "The Poet Speaks: A Reading and Interview with Sylvia Plath."

12. Plath, "Nick and the Candlestick" in *Ariel*, p. 37.

13. Plath, *The Collected Poems*, p. 294.

14. Plath, "The Night Dances" in *The Collected Poems*, p. 249.

15. Ibid.

16. Ibid.

◊

EAVAN BOLAND's most recent book of poems is *Against Love Poetry* (W.W. Norton & Company, 2001). She teaches at Stanford University and divides her time between California and Dublin, where she lives with her husband Kevin Casey. Her two daughters are Sarah, born in 1975, and Eavan Frances, born in 1978.

Pulse and Impulse:
The *Zuihitsu*

KIMIKO HAHN

black twig, rome, fuji, gala, granny smith, macintosh, red delicious—

Dove, Camay, Palmolive, Ivory, Dial—

January 1st *I was hoping to walk the dog in the Prospect Park meadow this morning, but the rain was coming down in sheets and she had to be dragged out just to pee. Funny how much she dislikes rain and baths but so readily jumps into messy puddles where possible. As long as it stinks.*

January 4th *Appointment with gynecologist this afternoon—PAP smear positive. Which is a negative thing.*

Quotes from Louise Glück's *Meadowlands*: "Such a mistake to want/clarity above all things."[1] "I'm sick of your world/that lets the outside disguise the inside."[2] "We look at the world, in childhood./The rest is memory."[3]

A person seeks models whether that model is used as someone to emulate or resist. For women, models are problematic because so few have been allowed to succeed. And to use the male as a model is also problematic because their experience—even if one could argue that their work is "universal" in symbolizing birth or loss—cannot accurately reflect what a girl learns about her body from that body and from culture. In fact, that is a problem with persona pieces that cross gender—how can a woman write from the body of a man, from a body that experiences erections? Or a man write from a woman's, one who conceives and gives birth? Who suckles? Is it possible? And how is the body contained in one's work apart from subject matter?

I began with my own soft but muscular body to seek words and a poetic—to seek models who would guide. My mother was a model for the intuitive process that I didn't consciously understand or appreciate until I began to understand my own process. The one

I trust. It is ironic that I couldn't consciously comprehend her powerful reliance on the unconscious. That I don't believe she did either. That to some extent it was cultural—"women are like that, less intellectual." Which is not true, and if intellectual in a different sense (not for this essay to determine)—so what. So much the better.

Emily Dickinson, Gertrude Stein, Louise Bogan, Elizabeth Bishop, H.D.—

So much the better I write from a very unconscious "place"—my therapist (no, my shamaness!) telling me my inside and outside reside very closely. How precious. How risky. How female?

Gertrude—how tender!

My mother died in a car accident seven years ago. My daughters were four and six. I was thirty-eight, and I had never felt as deeply as when I felt that loss. Never felt love or loss. Never felt. I began to understand missing *something* I had always missed. Something my mother couldn't give me because no mother can give a child what the mother gives in fairy tales. Which is one thing she did give me—fairy tales.

One important place I found inspiration was in the literature and lives of Japanese women who lived in the Heian Period (794–1185), considered the Golden Age of Japanese literature. Before this time, Japanese men wrote exclusively in Chinese and used Chinese conventions that over the course of anthologies became increasingly bloodless. (Similar to the West's use of Latin.) Because women were not permitted an education, a number of court women wrote in the vernacular—that is, in Japanese—which resulted in passionate and innovative work so rich that some men wrote in the female persona. The best-known works are Murasaki Shikibu's *The Tale of Genji* (the world's first psychological novel) and Sei Shōnagon's *The Pillow Book*. Both are models for their daring subject matter, aesthetic, and for the writer's position in society.

Little did I know that my mother was both the mother *and* stepmother in *Hansel and Gretel*.

January 5th   *I want to write poems that "answer" the quotes I garner from Louise's—even if completely out of context.*

Murasaki Shikibu, Sei Shōnagon, Ono no Komachi, Lady Ise...

When unhappy I lie down, cry, feel my whole body ripped open with sorrow. Delicious emotions because it is delicious to feel feelings. As when mother died it felt good to not feel numb but to lie down on the floor and weep.

So I began with my own soft but muscular body to seek words and a poetic—to seek models who would guide.

A form made popular during this time was the *zuihitsu*, of which *The Pillow Book* is an example. Donald Keene, in *Seeds in the Heart*, writes

> One genre that has no close European counterpart, *zuihitsu*, literally "following [the impulses of] the brush," and consisting of brief essays on random topics, has also had a sustained development.[4]

He continues later to describe this genre that proves to be difficult to define:

> The observations and reflection of the writer are presented with stylistic grace in such works, but above all, it is the personality of the writer that is likely to attract readers. An essay in a book of *zuihitsu* may be no more than an intriguing sentence or two, or it may extend over several pages. In the end, after reading a series of seemingly unrelated anecdotes or impressions, we may nevertheless feel a great sense of intimacy with the writer, much as if we had read his diary...[5]

Keene calls Sei Shōnagon's *Makura sōshi* ("pillow book"), which was written at the end of the tenth and the beginning of the eleventh centuries, "the most brilliant example"[6] of this genre. I respond to its spatial (as opposed to a journal chronological arrangement) quality that juxtaposes and makes no differentiation between an essay on the four seasons or "Sympathy Is the Most Splendid of All Qualities," court gossip or a list of "hateful things."

Why is it that the neighbors allow their dog and toddler to run in the common garden? I am not even sure which one is responsible for digging holes. We will see in the Spring if any of the bulbs survived their exuberance. I am glad to hear the delight but sorry to see even this muddy winter patch so worn. My annoyance sounds like the in-laws complaining that the girls always break something whenever we visit. Their busy little hands undoing or accidentally smashing this or that. Busy and delighted bodies.

The oldest is so full of her own delight—whether thumbing through catalogs for t-shirts and nail polishes or reporting some cliquish crime on the phone or writing an essay—that I sometimes forget how much she needs me. Her increasingly womanly body with a tiny child's face needs me.

January 7th *I am afraid to call the doctor. Finally afraid. Whenever I walk the dog I feel like I'm a little bit running away from home. The dog is the tether.*

The mother and evil stepmother. I accept that.

Another masterpiece of the *zuihitsu* is Kenkō's *Essays in Idleness, Tsurezuregusa*, which dates to the early 1400s. I particularly like the aesthetic he proposes: simplicity and irregularity. Virtues of poetry in general, though not ones I necessarily follow all the time. This austere Buddhist monk's point of view differed dramatically from the sometimes bitchy and always opinionated lady-in-waiting. I love both texts and only wish I had reached a level of classical Japanese where I could read them in the original.

Classical Japanese was not my undoing but certainly caused further humiliation. I can still talk Japanese baby talk. I can still teach my daughters baby words or the words to cue them in Japanese dances: fune (*boat*), tegami (*letter*), naku (*cry*)—*I can still feel the dances I learned in high school in my own limbs.*

The folk dances are the same dances we perform in July for the Buddhist festival commemorating our ancestors. We now dance them for mother.

My own *zuihitsu*, of which I have written about a half dozen, are not as miscellaneous as these predecessors—the form, yes, but not the kind of topical abandon. Mine are collected under a general theme such as "Possession" or the first 100 days after my mother's death or responding to a news article on hysterical blindness. The theme does not mean that each entry (what Keene calls "essay") is strictly about the topic. Rather, it is a kind of air current and what issues is very subjective, intuitive, and spontaneous—qualities I trust in my poetic process. When I edit, I try to maintain these three elements, as well as a clear voice.

So "Possession" encompasses paragraphs on free enterprise, a child's demands, a girl claiming a boy with threats to another girl, the supernatural, and so on. I imagine and include every possible element. A spatial collection. Suggestions of narrative.

I introduce this genre not so much because it was cultivated by a woman—though that is not unimportant to me or to this essay—but because the *zuihitsu* feels significant as a genre for women. It is by its own nature a fragmented anything. And fragmentation suits me because I love long pieces into which I can come and go as I please. Compartmentalized not unlike my own life of mother, wife, teacher…writer. Some friends who do not have the responsibility of children remark on how productive I am and how disciplined I must be. Yes—but not in order to write. I would do that all the time if I could. My discipline must come through for everything else: getting home around the time the children return home from school, shopping/cooking, and so on. So the fragments or the short sections in long pieces become the means to thrash around in—I was about to write "ideas or emotions"— themes. To make a mess. To lose the intellect.

Begin with your own soft but muscular body to seek words and a poetic—to seek fragments that will sustain.

I think of what we are left of Sappho's work—so ravaged by patriarchal flames yet still enduring. Endearing.

I love that phrase: "an intriguing sentence or two."

To invite the intellect back in for re-vision.

And by working in fragments—in themes—I do not need to adhere to a rational line of thought. I do not need to compromise a train of thought and, in such a way, can really explore raw material. Something about hysterical blindness can also comment on Asian American literature. A piece on Flaubert's relationship with a courtesan can contain something on losing my mother. A *zuihitsu* on losing my mother can contain a complaint about a professor in graduate school.

Further, a *zuihitsu* can include all those traits women have been assigned, usually with negative connotations: subjectivity, intuition, irrationality (what the short essays or lack of a formal structure might suggest). What is wrong with subjectivity anyway? Opinion, as we have experienced historically, is disguised as fact and document. So let me document my subjectivity and offer it, because it is fact. My fact. The fact of my experiences.

She told me I needed a cone biopsy and because I am not having any more children she will be "aggressive." I tried not to feel faint. I looked in her hands at the drawing of the vagina. I watched her point to the cervix and how she will cut.

I tell a friend a few days later, and she says she had a similar procedure a year ago and had also been afraid. I ask her why she didn't tell me. She says because it's not something one talks about. Meaning: there's an unknown connection to a sexually transmitted virus. I discover a number of women who have had this, but none had wanted to talk about it. Even the gynecologist does not know much—because it isn't something lethal to men there is not much research.

There are areas of our life where ambiguity can be lethal. Where we explore intuitively.

When I teach Introduction to Poetry I tell my students I want them to use a skill they already possess but which is not usually valued in the classroom—a skill akin to jay-walking or waking at night because something is wrong—an open window as a storm approaches. Intuition. I want them to use their intuition to analyze a poem. Or in the case of a workshop, use it to generate raw material. Intuition, like subjectivity, is not treated as a valid, responsible trait.

Where will she cut?

Where to edit?

What makes sense? What is not fragmented? What is whole? If whole, the object embodies potential fragments. And in each fragment, the whole—which, speaking of poetics, we know from that impossible to pronounce figure of speech, synecdoche.

Where is ambiguity a pleasure and where does it censure?

Irrationality is also not valued. But when working with, for example, juxtaposition, then the rational need not be sequential or comply to a conventional framework. The "logic" of a piece may be closer to an "illogical" train of thought—for which of course many have been rewarded. But I suggest celebrating it. Lose the mind in the creative process—hold it at bay until revision. Celebrate and bathe in these various air currents.

Miya, Rei, Kimi, Tomi—

Mother was so intuitive she seemed to disappear at times. As if thinking were not important, only trains of thought. Sometimes that disappearing was a way to survive other people's needs, and I imagine, to find her own self. I wish she could have been more present though. My need.

Somewhere there is a note on a Japanese aesthetic value called kaoru, fragrance. I have never been able to find the reference. Do I dare write to a former professor?

The other ten-year-old girls on Reiko's basketball team are also energetic and unfocused. It must be hormonal. They can barely stand still to listen to the coach. And are also entirely too polite. I'd like to see them get more aggressive with the ball. But when one jumps in the air to swish the ball—how stunning their bodies.

January 8th *It's my first husband's birthday. I'll send a card. How young we were. How old now this body that pumps iron three times a week. This body I did not love till after I turned forty—and told myself whatever is flawed is a flaw—not an issue of discipline. Not chocolate. What to tell my daughters?*

I know that male philosophers have omitted the body, *impure flesh*, from their philosophical work on soul, morality, ethics. That women philosophers have begun to insist on the body. Is this similar to a male poetic that sees creativity as real birth, a real male domain? Similar to a male poetic that uses science as a means to seek an objective theory? Rather than a dialectical vision that includes heart and mind—in Japanese, *kokoro* and *kotoba* (literally, words)?

I am still not sure how the body figures into a poetic as described over the past decade by a number of feminists. I find the possibilities in these "traits" which have been bound to the female body due to hormones and cradle. Still, this is a place to begin to claim what has been considered negative as not only positive but perhaps in fact *female*. And what is more female than our ability to conceive and give birth—when one's hormones are particularly wild?

Can these elements be part of a poetic?

January 11th *The youngest doesn't want me to go on a book tour. I gave her a notebook to write to me every day and report what she's done. We held one another. She calmed down.*

NOTES

1. Louise Glück, *Meadowlands*. Hopewell, New Jersey: The Ecco Press, 1996, p. 9.
2. Ibid., p. 37.
3. Ibid., p. 43.
4. Donald Keene, *Seeds in the Heart*. New York: Henry Holt & Company, 1993, p. 1.
5. Ibid., p. 9.
6. Ibid., p. 412.

◊

KIMIKO HAHN is the author of six collections of poetry: *The Artist's Daughter* (W.W. Norton & Company, 2002); *Mosquito and Ant* (W.W. Norton & Company, 1999); *Volatile* (Hanging Loose, 1999); *The Unbearable Heart* (Kaya Press, 1996), which was awarded an American Book Award; *Earshot* (Hanging Loose, 1992), which received the Theodore Roethke Memorial Poetry Prize and an Association of Asian American Studies Literature Award; and *AirPocket* (Hanging Loose, 1989). In 1995, she wrote ten portraits of women for the MTV special *Ain't Nuthin' but a She-Thing*, for which she also recorded the voice-overs. She has received fellowships from the National Endowment for the Arts, the New York Foundation for the Arts, and the Lila Wallace-Reader's Digest Fund. Hahn is a professor in the English department at Queens College/CUNY and the mother of Miyako, born in 1985, and Reiko, born in 1988.

And the Motherhood of Poetics

Susan Griffin | Berkeley, January 1999

Conception

The moment is not perceptible in any ordinary way. Just a slight shift in your body so elusive it hardly seems to exist. You would not even be able to say what you felt. Ordinary language seems to fail you. Still, even years later, you are drawn to find language here at the bare beginning, a second conception in words.

(*Epic*)

Considering the sentimentality that surrounds motherhood, it would be easy to overlook the awe that is part of the experience. An experience that, even in the barest physical terms, is epic. Though of course the word *epic* is usually associated with heroic images of war, which are in their own way sentimental.

Silences

As if there were a pause in parturition.

A caesura.

And you can only wait.

Still, you cannot take your attention away. Suspended as if at the pinnacle of a story, at each moment you feel yourself becoming a point in time. You are mesmerized by continuation.

And though you are eager to reach your destination, you are not hurried but calm. Held in the sway of these silences you rock along, a slumbering ballad, a line leaning into rhyme.

(*Significance*)

The titanic nature of the experience. The way that birth, for instance, places a mother at the boundary between two worlds. Facing two directions at once, she turns toward the beginning of life but also toward the possibility of death, which becomes suddenly very real to her. After a birth she is pitched to an extraordinary focus. The raw needs of her child are expressed in the visceral language of cries as she wakes at all hours of the night. Daily life as she has known it is halted, turned upside down, marshaled toward survival. Yet her life is charged with significance.

Nausea

But as the rocking motion deepens, you are jolted from every sense of the ordinary. The ballad is no longer predictably measured. You are out of balance, seasick, ill, and heaving. Still you will not jump ship. Gripped by the plot as it unfolds inside you, you must stay the course. Rising above the bilious, impenetrable misery, something determined in your mind, yet almost beyond your own will, is still set on the horizon, poised perfectly on a thin edge of light, as a suggestion of the future rises.

(*Form*)

Telling a story through which a culture remembers itself, the epic has been celebrated as the highest form of poetry. According to Isidore of Seville, writing in the sixth century A.D., even heroic meter surpasses every other rhythm.[1] The stateliness of the music has to mirror the gravity of the occasion, not just the gravity of warfare, but also the gravity of a narrative that defines a culture. The story renders the blood shed on the battlefield as sacrificial blood. The epic form an extension of this sacrifice. The bravery of the soldier, which has turned him into one of the gods, memorialized. Just as he gives his life for those who hear the story, those who listen make him eternal through memory.

Showing

Bit by bit as you swell, and the rocking slows to a pleasant lumber, you sense you are not alone. Someone who is made of your own substance is inside you. A silent reader with a different point of view. And this causes another revolution, not only in your body, but in your soul. Who exactly you are is not so clear to you any longer. Mathematics has shed its coherence. You are a couple and yet still indivisible. Two and still one.

As incipience ripens, you are becoming a sphere of contradictions in which nothing is logical and everything makes sense. A heavy, burdensome, sweet, satisfying roundness.

(*History*)

It has been suggested that in the shared psyche of our culture, the wounds of war mimic the blood of birth. Though the deepest wound of motherhood is not visible. That sense of girlhood freedom, of autonomy, of absolute independence that a young woman achieves at a certain age will be broken and then transformed by her child's need. Having put on the armor of the self, the armor must now be pierced. So that a greater body can be seen. And here is where the form of the epic is born. As in the *Iliad*, where each story, the story of Agamemnon, of Achilles or Patroculus, or of Helen and Paris, is cast into a larger canvas, the movement of history, she begins to sees her life as part of the larger story of generations. Everywhere connection becomes more evident to her.

Alchemy

Even your dreams seem to come from this roundness now. As you sleep, you give birth to stones and sheep. In your waking hours you feel yourself sinking into an endless image, a labyrinth of virgin births and fairy tale mothers in which you are lost, but also where you are the queen. You are becoming mythological. The maternal savior. The Monstrous Mother. Chimerical, like a changeling you possess magical powers that possess you too as the story inside you stretches your body to gigantic proportions.

(*Erasure*)

But the epic is often turned to other purposes. The glorification of empire, for example. In the service of that goal, the poetry of warfare erases the real experience of soldiers, the terror, the brutality, the betrayal replacing all this with an idealization of war. Similarly, there is a poetry of motherhood that replaces the expansion of awareness, which is part of motherhood, with diminishment. A mother is supposed to erase herself, her own needs, her own thoughts for her family. In this way the epic of motherhood is reduced to an uninteresting cliché.

Quickening

What is that? A movement inside you. Your belly forms a wave, a slight rise, a hill. A foot, perhaps, or a knee, a small arm. And though this is exactly what you had been told would happen, you are astonished. You feel thrilled.

A very precise thrill. Not like any other. No single simile will do. Only a chain. A mysterious chemistry of comparisons. The sight of land on the horizon, the fin of a marvelous creature cresting the water, the glimpse of a long lost love strolling the dock, that piece of evidence which finally proves that your version of events was right all along, a jack in the box, a surprise visit, a rosebud opened slightly by a small wind, a rabbit fleeting through tall grass. The list is infinite. This little motion, the mother of all metaphor.

(Parody)

Two decades I wrote "The Perfect Mother" almost as a parody of conventional ideas of motherhood.

> The perfect mother lets the cat
> Sleep on her head. The
> children laugh.
> Where is she?
> She is not in the sandbox
> She is not carefully ironing the starched
> ruffles of a Sunday dress.
> What does she say?
> She doesn't speak.
> Her head is under the cat and
> like the cat, she sleeps.[2]

Though these lines evoke and mock the dull poetics of conventional motherhood, another force altogether sleeps inside these words.

Sounding

Not so much what you hear yourself but what you imagine the one inside hears. The words would have to pass through water. Is there the faintest hint of memory somewhere in your imagination? What you heard yourself when you were floating in your mother's womb. No sense to the words. But the words a palpable force, making waves around you, sounding in you. Patterns of nonsense steadily stitched into your existence.

(*Voice*)

The language moves in a different direction than the content. It is uncontained and fero-cious. A ferocity that comes in part from the tension between convention and the rebel-lion expressed in the poem. But there is another, less obvious source. The key can be found in a shift that occurs from the second to the third stanza. Here the voice of the narrator yields to the voices of the perfect mother's children:

> Where shall we go? We ask the perfect
> mother. What
> do you want of us? She is no
> where to be found.
> Not in the cookie jar
> we have broken to bits
> not under the shiny kitchen floor
> not on our lips.[3]

Labor

And now another powerful sound sweeps you away like a wave. At first subtle then slowly a force fills every inch of space or even imagined space. This is your voice. Though you have no memory of crying out and think the sound might even belong to someone else, the power of it makes you believe you have flown into the air before you float back down in the soundless moment between one wave and another.

(*Counterpoint*)

The slightly menacing quality of these lines describe the erasure of the mother. But the lines have an unruliness that acts in counterpoint to the menace. Yes, it is true that the children are almost frightening, like surreal Katzenjammer kids, unpredictable in their naughtiness.

> What does it matter if
> they are hatching plots, if
> in their waking dreams
> the poor cat is trapped
> its hair
> standing on end?[4]

But the voice of the children is also madcap, zany, as if teetering over the edge of impossi-ble meanings. The tone of the voice expresses an elemental exuberance. Though there are costs to this vitality—the cookie jar has spilled and broken—the range of possibility in the poem enlarges with the mere evocation of a sensibility that is as yet untamed.

Crowning

You can neither see it nor feel it. Covered in sweat, aching and tired, you are so mired in the rhythm of labor, you do not witness the moment. But the others witness, crying out together because they have glimpsed a new roundness coming out of you.

(*The Image*)

Then finally one more shift occurs in the poem. Though the last lines are bleak, they are also electric:

> Here we are transfixed,
> mourning the perfect mother, and she
> is caught in the trapped cat
> of her children's dreams.[5]

The transfixion here is in part caused by a conflict: the conflict between the unrealistic wishes of children for an impossible perfection, the desire for a mother who gives everything and makes no demands, and the rebellion. But the image of the trapped cat that appears earlier changes its nature here with the mother suddenly inside both the cat and her children's dreams.

Birth

You are still in a kind of shock when the infant slides out of you into the doctor's hand. Until she is put on your chest, her face turned toward yours and you look into her eyes. At that moment you understand that another person has come to exist who was not here before. That she has come out of your body. In the days that follow, vocabulary swims in your mind. Beginning with the word *birth*, which as it expands seems almost infinite, reshaping everyone and everything in its path, all the words you know have become fluid. You have almost lost the capacity to speak.

(*Mood*)

And that the mother is now inside the children's dream is echoed by the convergence of both the narrator's voice and children's voice in one sentence. From this new configuration the sense emerges that both children and mother, like the cat, are trapped by a stereotype from which both dream to be free. This dream, of necessity, is implied rather than stated. But its power can be felt all the more precisely because it seems to be more mood than statement.

Night Feeding

So tired you have lost all attempt at order or reason, you have slipped into the elemental, the inchoate; your attention shaped by cries, your body filling with milk at the sound, every thought tuned to what is simple, food, warmth, sleep, still larger thoughts wash over you, seize you, shake you making the simple less simple than it seems.

(*Language*)

The mood here is actually heroic because what is at stake is not only physical survival but the survival of souls in search of the epic poetic of motherhood. So with a ferocious effort, the same ferocity children have in their eagerness to be alive and live fully, another meaning forces its way into language.

Lullaby

The havoc of need and the fear of death, a monster at the edge of your shared world, as the night encroaches, you rock together again, the waves of a song soothing you both.

(*Resonance*)

The epic as the story of the heroic process through which we recognize the existence and hear the resonance of other lives through love. To put this into words. And this too would be part of the same epic. That as a mother watches language begin in her child's life, with her child's first words, language is reborn in her.

Patty Cake

As you say the words, she watches you. Then she says what you say. Back and forth. Back and forth. *Patty cake, patty cake. Baker's man.* Neither of you know what it means really. And then, you both know perfectly well what it all means, as you laugh and say the words together, marveling at the symmetry in the rhyme, the meeting of your hands.

NOTES

1. Isidore Seville, *Etymologiae*, as cited in *The New Princeton Encyclopedia of Poetry and Poetics*, ed. Alex Preminger, T.V.F. Brogan, et al. Princeton, New Jersey: Princeton University Press, 1993, p. 524: "...because in it the affairs of and deeds of brave men are narrated (for heroes are spoken of as men practically supernatural and worthy of heaven by account of their wisdom and bravery) and this meter precedes others in status."

2. Susan Griffin, "The Perfect Mother" in *Bending Home, Selected and New Poems 1967–1998.* Port Townsend, Washington: Copper Canyon Press, 1998, p. 83.

3. Ibid.

4. Ibid.

5. Ibid.

◊

SUSAN GRIFFIN is a writer and poet. Her latest work, *The Book of the Courtesans, a Catalogue of Their Virtues,* was published by Broadway Books (Random House, 2001). Other works include *Woman and Nature* (Sierra Club Books, 2000), *A Chorus of Stones: The Private Life of War* (Doubleday, 1992), *What Her Body Thought* (Harper San Francisco, 1998), and *Poems Selected and New 1967–1998* (Copper Canyon Press, 1998). Her essays on gender and society were collected in *The Eros of Everyday Life* (Doubleday, 1995). Named by the *Utne Reader* as one of a hundred important visionaries for the new millennium, she has been the recipient of an NEA grant, a MacArthur Grant for Peace and International Cooperation, and an Emmy award for her play, *Voices.* Griffin lectures widely in the United States and also teaches privately from her home in Berkeley, California. Her daughter, Chloe Andrews, born in 1968, is mother to Sophie and Jasper, born in 1997 and 2002.

Elaborations of Between:
The Interpolation of a Child into a Writer's Poetics

The Madonna and Child of Duccio di Buoninsegna's *Madonna Rucellai* [1] repose in calm, the mass of her darkly robed figure and his lighter, smaller one enthroned in iconic, anisotropic space, only slightly wrenched from the flat Byzantine picture plane. We can tell from bodily locations that we are meant to understand that he is sitting on her lap, neither suckling nor sleeping, gazing into space. The perspectival strategies, however, are insufficient to create the representation of an actual lap; he is hovering before her, or embedded within her, or gracing the surface of her robe, while small, adult angels arranged vertically on either side of her throne kneel in space, one above the other. The nearly flat human shapes stylized in gold lines don't ask us to take this Madonna and Child as any particular mother and infant living in the three-dimensional world we consider our own, nor do the artist's pictorial devices allow us to include ourselves in their world. On the contrary, the stilled aggregate of figures emphasizes their unknowable nature, their dedication to that which cannot be expressed. They float remotely in a magical [2] expanse where objects and space are not systematized. So it doesn't trouble us that the baby is unusually quiescent for a baby, any baby we've ever known, and that the mother rests undisturbed, as rarely happens with a wide awake, non-feeding child in lap.

Well into the Renaissance, when painters had gradually learned to create illusionary space in which to depict naturalistic phenomena, the Madonna and Child of Bellini's *Sacra Conversazione*,[3] like Duccio's, also sit becalmed, surrounded by holy figures. But our relationship to this set of figures, who have been rendered so individually as to seem modeled on actual people in Bellini's neighborhood, is entirely changed, as we now find ourselves part of their world; or, in fact, only one of us, me, my own single point of view, is drawn into their domain by means of geometrically rationalized perspective. As I stand before the realistically rounded figures of mother and infant, who are just as still as Duccio's figures, I wonder about them: each, disengaged from the other, gazes meditatively away into space, a space in which Bellini has defined the viewer's relationship to his subjects; the mother is doing nothing at all in response to any real infant energy. And I wonder, too, about the experience of the painter who represented them. The infant looks true to life, like dozens of babies I've known, but nevertheless is posed on his mother's lap, balancing adroitly on one leg, raising the other with foot poised in space, as no actual baby might do. The realism of the painting makes me, a mother myself, uncomfortable with their unreal relations. I know that, as in Duccio's painting, the disengaged stillness of Bellini's Madonna and Child is meant to convey the sacredness of the subject. But Bellini, by positioning his embodiment of the sacred within range of my own present view, seemingly within my physical reach, has nullified the mystery of distance. The naturalistic presence of his mother and child, like those in countless similar Renaissance paintings, fails to convince us of their reality at the same time as it dulls the aura of the sacred: "...perspective seals off religious art from the realm of the magical."[4] In fact, Bellini's pair seems to have been painted by someone who has never taken care of a baby. A living mother and baby are not still, not fixed in immobile union. The space between mother and child is a sea of perpetual activity, of nurture and contention.

The events of pregnancy and childbirth are replete with potential experience that belong to the birth mother alone. "Nature creates similarities. One need only think of mimicry. The highest capacity for producing similarities is man's."[5] Walter Benjamin was referring to the production of "non-sensuous similarities," in particular, of art. But the highest capacity for producing sensuous similarities—that is, another living likeness—is woman's.[6] When the birth event is over, however, biological motherhood emerges as a particular case of caring. Any able person—father, relative, step-parent, and so on—can assume the personal and voluntary obligations of mothering, parenting the newborn. The birth mother, therefore, with her particular biologically determined capacities, has a special, but not exclusive, status as a caregiver. Nevertheless, I will continue in this essay to speak of "mothers" and "mothering," since my own knowledge of the topic is that of a biological and primary caregiving mother.

All caring and nurturing involve, along with active physical labor, responsibility and response. At the outset, all parenting involves mimicry, the initial communication between the infant and the world culture to which it suddenly belongs, and mutual projection, the unconscious confusion of selves. Mothering requires openness to the intermediate flow between mother and infant and the necessity for both to swim in the flood of signs, in the intersubjective flux of communication.

◊

In *Perspective as Symbolic Form,* Erwin Panofsky argues that when the artistic problems of an epoch have been exhausted, there will occur a "great recoil, or perhaps better, a reversal of direction" during which we look back to more "primitive" models of art.[7] We may be in the midst of such a recoil just now. Panofsky demonstrates his theory by examining how the spatial systems of historical eras articulate the world visions particular to an era and the systems of belief that inform them. He focuses on, among other things, the contrast between the pre-perspectival notion of "tactical space" and the mathematically rationalized space that emerged during the Renaissance.

Within the pre-perspectival orders that prevail in Duccio's painting, the viewer senses "tactical space," the *tastraum* (literally translated as "touch room"), which embodies the effects of perceptual, or psychophysiological, space. That is, in the *tastraum* there is "no strict homogeneity of position and direction; each place has its own mode and its own value,"[8] whereas, "exact perspectival construction is a systematic abstraction from the structure of this psychophysiological space."[9] Perspective draws "this world of things, an autonomous world confronting the individual, into the eye,"[10] the single eye, the dominating eye of the autonomous viewer. The world is organized into rationalized, controlled, mathematically determined segments in relation to the one viewer, my own eye, myself.

The space existing between a mother and her newborn, however, resembles less that of perspectival order with its one-way autonomous control, and more that of the *tastraum.* Between the mother and newborn lies the psychophysiological expanse of mutual ignorance and a pressingly full immediacy to negotiate, test, intuit, feel, cross with signals, back and forth, back and forth. Mother and infant begin communication without a common language or the contract of reason, but with sensuous contact as the only medium of exchange. The terms of that exchange, constantly interpenetrating in the newly constructed space between them, undoes the mother's oneness, violates her boundaries, and abruptly wrenches her perspective from the singular to the multiple. Nearly a millennium's worth of naturalistic Madonna and Child images, along with other cultural messages, may have left the new mother with some misconceptions about what mothering is going to be like. Perhaps easy, peaceful, everything under control, no problem. The familiar images, constructed with rationalized perspective, may have misled her.

> For it is not only the effect of perspectival construction, but indeed its intended purpose, to realize in the representation of space precisely that homogeneity and boundlessness *foreign to the direct experience* of that space.[11]

The unprepared mother at first finds direct experience of this new space unfathomable, with herself and the infant seemingly its poles or its boundaries, boundaries that are unstable, always in motion, and perpetually impinged upon by one or the other and by the suddenly recontextualized contents of surrounding space. She's now permanently a party to this new arrangement, and, as she is subject to its derationalized procedures and chaotic orders, nothing's the same.

◊

My early pre-motherhood writing had also been diffuse, subjectless, and often anisotropic. Those first efforts were based in part on a desire to convey the remembered effect of my own prelinguistic existence based on what seems to be an unusually large and detailed pool of infant and early childhood memories. I wanted to convey in writing my vividly recollected sense of "prelinguistic thought" and "preconceptual language," as I thought of it when I first began writing, the language of phenomena, of sensation, gesture, and, strangely, of my own mind, lifted out of its transfixed body. I remembered my infant mind as an equivalent actor along with light, temperature, dust motes, breezes, the texture of my blanket, the taste of my thumb, and so on, a kind of thought which seemed to know a world whose orders were, in retrospect, not yet influenced by the logos.

However, while I was making these early attempts, I was unaware, because of personal circumstances, of the more radical currents in twentieth century literature that might have confirmed the legitimacy of my initial impulses. The only poem available to me at the time was the canonical model. So I tried for nearly fifteen years on and off (with life frequently interrupting the effort) to "correct" my writing from what I feared was mere material, an apersonal sea of words referring every which way, into a regular or real poem, as I then thought of it. Such a poem would be a lyric with line breaks, regularized rhythm, a melodious pattern of sound and summarizing visual images, the entire work unified by means of a central "I" which progresses toward a moment of revelation at the conclusion of the poem, at which point its intended meaning becomes clear to all readers.

Although I was never interested in a literary entity called "myself" or my personal psychosocial experience as a possible subject of my writing, I was, nevertheless, before I became a mother, comfortably "me," an autonomous, individual observer of "the world." In the world which constructed me, the western world, a modern young woman could arrive at adulthood with her mind, her self, organized more or less along Cartesian lines, with the surrounding domain managed from an unconsciously mathematized single point in the surrounding grid of space. I knew who I was because I was here, and everything else, established by my coordinates, was comfortably somewhere else, situated in increasing degrees of there. The boundaries were clear, and I could withdraw into my solitary fastness of silence to observe, think, read, and dream from my own point of view.

For the first few weeks after my daughter, Ariana, was born, I felt as if I were accommodating an entertaining but slightly fretful houseguest. You enjoy, serve, finally become weary with company, crave your solitude, and watch, at last, as the guest duly leaves.

One morning while changing the hundredth or so diaper, just about when those tolerable few weeks should be up, I was stunned to realize that this guest would not be leaving. I stopped where I stood, staring at the tiny, contorted, shrieking figure, and realized that this was not a guest at all, but something alien that seemed to have permanently attached itself to me. The cool austerity of my singular perspective erupted into excess, and the silence was full of noise.

> Where was I?   Falling into paralogical
> esthesia: the great instrument by which
> certainty has been given to precedents is a volley of pleas.[12]

From one second to the next, I felt the rupture of my personal boundaries, the conquering of my keep of quietude, the assault on the solitary, inner-directed self I hadn't even realized I possessed. My body was flooded with the chemical of emergent horror: how could I even know who I was, or what I was thinking, or what I wanted to do if I weren't able to occupy my single point alone, if I had to share it with another person? Could there possibly be any recourse, any means that would allow me to keep my self intact? Or could I possibly ever learn to give it up? Willingly relinquish my self...indulgence, absorption, direction?

It was clear that she suffered: she screamed, turned red, sleeplessly cried and cried in wordless despair as I fed, changed, burped, fed again, serenaded, and rocked her, and finally, clasping her to me, walked her back and forth across the same patch of floor for eight hours at a time, the only tactic that soothed her. The doctor said it was colic, but what was that? Just a vague diagnosis without a specific treatment, a word, not a solution. In desperation, I held her limp little body on my lap, turned her crumpled face toward mine, and addressed her absurdly, "What is it, what do you want, little baby? Tell me, just tell me."

The effort to parent, to give the infant comfort and well-being, involves guessing, conjuring, inventing, reading. But one is trying to read the signally indecipherable, the inexpressible, the uncompromising; you are reading another living being. Lost in the thick intervening darkness that you labor to breach, you improvise meaning. "The point at which you read each word (the only point there is), two minds share a larger whole."[13]

Share or contend for. The act of reading an infant is a reading of rupture, interior and peripheral. In the act of decoding its cries, its sighs, your efforts blur the distinction between writer and reader. You are wondrously absorbed into the fabulous chasm between mutual output and input. And you want to escape the struggle by establishing your meaning: "Now it's night and night means sleep." At the same time, you are troubled with the sense that construing is always constructing. Are you unfairly transgressing, over-interpreting, mindlessly or selfishly dominating? Are you reading? or writing? or are they the same? This mutual process is never simply a two-way trading of signals, but is perpetually interrupted and expanded by exterior, uncontrollable phenomena. You rock the infant for an hour and finally convince it to sleep. At last you can rest, maybe take a shower; a truck roars by; the baby's awake and you're back at work. You live together in a chaotic, directionless, ungovernable universe where the mother, at least, is very tired.[14]

So it was difficult. And yet, and yet...when she was at peace, nothing on earth had ever been so fascinating as this inscrutable wisp of a creature. Her frail velvety body, remoteness still shadowing her, was that of a vivid but circumspect emissary from incalculable dimensions, her silvery eyes looking in from stellar clouds, her anemone limbs still fractionally waving as if in the mild currents of an amniotic sea. And her intelligence: there, huge, still, and ready.

A mother's confrontation with the sensuousness of this other intelligence, with its thoughtful emanations devoid of words, makes her witness to a distanced world, unlit, cryptic, rationally illegible. The experience of its iconic remoteness provokes—or did in me, in any case—a sense of being in the presence of the inexpressible in the same way that Duccio's painting does. We can look at it, but not into it. We can't see through its opaque yet tangible presence, but nevertheless sense significance: there is the effect of meaning. As I looked upon remoteness while gazing into her eyes, particularly while she was feeding, she would lock my eyes into her gaze, and with elaborate theatricality, slowly, almost ritually, raise and lower her eyelids without breaking the gaze, her eyes glimmering with merriment as if to disclose voluminously, steadily, without prejudice, from the poised heart of her intelligence.

Albrecht Dürer, an admirer of Bellini, said of perspective: "...the first is the eye that sees, the second is the object seen, the third is the distance between them." But, continues Panofsky, "then it [perspective] in turn abolishes this distance."[15]

The eyes and being of this other, fixing the mother's in ecstatic mutual absorption, recover the distance. I forgot myself for hours at a time. For months, we were never apart, and within our domain of intimacy, as she grew and changed and became mobile, I followed her at close quarters with my eyes and often with a camera.

In "The Work of Art in the Age of Mechanical Reproduction," Benjamin writes of the capacities of film to open up space.

> By close-ups of the things around us, by focusing on hidden details of familiar objects, by exploring the commonplace milieus under the ingenious guidance of the camera, the film, on the one hand, extends our comprehension of the necessities which rule our lives; on the other hand, it manages to assure us of an immense and unexpected field of action.... With the close-up, space expands; with slow motion, movement is extended.[16]

The mother/child relationship is already one of close-up, the perceptual intimacy of body to body and moment by moment surveillance, as the child feeds, smiles, begins to gesture, turn over, sit, crawl. Details of the baby's fingernails, eyelashes, and skin, as well as the dangers in its way, edges, corners, stairs, all occupy the extensivity of slow motion, and within that expanse, mimesis flourishes. As the infant ages into a child and begins to participate in the canon of language, the distance slowly fills up as mimesis and projection take its place. The initial instances of mimesis gradually proliferate into a dense web of interconnectedness that never dissolves from the lives and consciousness of either.

Unlike the unreal, manageable infant of Bellini's naturalistic Madonna and Child, an actual infant is live Will. Active disrupter, ferocious contender, at first, when tiny, it trembled, squirmed, and thrashed; a little later, equipped with more sophisticated motor function, it clawed, tore at my hair, bit my nipples (with rakish laughter), and wrestled itself into preferred positions.

Space, however extensive, was never big enough for both of us. Nor time. A book in my lap reminded her that a lap was a comfy place to play; just as she wanted to be fed, I wanted to sleep. As we continued to share and contend for space and time, control emerged as the central issue, or, for me, learning to accommodate loss of control. Unlike the arrangement depicted in Bellini's painting of the large calm mother with small passive child, one's own physically diminutive child often seemed to possess the larger will by far, and with it the power to determine nearly every quotidian thing. I, the adult, the one with skills, knowledge, and sense, struggled for every inch of ground: you have to wear shoes when it's cold, you can't climb out the window, you have to sit in your car seat, I have to go to work, I can't stay awake any longer, and no, you can't have all the cookies in the supermarket.

◊

The traditional notion of Narcissus as model for the artist, in which the reflection of the artist is as much a part of mimesis as the phenomena the artist works to depict, prevailed throughout my early years of writing. When Ariana was about four, I began to write again, and as I continued to try to wrench my language into poems of direct experience expressed from a single point of view, I felt increasing dissatisfaction with the results. Although I didn't consciously recognize it at the time, the effort to achieve a "correct" poem now involved an additional difficulty as I sensed how thoroughly my former arrangement with the world, myself at its defining center, had been reconfigured: the model of Narcissus could no longer represent me, if ever it had. I was not Narcissus; no singular reflection shimmered back at me. Even with only one child, the crucial disruption is effected. The reflection of the mother-artist is disordered, and her once singular identity, now perpetually projected back and forth between herself and her child, is multiplied into ripples, strings, twists, meshes. For those mothers with more than one child, the disruption of singular identity must result in even more complex patterns. Indeed, the experience of parent to child can feel arbitrary and clinching at the same time that it's unsettled and inflecting, much like the relationship of the signifier to the signified. In the gap, the precarious negotiation of difference, always mobile, always based on minutiae, constantly persists.

Gradually I decided that there was something fundamentally amiss in my approach to my writing and determined not to write again until I could face the work from a different stance. The resolution made, I occupied myself for about two years with work on a non-fiction book about mothers; its ostensible purpose was to address the question, How can something as natural as mothering be so difficult? I interviewed eighty mothers and pondered their stories alongside my own experience. Eventually, an emerging recognition of the immense discrepancy in character between the slow-motion psychophysiological mother/child topos and the clock-timed, rationalized dominion of the technologized marketplace began to offer suggestions of a new beginning for my writing. Although I continued for a while to work on the nonfiction book, more and more I wanted to pitch my poetry into this volatile tract between the frantically rigid, projectilely rent and scored spaces of the sociopolitical structures of the marketplace outside, and the tensible conjunction of the sensuous mother/child relationship, of hunger, tears, saliva, sleep, goop, untamed emotion, and fascination with and fear of the new that characterize the inside domain where nurture takes place. The undeniable—indeed, the utterly unavoidable—legitimacy of this natural, uncontrollable world of bodily fluids and intense emotion at last enabled me to question the authority of the given structures of the outside world, including its representative orders of literature and language.

I looked back at first to Charles Olson's conception of the poem as a field of energy and found it suggestive, but also identified as a hindrance the linearity implied in his statement that "ONE PERCEPTION MUST IMMEDIATELY AND DIRECTLY LEAD TO A FURTHER PERCEPTION,"[17] not to mention the insistent, authoritarian tone of his caps. And I immersed myself in Gertrude Stein. I was curious about her "sense of a space of time...that is filled with moving,"[18] provoked by her enigmatic statement in "How Writing is Written" that "the thing has got to the point where poetry and prose have to concern themselves with the static thing. That is up to you."[19] I experienced that "you" as an engaging provocation. Poetry and prose were not divided, so the rules, or the breaking of rules, that applied to the one also applied to the other. By "static" did she mean "still?" Atemporal, and therefore spatial? And if so, what could a spatial writing be, especially given the apparently indelible linear drive of the simple declarative sentence, like the discharge of a shotgun—thing, action, thing—subject, verb, object—at the foundation of all normative English grammar? Finally I turned back to my own writing and confronted what I had considered its weaknesses and deficiencies, the errors of its ways. Now I had the means to question the authority that had seemed so unfortunately to classify my literary idiosyncrasies as problems. Could these problems perhaps be possibilities? At just around this time, I had the good fortune to study with Robert Duncan, who unequivocally confirmed the validity of such an approach in his lectures as well as in his own poetics. He emphasized particularly how his misaligned eyes with their error of sight had given him "double vision" in poetry. One's difficulties could be one's gifts, limitations that might let one see in a particular way.

In my own case, then, could the absence of strong central perspective expand rather than nullify the poem? Could "weakness" in language usage and literary form provoke? Could a want of dominance, a controlling narrator, a prevailing scheme of imagery, or a chief purpose serve to open the poem up to estranged conditions that might cause it to fly apart into new possibilities? Could a poem be "spatial" instead of "temporal?" And most particularly, with the loss of a naturalistic, psychologically engaging "I" to guide the reader toward the closing moment of the poem's epiphanic meaning, could distance be returned to the poem, the same quality of distance that rationalized perspective and a Cartesian world view had gradually painted out of art during the Renaissance? Would it be possible to recover in a poem the same mysterious opacity of earlier art forms that we find in Duccio's painting, a physicality that engages its spectator-readers with a demand to invest themselves, with both their knowledge and the limits of that knowledge, in its effect of meaning? With those questions, I finally began to find my way in writing.

◊

As the age of mechanical reproduction mutates into the present one of electronic confluence with its invisible technical and neural networks woven together across enigmatic tracts, is it possible that those responsible for direct, personal caregiving have a particularly apposite standpoint for the making of contemporary public art?[20] Those weavings entwine us in a post-perspectival world space in which identity is fluid, authority fractured or inscrutable, control diffused, and position crucial, a world in which stem cell experiments show that a change in the location of a cell can alter and determine its identity, and when, in the relation between human and machine, "It is not clear who makes and who is made."[21] As art recoils from the Renaissance construction of space and its concomitant ideologies, the caregiver artist is configured not as individual visionary, but as participant in a miraculous act, the act of creating non-sensuous similarities, aesthetic acts recounting the inconsistent textures and events among subjective admixtures and their positions: marvels whose surfaces are saturated with distance.

NOTES

1. *Madonna Rucellai*, Duccio di Buoninsegna, c. 1285, Uffizi Gallery, Florence.

2. I am using a definition of magic which has not to do with practices or beliefs associated with the supernatural, but which describes phenomena not yet confirmed by empirical evidence. An example of "magic" prior to 1923, then, would have been the notion that light can assume the properties of either a wave or a particle—that is, before Louis de Broglie conjectured and C.J. Davisson and L.H. Germer demonstrated that, in fact, it can. Though linear, rational language and instruments of investigation as we now know them fail to present an adequate account of non-rational means of knowing, that failure does not necessarily preclude the possibility of such a case being made at some point in the future. From this point of view, there is nothing particularly "magical" about magic.

3. *Sacra Conversazione*, Giovanni Bellini, 1505, San Zaccaria, Venice.

4. Erwin Panofsky, *Perspective as Symbolic Form*. New York: Zone Books, 1997, p. 72.

5. Walter Benjamin, "On the Mimetic Faculty" in *Reflections*. New York: Schocken Books, 1986, p. 331.

6. For many years the argument was made that women expended all their creative energy in reproduction and therefore were unable to make art, particularly "high" art. Such notions are now fundamentally complicated by the resources of biotechnology, such as the gestation of embryos not originating in the birth mother and the recent cloning of mammals.

7. Panofsky, *Perspective as Symbolic Form*, p. 47.

8. Ernst Cassierer, *Philosophy of Symbolic Forms: Mythical Thought*, Volume 2, trans. Ralph Mannheim. New Haven: Yale University Press, 1955; quoted in Panofsky, *Perspective as Symbolic Form*, p. 30.

9. Ibid.

10. Ibid., p. 67.

11. Ibid., p. 31, my emphasis.

12. Mary Margaret Sloan, "On Method: Near and Far" in a forthcoming book. Bolinas, California: Avenue B, 2003.

13. Ron Silliman, *What*. Great Barrington, Maine: The Figures, 1988, p. 40.

14. The difficulty of bridging the gap between mother and baby is possibly exaggerated by the mother's particular temperament and circumstances, both by the degree to which her psychological individuality has been consolidated by her cultural surroundings, and also to the extent that she faces the parenting task as an individual, that is, alone, without physical help or the guidance of communal know-how passed on by oral traditions from one generation of mothers to the next.

15. Panofsky, *Perspective as Symbolic Form*, p. 67.

16. Walter Benjamin, "The Work of Art in the Age of Mechanical Reproduction" in *Illuminations*. New York: Schocken Books, 1969, p. 236.

17. Charles Olson, "Projective Verse" in *Selected Writings*, ed. Robert Creeley. New York: New Directions, 1966, p. 17. For additional discussion of the influence of Olson on women innovative writers, see Kathleen Fraser's essay "Translating the unspeakable: Visual poetics, as projected through Olson's 'field' into current female writing practice" in *translating the unspeakable: Poetry and the Innovative Necessity*. Tuscaloosa: The University of Alabama Press, 2000.

18. Gertrude Stein, "The Gradual Making of Americans" in *Selected Writings*, ed. Carl Van Vechten. New York: Random House, 1962, p. 258.

19. Gertrude Stein, "How Writing is Written" in *How Writing is Written*, ed. Robert Bartlett Haas. Los Angeles: Black Sparrow Press, 1972, p. 160.

20. This suggestion of course applies also to the many men now involved in direct caregiving. It should also be noted that the mother-artist has always been productive, but that the artifacts she has produced, pottery, weaving, and other domestic goods, have only recently and occasionally been recognized as legitimate art in the official institutions of art.

21. Donna J. Harraway, *Simians, Cyborgs, and Women: The Reinvention of Nature*. New York: Routledge, 1991, p. 177.

◊

MARY MARGARET SLOAN is the author of three books of poetry, one forthcoming from Avenue B in 2003, *The Said Lands, Islands, and Premises* (Chax Press, 1995), and *Infiltration* (Queriendo Press, 1989). She edited the anthology *Moving Borders: Three Decades of Innovative Writing by Women* (Talisman House, 1998). Her work has appeared in numerous magazines and has been anthologized in *Primary Trouble: An Anthology of Contemporary American Poetry* (Talisman House, 1996) and *The Art of Practice: 45 Contemporary Poets* (Potes & Poets Press, 1994). After living for many years in San Francisco, she has recently moved to Chicago, where she teaches at the University of Chicago and at the School of the Art Institute of Chicago. Her partner is Larry Casalino and her daughter, Ariana, was born in Melbourne, Australia, in 1971.

The Writing Being

Laura Moriarty

Ob(litera)tion

The writing being considered here exists as both foreground and background.

"In it, the partial mother declares her omniscience but I am thinking about extravaganzas as unfolding in my other left hand, the one that will always be free and invisible to her grasp."[1]

There is an opening, an emptying, a making available, an including, an organizing, a proposing, an asserting, a providing of context, and a taking care of business.

The writer foregrounds her resistance to the fact of her obliteration.

The background is also obliteration. She calls this the world.

Beyond their having been written at the same time, there are connections between *The Literal World* (Day) and *The Case* (Moriarty). Both have to do with birth, death, the experience of new motherhood, and a consideration of thought and identity, perhaps thought as identity.

"The world is everything that is the case."[2]

The world is the convention; the case is the problem.

In Western Civilization, where the writing being (traditionally) must be able to privilege writing and thinking over other concerns (who is, in short, a gentleman), the writing mother obliterates the conventions of what the writing being is each time she writes.

Her strategy is relational.

"Okay. Come at me from any direction."[3]

The writing being takes up space and time that are shared by other entities or activities.

The usefulness of the experience of obliteration is in the potential for new connections in the time after, if there is time after.

The writing being is so occupied with being that the writing is forgotten. Writing is then rewritten from a fresh perspective.

The writing being read in this case is written under duress, at times that are difficult to anticipate and seem barely to exist while they are going on.

The writer can't think without being interrupted.

"One would have had to have known the ironies of autarchy to understand the pictures in this particular book."[4]

The interruption, the discontinuity becomes both subject and object of the work.

In several hours' time the writer has performed various tasks including writing the sentence:

Writing is not a gender-neutral activity, nor should it be.

"Take beginning: In an age of comic genitalia, I find myself funny all the time, that is, to the extent that I find myself."[5]

The slippage now commonly perceived to exist in the meanings of words exists also in the identity of persons.

"It is like every case in which the roles of the participants merge. They hold onto their identities, returning to their imagined security at the slightest provocation. This is where she has them. During the transition, information comes out. Her own loss of identity hastens the process. She is careless of her safety. She never feels safe ... When most lost in the role, when most defenseless and overcome, something appears."[6]

A writing is proposed that is not (contemptuously) detached or designed for use by one able to ignore the vicissitudes of life.

The writer proposes to make connections between varying poetics and between discourses.

"Our Commonality"[7]

She is attached.

She celebrates the vicissitudes.

The work is harsh, hilarious, demanding, firm, knowing, and enduring.

The writing being proposed includes aging and illness. It includes death.

In the game of this writing winning is redefined.

"'Maze' where the object is to be/At the same place as yourself/At the same time"[8]

The writing being considered here routinely outrages the perceived limits of the writer's identity.

"open to the present/disheveled, she"[9]

The outrage occurs not only because of the identity of the writer, but because of her lack of identity—because of the obliterated identity of the writer and of the writing.

"In an odd combination of hurry and languor (called attention) my goal is to unfill. Memory is not a question of neatness, or a noise I remember making; I'm a nomad in territories of my own devise and my maxims have a retroactive taste."[10]

The writing being admits congruence with both the obliterated and the empowered.

"These terms are not addressed to someone else."[11]

The writing (mother) creates the citizen.

The writing being done here is imagined in relation to another person whose claims on the writer are generic and absolute.

This person is, for example, the newly created mother.

"Soft but implacable"[12]

The writing listens.

The writing being "reorients [her] perspective in order to accommodate that of [her] interlocutor."[13]

Movement is incessant. There is relief (for writer and reader) from making decisions about what to do—that being clearly to take care of whatever needs to be done next.

There is scrutiny. It is direct and exhaustive.

The being in the writing being takes over, again.

Attention and tension are wrung out of the writer by an ongoing project, which at times is the most pleasurable part of life.

"Thank you, this chaos was wonderful."[14]

In the genre of this writing, waking is relentless and attention is constant.

"I can't possibly be awake now."[15]

The writing being done in the postmodern family may be done by any member performing any familial role.

The writer's (mother's) role in the family is not necessarily fulfilled by one person consistently.

The writer doesn't have to be a mother to be a mother.

If one is inscribed (determined) to some extent by one's mother, then the work of the writing mother lays bare the context and motive for this rendering.

The mother you read, etc.

"'Use notebooks,' she said, forgetting my lexical limitations. I wanted to describe my inner self as a house, lived in by generations yet full of debris peculiarly my own. But at the end of the day, it seemed to go without saying: shut the door, good-night, good-night."[16]

Nothing is obliterated finally but time and identity. Identity is overrated. There is always less time and more work. The writing being/other mothers. Each one does it differently, but the activity is the same. The blur is where the action occurs. She writes the world.

"something appears"

In "Narratives from the Crib," Jean Day uses the first person to write into a being's initial experience of life. In this work there is a combining of the writer's perception, infant development, and mother development. Observing, imagining, and wording the think-ing is the procedure. It comes out in prose.

"Syntactically, it's a question of accumulation, I hear them and am always adding to what I've already sung."[17]

The humor and intensity of the writing evoke the qualities of the infant milieu. "So my body rises ever near completion, or is it pure distraction?"[18]

It is a work about the discovery of being shared by mother and child. "Narrative" lacks sentimentality. "Sentiment? That's next year, I think…"[19]

The experience is given as a formative one. "…in the genre of day there are no originals."[20] In the form, the category, of the experience of the world there is no beginning. The world, the experience, and the form are ongoing.

The work is written in relation to *Narratives from the Crib*, edited by Katherine Nelson, a multidisciplinary collection of studies of the development of a particular infant. One of the conclusions of this research is that children mature in a far more complex and verbal way than had been imagined. This is also true of mothers.

Day's narrative is one of physical and mental growth in a situation of intense but ordinary intimacy. In any caregiving situation, there may be a shadow "I," whose needs and con-cerns exist as a being in the consciousness of the caregiver—in this case, the mother. She creates the story the "I" narrates.

A thrilling intimacy is presented in elaborate sentences. "Narrative" makes a connection with the reader, who probably grew up and had a mother, which simultaneously becomes a fascinating commentary about thinking and awareness.

"If the mind comes barreling past my window, how can *I* be *its* subject?"[21]

The blending of mother/child, writer/reader, subject/object is accomplished seamlessly with a prose style that is light and persuasive in its questions and observations about being.

The use of "I" in these narratives is not unlike Stein's use of "I" in *The Autobiography of Alice B. Toklas*, but seems less highhanded. These "I's" have in common that they are about intimacy and love as world-producing and world-altering experiences.

"Yet clearly, in this excess of timelessness between her coming and going, I am."[22] There is information here about love and dependency, the nature of childhood and of caregiving. The symbiosis of the thinking child and the writing mother is very compelling. Point of view stays grammatically the same, but seems to shift in the heady environment of new life. "Desperate for affection, the padding ghosts had been plying me with products; now they were crowding my world with their bobbing things."[23]

The writer evokes the parents (ghosts) emoting toward the child remembering the movements of the parents and others, as well as the movements of objects "they" set in motion to engage and develop his (her) attention. "Desperation" is involved. The stakes are high. The entire world whirls around this moment. But the intensity is also undercut by the formal hilarity of the diction. "Here they saw themselves in need of metaphor and *I* came along, a virtuosic index of their changing conceptions of closure—*and* secured at the end of a rope."[24]

"Narratives from the Crib" asserts a mellifluous, considered diction in a persuasive display of postmodern writing and mothering. Jean Day's engagement with language, being, grammar, love, childhood, parenthood, as well as, implicitly, sheer mental and physical endurance are present in every line. *The Literal World* demonstrates that the best way to deal with the issue of writing and motherhood is to write.

Summarily

The writing being figures it close to the limit of what seems acceptable and then edges past that limit. She creates an environment of agreement so compelling that the option for an even greater outrage of limits is perceived as inevitable by almost everyone involved in the situation (the world). The case. Those not in agreement complain that if this writing being is even imagined (literally) everything will change and things formerly sneered at will seem central. But they are too late—she has always already existed.

"Then I wake up, already in a position for play, and turn my eager ear to the door. The sociolect (that stream of 'babblers' calling for years from the sky) is in progress, just waiting for the paradigm shift two points off the starboard bow. I am inconceivably hungry..."[25]

NOTES

1. Jean Day, "Narratives from the Crib" in *The Literal World*. Berkeley, California: Atelos, 1998, p. 93.

2. Ludwig Wittgenstein, *Tractatus Logico-Philosophicus*, trans. C.K. Ogden. London: Routledge & Kegan Ltd., 1983, p. 1.

3. Laura Moriarty, "Puppet Light" in *The Case*. Oakland, California: O Books, 1999, p. 45.

4. Day, *The Literal World*, p. 93.

5. Ibid., p. 99.

6. Moriarty, *The Case*, p. 19.

7. Jerry Estrin, "Our Commonality" in *Avec #7*, ed. Norma Cole, 1994.

8. Moriarty, *The Case*, p. 55.

9. Ibid., p. 43.

10. Day, *The Literal World*, p. 101.

11. Moriarty, *The Case*, p. 45.

12. Ibid., p. 51.

13. Gemma Corradi Fiumara, *The Metaphoric Process*. New York: Routledge, 1995, p. 82.

14. Day, *The Literal World*, p. 99.

15. Moriarty, *The Case*, p. 63.

16. Day, *The Literal World*, p. 98.

17. Ibid., p. 93.

18. Ibid.

19. Ibid.

20. Ibid., p. 102.

21. Ibid., p. 95.

22. Ibid.

23. Ibid., p. 96.

24. Ibid., p. 102.

25. Ibid., p. 100.

◊

LAURA MORIARTY is the author of ten books of poetry, including *Nude Memoir* (Krupskaya, 2000), *Rondeaux* (Roof, 1990), *like roads* (Kelsey St. Press, 1990), *Symmetry* (Avec, 1996), *Spicer's City* (Poetry New York, 1998), and *The Case* (O Books, 1999), as well as *Cunning*, a short novel (Spuyten Duyvil, 1998). She was the Archives Director for the Poetry Center and American Poetry Archives at San Francisco State University from 1986 to 1997. She received a Poetry Center Book Award in 1984 for *Persia* (Chance Additions, 1983). She is currently Acquisition and Marketing Director of Small Press Distribution in Berkeley, California. Her step-daughter, Columbine Robinson, was born in 1984.

Radiance in the Story Lattice

PATRICIA DIENSTFREY

I.

The story as a form that we inherit and pass down claimed a hold on my writing when my children were very young. My sons were two, three, and four years old when writing became a way of reseeing the world and of looking for a lost balance. Although my imbalance seemed to be "existential," it also seemed specific to my situation as a mother. At home during the day, in sole charge of three children's lives, I felt cut off from the adult work-world, which now seemed to me strangely "mothered" with its agendas and social lunches. And the story, which I associated with a childhood sense of wonder and later, with a more adult sense of a plan at work in the universe, when I sat down to write, was no longer in place. My ideas, feelings, words had nothing to refer to. The story, the reliable thing, so taken for granted, had fallen apart.

Writing, then, became a search for a usable form. I hadn't heard of Ezra Pound's "emotion is an organizer of form"[1] or of Walter Benjamin's narration-through-juxtaposition.[2] It was the seventies and, looking back, I can see that I was turning over poetics issues that were in the air and would be developed in the eighties and nineties in debates over the agency in writing of desire, logos, eros, grammar, syntax, the body.

My conceptual framework, shaped by a Protestant upbringing, nineteenth-century novels, and college literature courses, was basically progressive and linear. I became more interested in circular, broken, and ephemeral patterns, in phenomena like "light" and "presence," and in darker, less hopeful views than those I had absorbed from my father's daily Bible readings before breakfast. I read Robbe-Grillet's short phenomenological pieces in a little book called *Snapshots*, and felt especially drawn to one entitled "The Shore," which braided four periodicities—the ripplings of ocean waves, the straight lines of sunlight, the movements of three children walking on a beach, and the resonance of their voices in banal conversation—into a seamless narrative. I also read Nathalie Sarraute's prose-poems in a slim volume, *Tropisms*, which she locates in a time that is "no longer the time of real life, but of a hugely amplified present."[3] Here, she writes, we experience events closer to the "secret source of our existence in what might be called its nascent state."[4] In both books, writing created an adequate stability, not through plot but through continual reorientation toward an invisible point, or source. What was "happening" could be light itself, or tidal shifts, or fleeting sensations in the body caused by passing emotions.

With children playing around me, I had a sense of overlapping times. The sunlight that came through the windows seemed to combine its energy with theirs, and to open up the walls. In this air, it was possible to be in the room with them and back in my own childhood playing on the landing of the attic stairs with my doll. Here light from two narrow windows provided everything we needed—landscapes and dramas—which, I suppose (given a basic emotional tone that accompanies memories of this time in my childhood), were of protection and punishment. Nothing in my play, or in the stories I made up, was separate from the presence of my mother moving around downstairs, always close, on the other side of something like a membrane that breathed throughout the house.

I became interested in the work of Carl Jung, especially in an early book, *The Psychology of Dementia Praecox*, his analysis of a patient called Babette S. who was confined to the Burghölzi Asylum in Switzerland. He kept records of her "stereotypies," which he defined as a "constant reproduction of a certain activity" that, through its "strong feeling-tone [engraves the] various phases of the process on our memory."[5] With Babette, these "feeling-tones" took the form of phrases such as "Naples and I must supply the whole world with macaroni," "I saw the book terribly high above the town-hall grounds covered with white sugar," "we are also the lilac-new-red sea-wonder."[6] It was Jung's work to make diagnostic sense of her images, but I felt free to be drawn to the aesthetics of her mutterings and the connections she might be making in a less lonely world.

In time, I came across the work of Jung's student, Marie-Louise von Franz, her studies of psychological projection in a volume entitled *Projection and Re-Collection in Jungian Psychology: Reflections of the Soul*. Here she presents two Jungian hypotheses that significantly modify the story's linearity. One is that dreams draw on future events as well as past, which results in their temporal collisions while, at the same time, they maintain a narrative. Another proposes a phenomenal world in the form of a lattice, which Jung describes as a "fourth mirror relation [based on] the same element as light in physics."[7] Here, he writes, number is "the predestined instrument...for apprehending an already existing, but still unknown…'orderedness,'" which *"may well be the most primitive element of order in the human mind"* (Jung's italics).[8] Von Franz continues to define Jung's theory:

> In the deepest levels of the objective psyche there is probably an *acausal orderedness with a numerical structure* that is equally valid both for the psyche and for matter. There in the lattice patterns of the numerical field, psyche and matter, we may conjecture, are continuously mirroring each other, whereas in synchronistic events we become aware of this mirror-relation only exceptionally and then as specific happenings pregnant with meaning.[9]

Concepts of light-like structures, of a mirror relationship between solid matter and the immaterial mind or soul, and of an "acausal orderedness" presented themselves as shaping elements for a revised story form. A lattice field also suggested new ways of reading. Its synchronicities helped me understand the power of myths, for instance, to involve readers as co-creators of human experience and as witnesses. This was a power available to a Hellenic priestess, a Renaissance playgoer, a twentieth-century school child. In a lattice order, Olympian gods and earthly mortals, alike, could be seen as "mere props," as Sarraute puts it in *Tropisms*, for patterned movements "which are inherent in everybody and can take place in anybody at any moment."[10]

Magic was in the air some mornings in my children's play, the ways stories flowed without a break from their imaginations into heroes and props: "It's a fire! You be the engine. I'll be the fireman…(siren sounds)…" While they played, I could sit with a second cup of coffee and read for a while. A book that suited these mornings in uncanny ways was Jean Genet's first novel, *Our Lady of the Flowers*, written when he was an inmate of Mettray Penitentiary Colony outside of Paris. It set into relationship our circumscribed lives, his as a prisoner, mine as a mother bound by her choices, and the children's as creators of adventures that wildly transcended their abilities to carry them out (my reflection on their play, not theirs). And so we lived, like Sarraute's characters, not in the time of real life but in a "hugely amplified present." I could believe that, as adults, Genet and I inhabited a less bounded space, having submitted to another kind of restraint, love. Mine committed me to my children and my marriage and his to his homosexual infatuations as an adolescent living in a prison inhabited exclusively by males. "Thus," he writes, "I lived in the midst of an infinity of holes in the form of men."[11] His image of men as holes formed a compression, a radiance, a postmodern desire that destroys its object, a presence-in-absence. There was much in Genet's writing that, given the hold that linearity still had on my mind, I found liberating.

The image also suggested a metaphysics of the eroticized body, Genet's own, which he transformed into writing by dividing it into halves—male and female, Darling and Divine—a couple he paired under his prison blanket. "It's a good thing," he observes, "that I have raised egoistic masturbation to the dignity of a cult."[12] And so he gives birth to generations of events. His writing process suggested a connection between his sexual creations and my own. But on this subject, Genet draws a crucial distinction when he acknowledges that his creative process is inherently perverse, seeing that his female Divine is, to her distress, really a man in a skirt, and Darling, his virile male, is transmuted by an act of willful bloodshed, into a virgin, Our Lady of the Flowers.

I read Genet's "novel" (which he knew wasn't one except for marketing purposes) as a lyric poem. The writer of *Our Lady of the Flowers* is a poet, a scholar of language, and a lover of words, of their sounds, which he interrupts his writing to recall:

> But what is to be said of one of the strangest of poetic phenomena: that the whole world—and the most terribly dismal part of it, the blackest, most charred, dry to the point of Jansenism, the severe, naked world of factory workers—is entwined with marvels, the popular songs lost in the wind...sung by the grave mouths of workers which utter such words as: succumb...cottage...marble...sweethearts...dear...love...jewels... crown...oh my queen...dear stranger...gilded room...flowered basket...treasure of flesh...golden waning...[13]

While Genet is captured by words' sensuous qualities, Italo Calvino, in *Six Memos for the Millennium*, describes other claims words may make on a writer's passions. "There are those," he writes, "who hold that the word is the way of attaining the substance of the world, the final, unique, and absolute substance."[14] There are others who use the word as an approach to things, not in their substance, but in "their infinite variety, touching on their inexhaustibly multiform surface."[15] For still others, words enter experience as ideas, images, thoughts, spiritual feelings that "follow each other so quickly that they seem simultaneous."[16]

For years, I attempted to make a writing of an experience of a word that came to me as narratives that clustered in a way that seemed simultaneous. It arose in response to something I saw outside a glassed-in porch off the kitchen of our New England ground floor flat when I was two years old. The experience was of knowing a word before I could talk. My view was of bare trees against an overcast winter sky, a railroad trestle on a snow-covered embankment, and the afternoon train going by, the passengers facing ahead in the windows.

Then a boy and girl appeared on a chase, both bundled in blue snowsuits and red scarves, like animated Doppler effects. A little struggle, and they collapsed, the boy on top of the girl. He pinned her into the bank, scooped up snow and rubbed it around her face, while she twisted back and forth under him, laughing, snow coming out of her mouth. The word, which I breathed out in excitement, was "romance," on the glass an "O" suspended over the scene. The thrill of the chase and struggle became an urge to tell my mother this story I had no language for and sent me running across the porch to the kitchen door. She was sitting ironing at a table mangle, her lap draped in warm bed sheets. In steam from a kettle on the stove, she looked as if she were made of marble; and the sheet that hung down from her lap looked like a curtain drawn across the entrance to an oracle. I was on the threshold of another place and time.

A few years ago, I came across an account of an experience that reminded me of my own. The similarities strike me as amazing. The account appeared in Walter Benjamin's memoir/essay, "A Berlin Chronicle." His word originated in a Berlin park where, as a three-year-old, he was brought on afternoon outings by his grim nursemaid. The site of the word's emergence was a maze around statues of Frederick William II and Queen Louise "rising sheer from the flowerbeds." This embankment was, he recalls:

> ...but a few yards from the strangest place in the city. At that time, it is true, it must have corresponded more than closely to what was waiting behind it...the haunts of that Ariadne in whose proximity I learned for the first time (and was never entirely to forget) something that made instantly comprehensible a word that at scarcely three I cannot have known: love.[17]

The place in which the childhood word was made "comprehensible" was a brothel in an immediately adjacent section of the city called the Wedding Quarter. A significant part of Benjamin's education as a middle-class German youth occurred "under the auspices of prostitution."[18] "Publicly accosting a whore in the street," he writes, was an event of "almost unequaled fascination."[19] On the site, then, of the three-year-old's "haunts of...Ariadne" he writes, he penetrated to the:

> innermost place of the Minotaur's chamber.... *This* mythological monster had three heads: those of the occupants of the small brothel on Rue de la Harpe, in which, summoning my last reserves of strength (and not entirely without Ariadne's thread), I set my foot.[20]

My word "romance" threaded its way through my girlhood in comic books and movie magazines, which I snuck into the house and hid under sweaters in my closet. But its meaning changed during adolescence. Like Benjamin's "love," my word enacted a connection between my two-year-old self and my expanding social and intellectual world as a college student in Cambridge, Massachusetts. It encompassed a cycle that linked that winter I was learning to talk with my fascinated adolescent encounters with boys during a summer on the South Shore of Boston, where I worked as a waitress in a resort hotel. The situation brought together a number of correspondences: the crystalline aspects of snow and a beach; the atmosphere of transience that surrounds a passenger train and a hotel; early boy-girl tussles and play and adolescent flirtations and sparrings. Many of these at the hotel were "under the auspices" of a group of young bartenders of clean-cut good looks, who competed with each other for sexual "points" and clipped small amounts daily from the profits. Now, like Benjamin, I was no longer a child looking on. I began to spend my time off with a man who lived in town—a fighting, storytelling Irish fireman true to a New England "type," to which he brought modesty and ease. There was a romance, a conception, and a pregnancy; a plane trip; Kelly Girl temp jobs on the West Coast; meetings with an adoption worker; a birth and giving up of the baby, a girl, each of us leaving the hospital a few hours apart to live separate lives.

I admit to deeply conflicted feelings surrounding the differences in Benjamin's and my experiences—the difference between a brothel and an adoption agency, for instance, when the institution of marriage is missing. They could inspire a diatribe, a harangue. Issues of gender inequality have committed me to work for change wherever I can. But my engagement with poetry, as it involves working with words, has refused these priorities. This has been a rejection not just of the mind, but of the body. A response to a word—its sound, meaning, use, origins—feels like an entrance into its world, its history. This engagement feels like definition at work, which seems, in itself, enough.

II.

"Let them read on my gravestone he founded an institute for the study of the prenatal life of the child."[21] The words are Velimir Khlebnikov's, the twentieth-century Russian Futurist poet, linguist, natural scientist, and mathematician. What might come out of such an institution? Infancy has been a subject of scholarly studies of history and language in recent decades, in closely written works that seem to weigh every word, but which sometimes confuse "conception" and "birth." In its name only, an Institute for the Study of the Prenatal Life of a Child would bring more clarification to this field, more sensitivity, rigor, and nuance to further investigations.

It might answer a question that fascinates me, one that is not separate in my mind from questions that involve writing and art: Why do so many children, across cultures, draw similar figures in their first play with a pencil or crayon? After the initial scribbles, the first controlled lines curve and close into ovals. Soon after, children add linear segments that break the perimeter, composing a radiant figure that looks like a paramecium, zygote, or sun.

Edward Edinger refers to these pictures in *Ego and Archetype* as possible representations of the evolution of the human figure and of Plato's idea of an "original round man."[22] One day, looking at this shape drawn by one of my sons, I stood behind him with my hands on his shoulders. His arms, his whole body, still had an infant roundness to them, so that his picture suggested a "snapshot" of him, but in a not-of-this-world light. An article in the *New York Times* "Science Times" in the 1990s suggested that light by which images could be formed on an embryo's retinal screen may be carried in the blood by hemoglobin.[23] Are babies born with a sense of form? This form? A memory of it? A visual memory? A desire to make it? A desire to reproduce it on a separate, facing surface? To see it? To see it again in a new time and context? To begin using it?

Khlebnikov kept notebooks of words and phonemes on pages filled with letters and algebraic signs. Letter sounds were represented as living agents in a "dictionary of the spatial world":

> So then, from our landing on the staircase of thinkers, it has become clear that the simple bodies of a language—the sounds of the alphabet—are the names of various aspects of space, an enumeration of the events of its life.[24]

An idea of formative movements interior to vowel sounds made its way into my writing in a book entitled *The Woman Without Experiences*:[25]

                ... ... Sound. ... ...
                ... ... Wound. ...
            ... ... Round. ...   .
            ... ...
            ... ... Found. ...
            ... ...
        ... ... Bound. ... ...
            ... ...

The ellipses are a lattice field of marks on a page that represent what is missing there, evoking what Jung calls an "acausal orderedness." The *o* and *u*, paired, create a synesthesia that is "round" to my ear. And the laying out here of these metaphors employs a common storywriting strategy that is missing in the book. Still, the figure illustrates a narrative: a mother is bursting through a doorway into a room in response to her child's cry—his cookie has fallen on the floor and broken. It's a wail of pure loss born of his perspective, and it has brought her running with her arms out to gather him up and make things better. The lattice figure could be cut from this setting and given a title like "The Threshold" or "On the Staircase of Thinkers." Such shifts and movements recall Benjamin's "narration-through-juxtaposition" writing procedures, in which fragments may be related to each other in different ways, depending on the preferences of the writer who has collected the pieces. Such a composition might be seen as an assemblage of starting points, each fragment having its own. In this context, elements of a writing—a title, word, sentence—can be clustered in varying arrangements, or set apart to stand alone.

Khlebnikov believed it theoretically possible to create a language that would, through sounds' formal properties, change institutions and assure world peace. Toward this end, he kept notes on the characteristics of letters and syllables, publishing essays under titles such as "Z and Its Environs" and syllable poems such as "Here is the way the syllable *so* is a field," which begins:

> Here is the way the syllable *so* [with] is a field that encompasses *son* [sleep], *solntse* [sun], *solod* [malt], *slovo* [word], *sladkii* [sweet], *soi* [clan; Macedonian dial.], *sad* [garden], *selod* [settlement], *sol'* [salt], *slyt'* [to be reputed], *syn* [son].[26]

Below is a drawing that he inserts to follow his *so* poem:[27]

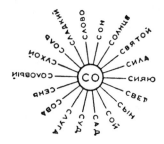

◊

The words that I have chosen in order to talk about form—"romance" and "radiance"—come from my experience. At times, while I was struggling with questions as a writer, my children *illustrated* radiance as a starting point in a slightly changed—familiar, unfamiliar—environment. Special interactions in our daily life illuminated, as Calvino writes certain words do, the visible trace of the invisible thing. I held them and gave them orders. Yet I was working with a world beyond my powers to control, or even touch. We enacted a life that I think the halos in Christmas nativity scenes stand for, revealing the family members (and, in some cultures, the animals and shepherds) to be, each one, a separate entity and, at the same time a member of an encompassing whole.

◊

A Poetics and Its Environs

The story form, as it has evolved for me, is made up of radiant parts, but what relates them and gives them meaning remains mysterious. Life, from day to day, drops clues to this mystery. This is a structure I can work with as a writer—and I am not alone. Many contemporary poets negotiate this territory, writing from it in different, sometimes signature forms. It is a situation that has opened up poetry to many kinds of experiment and to contingent issues. Perhaps in the future, in some Khlebnikovian field of research, these may incorporate more far-reaching explorations of Sarraute's events experienced closer to a "secret source of our existence"; of Jung's number as an "instrument" for apprehending a primitive order in the human mind; and of formal beginnings in prenatal life that continue through infancy and childhood play into art, writing, scholarship, and institutions.

NOTES

1. Hugh Kenner, *The Pound Era*. Berkeley, California: University of California Press, 1971, pp. 145–146.

2. Michael André Bernstein, "Walter Benjamin" in *Five Portraits*. Evanston: Northwestern University Press, 2000, p. 95. "Narration-through-juxtaposition" is a term Bernstein applies to Benjamin's narrative methods, which I found true to my own readings of Benjamin's assemblage procedures; this is the spirit in which I have used the term here.

3. Nathalie Sarraute, *Tropisms*, trans. Maria Jolas. New York: George Braziller, 1963, p. vii.

4. Ibid., p. vi.

5. Carl Jung, *The Psychology of Dementia Praecox*, trans. R.F.C. Hull. Princeton, New Jersey: Bollingen Series, Princeton University Press, 1960, p. 92.

6. Ibid., pp. 100–104.

7. Marie-Louise von Franz, *Projection and Re-Collection in Jungian Psychology: Reflections of the Soul*, trans. William H. Kennedy. La Salle, Illinois, and London: Open Court, 1980, p. 195.

8. Ibid.

9. Ibid.

10. Sarraute, *Tropisms*, p. vii.

11. Jean Genet, *Our Lady of the Flowers*, trans. Bernard Frechtman. Great Britain: Panther, 1966, p. 164.

12. Ibid., p. 124.

13. Ibid., p. 192.

14. Italo Calvino, *Six Memos for the Next Millennium*. New York: Vintage Books, 1993, p. 76.

15. Ibid., p. 77.

16. Ibid., p. 42.

17. Walter Benjamin, *Reflections: Essays, Aphorisms, Autobiographical Writings*, trans. Edmund Jephcott. New York: Schocken Books, 1978, p. 4.

18. Ibid., p. 11.

19. Ibid.

20. Ibid., p. 9.

21. Velimir Khlebnikov, *Collected Works of Velimir Khlebnikov, Volume I: Letters and Theoretical Writings*, trans. Paul Schmidt. Cambridge: Harvard University Press, 1987, p. 196.

22. Edward Edinger, *Ego and Archetype: Individuation and the Religious Function of the Psyche*. New York: Penguin Books, 1972, p. 9.

23. Sandra Blakeslee, "Surprising Theory on the Body Clock: Illuminate the Knee," *New York Times*, January 16, 1998, "Science Times" section, p. A1.

24. Khlebnikov, *Collected Works*, p. 367.

25. Patricia Dienstfrey, *The Woman Without Experiences*. Berkeley, California: Kelsey St. Press, 1995, p. 88.

26. Khlebnikov, *Collected Works*, p. 272.

27. Ibid., p. 272. Note: *C* in Khlebnikov's list of consonants is represented in the translation as "C [*s*]." Illustration reprinted with permission Harvard University Press. From 1912–1913 *Neizdannye proizvedeniia*. Moscow, Khudozhestvennaia literatura, 1940.

◊

PATRICIA DIENSTFREY is a co-founder of Kelsey St. Press, established in 1974 to publish innovative writing by women. Her book of prose-poetry, *The Woman Without Experiences* (Kelsey St. Press, 1995), was winner of the 1995 American Award for Fiction. Selected work appears in *Moving Borders: Three Decades of Innovative Writing by Women* (Talisman House, 1997). She lives with her husband, Ted, in Berkeley, California, at scattered distances from their three sons, Aaron, Andrew, and Tobias, who were born in 1967, 1968, and 1970.

Parallel Play

CARLA HARRYMAN | 1998

Parallel

A thorn in the side.

My interest in stock phrases and subgenres is partly related to the baffling concealment I sense within their too-obvious self-presentations. The potential confusion brought about by multiple desires of the writer—to understand, to change, and to replace "the world" with fantasy—is also put into critical play in my work. The goals of the writing are built on sometimes contradictory or competing claims, which manifest themselves in shifts of style and genre within individual texts. I want the claims to work themselves out transformatively.

Mother's delicate parts.

I am interested, for instance, in the erotic and intellectual desires of the autonomous adult as they compete with the requirements of being a parent in a culture that still imagines the fiction of "white bread/bred" motherhood as normative. This fiction of motherhood not only de-eroticizes women who are mothers, but also conditions others to think of mothers as those subjects whose imaginations are absorbed only in their children. There is then something dangerous (it feels dangerous, in any case) about the exploration of the erotic imagination through and in writing from this "maternal" circumstance.

Assortment of tongues.

The cultural anxiety about keeping the adult eros separate from the child is not necessarily as deep or basic as the anxiety over the child's witnessing the primal scene even if these anxieties are related.

Play

Scene I: A charming and a not so charming story

JACQUES LACAN:

The little girl I mentioned earlier, who wasn't particularly awful, found refuge in a country garden, where she became very peaceably absorbed, at an age when she was scarcely walking on her feet, in the application of a good-sized stone to the skull of a little playmate from next door, who was the person around whom she constructed her first identifications. The deed of Cain does not require very great motor sophistication to come to pass in the most spontaneous, I must even say the most triumphant, of fashions. She had no sense of guilt—Me break Francis head. *She spoke that with assurance and peace of mind. Nonetheless, I still don't predict a criminal future for her. She simply displayed the most fundamental structure of the human being on the imaginary plane—to destroy the person who is the site of alienation.*[1]

NATHALIE SARRAUTE:

It is not only my mother who is absent from that house.[2]

CARLA HARRYMAN:

My then seven-year-old son found himself flat on the sidewalk in the school yard one day, as a friend seated on the small of his back held his head between his hands and with a melancholy repetitiveness pounded it into the cement sidewalk. I was the only adult witness of this act, and I might not have been there at all had I not arrived at school early that day for a meeting. As I pulled the child away, my son declared in a rather affectless tone that they were no longer friends. This event did indeed mark the end of a nearly three-year friendship between them. It is not one

The cultural anxiety about keeping the adult eros separate from the child is not necessarily as deep or basic as the anxiety over the child's witnessing the primal scene even if these anxieties are related. Sometimes I imagine this primal fear as the key concoction of a bad script. The fear that a mother's sexuality will dominate or control a child may also be part of this script. In the script, fantasies of masculine aggression are projected onto the mother's body and are concealed by stock phrases such as "primal scene" and "mother's sexuality will dominate or control the child."

A queen bee in a log jam.

A friend of mine recently taught one of my anthologized poems[3] to high school students in her course on poetics. The poem, a satire of Sade's *120 Days of Sodom*, probably could not have been taught in a public school. "The ventriloquist plunges his hand into her ass and pulls it out screaming, minus a finger," is one of the lines in the poem. When I was asked to visit the class (members of which are friends of my son who attends the same school) and discuss my writings, I decided to read from and discuss a prose section of the same piece in which I make use of Sade's *Philosophy in the Bedroom*. I very much appreciated my friend's ability to sanction in her classroom writing with sexual content created by a woman. It is important to allow young people access to sophisticated literature by women, including literature with sexual content. Of course, the sophistication of the teacher and her ability to speak to the students as individual readers of such a text is equally important.

that I had the heart to encourage after my insistence that the school and the parents speak to the attacking child purposefully about his actions resulted in the suggestion that I had exaggerated the event. This is not a charming story.

Above and beyond the psychological fact of aggression is the manner in which it is understood and addressed. Clearly humiliation—the children's, the school's, the parents'—controlled the event. It was a humiliation (underscored by fear of repercussions) born of a lack of adult presence in combination with the attendant presence of the mother, who, in this case, does not fit into the correct category of adult. But I am quite confident that the humiliation—the humiliation of language, the suggestion of "exaggeration," would have not been passed on to me had I been the child's father. Why? The father would have been assumed to be already suffering the humiliation of his son's inability to defend himself. In other words, the underlying question involves a subliminal cultural understanding about boys fighting, and it goes something like: had our son picked a fight without being able to defend himself? It is the father who is responsible to the son for the narrative of attack and defense. Thus, the father would have already been punished for his child being attacked and his child's potential culpability, for in not preparing his child for the fight, he shares in the child's shortcomings. Over and over again it is their culpability in relationship to gendered narratives that grants men "objectivity" as witnesses. It is a ubiquitous cultural belief that women cannot be objective in matters concerning their children and that men can. And yet in some respect, the most fundamental problem here was economic; the school was poor, and there was no one being paid to supervise the children playing outdoors at that time. The effects of lack of money, however, yield an

This is not simply about some superficial notion of health, as if teaching poetry were a nutrition class. It is about honesty and human sexuality and children's and particularly teenagers' concern with honesty. One aspect of honesty withheld from children is that concerning the adult—particularly any woman's—erotic imagination. The withholding of this kind of information from teenagers contributes to their feelings of being outcasts.

Grazing on mystification tables of log's rhythms.

In my other two essays on the subject of motherhood, I have focused on how I learned to write while being a mother: I discuss learning how to manipulate the time of the writing so that it is a response to lived time with a child and to the world experiences that enter the time spent in proximity to the child. Now that my child is a teenager, those startling moments when the child's voice shot through the enveloped time of the writing-mother with a terse report or demand from his vivid world, is no longer a defining event of the writing. His time is much closer to adult time, and so another time has returned to me. In this time, I am interested in thinking about the way my own intellectual interests condition me as an artist, as they do and don't influence the child, who now in many respects has his own life.

Writing is about time: fable, mannerism, shovel.

I want to insert something into the world as an object, or thing, a communication and a complex fact or act—something that cannot be easily taken back. Writing is an intervention of which the full *emotionally symbolic world of humiliation catalyzed by the presence of the mother. Does not this power to humiliate touch upon the domain of the* femme fatale?

Scene II: Book jacket summary of a detective novel in which the femme fatale is assigned the role of detective

BOOK JACKET SUMMARY:

There is a gathering of women poets who write poems primarily about the betrayals of men.[4] One evening, someone in the group declares that we "are all writing about the same man." Everyone agrees. Now the question is, who is the man? What does it mean that we are all writing about the same man? Is it Don Juan? It becomes apparent that there are two male deities: one of them is Papa, who is present everywhere, and the other is Don Juan, whose presence is not panoptic and metaphoric, but fragmentary, corporeal, and metonymic. Have we been betrayed? We have known for a long time that Don Juan and Papa are at odds, even if we just now realize that our feelings of betrayal occur in respect to each of these characters: the protector and the violator. Each keeps us in a savage state of sexual need. Each one of us sees the other as a femme fatale in a detective novel. But we have an organization! We are all present at once. The woman whose father's wrath falls on her as her lover betrays her for one of her friends. The woman, who loyal to her father's wrath, refuses the betrayer of her friend. She who has a family and she who no longer has one. The femme fatale *becomes the detective. The object has become the agent who is to investigate these feelings of betrayal, which are the invisible scars of endured sexual need. The sign on our agency door reads "Mothers of Invention." We are accused of copyright or*

consequences cannot be anticipated. The full consequences to my child of my life as a writer also
cannot be anticipated.

Never fully namable or objective.

Language creates things, says Jacques Lacan. In the
realm of the child separating from the mother,
the acquisition of language on the part of the child
makes the mother into an object.

She is a thick truck in heavy snow.

Of course, the construction of dangerous women
in other social discourses surrounds us familiarly
and continuously. In the classic *noire* detective
novel, the *femme fatale* is the object of desire of the
detective and other men whom she manipulates to
such a degree that mayhem is created.

Renegade pink geraniums in a flower box.

Abigail Child's film *Mayhem* is a brilliant decon-
struction of this genre. Focusing on the *noire* heroine's anxiety as it is produced by male violence and
the heroine's unrepressed sexuality, Child not only
critiques but subverts the *noire* conventions. Her
subversion would not be complete, however, without the film's pasted-on happy ending: found
footage of a playfully pornographic narrative of two
women making love with a goofy-looking "robber"
masturbating at the fringes of their pleasure-mak-
ing scene. Child's film explores specific generic fantasies related to questions of sexual repression and
the nature of violence that exists not only in art but
in the "real" world.

Gossip and die in a bed of money.

patent infringement—finally we have entered the real
world of lawsuits. Our business is solidified, even if this
side issue distracts us from our more noble cause. Our sus-
picion is this: Don Juan and Papa are secretly in cahoots.
They may even be The Same Man. The worst of it is that all
of our children have been born under the sign of the same
man… What is a poet to do?

NATHALIE SARRAUTE:

My father is the only one who remains present every-
where.[5]

Scene III: To speak to a child as if one lives in a matriarchal society is probably impossible, for example[6]

PLAIN JANE:

The mother becomes very nervous about what she is saying,
because she has formed herself as a sociological entity and
is in conflict then with the aesthetic. When her writing is
not aesthetic, it seems distracted, an emanation from a
queen with no country or a woman senator in an all-male
assembly, or a revolutionary without a purpose. It begs
questions and opens itself to attacks. The language of
poetry falls away. She is left with a few questions about
those things one lives in and out of books. She is told she
ought not to have a picture on her book jacket with her
child because it would define her negatively as an author.
She is told great women poets do not have children. She
says fuck you and wishes later that she had made a more
comical response, borrowing from Chandler's detective
Marlowe's edgy ruminations and quips. She possesses
a radical sense of freedom even if she does feel a little
hurt. Like Marlowe, she closes herself in her office and

At this very moment, there is "mayhem" in the U.S. government played out in the cartoon of the U.S. Congress's attempt at a *coup d'état* over the President's sexual misconduct and the politically condoned murders of the people of Baghdad. There is no Congress who has yet considered impeaching a president for illegally conducting war.

Sometimes one wishes to stay in bed.

My interest in Child, my condemnation of the attacks on Baghdad, that I read a book titled *Psychoanalysis and the Family* and my faithful love of *Go Dogs Go*, my disdain and fury at the "moral" right's attempted *coup* using a young woman for bait which they hook into each citizen's mouth with neither approbation or consent, certainly is to my child as present and powerful as the events in and of themselves. I am a camera (object) that casts a lens onto the world separate from the child but close to him. He knows how to use a camera.

Groaning sheets turn to flags.

Because I am interested in questions of power, I cannot ignore that my child is growing up in *this* world. I describe the world through the demonstration of my interests. He knows also that I spend much of my time working: that I am at this time in his life, at least, "a producer." He and I have a relationship that is increasingly decided by work as he gets older. Until recently, he was less aware of my relationship to him through my relationship to work. In my other two essays on the subject of art and motherhood, I intercut his interruptions verbatim as I worked on the essays. My approach to art-making changed at *contemplates whether or not she should answer the phone. Your son is missing homework assignments. He is resistant to grammar. Even though she is not particularly resistant to grammar, she is certain he acquired the resistance from her. For she is resistant to placement. Sometimes she is accused of obduracy. And closes the blinds to her office. Sleeps on the couch. Doesn't dust. The only aesthetic objects in her office are the bottle of Maker's Mark and a decanter as sleek as modernity itself. Everything else from keyboard to whisky glass, which she mostly uses for water, fills her room with plain jane functionality that signals the presence of a proprietor mostly stuck in her head.*

Scene IV: Book jacket detective novel summary: in which the femme fatale and the mother turn out to be the same woman

How does the mother become the mother? She is a mess. Not because of anything she has done or even said. But because mothers are the shadows of children in novels and in theories about the family and in theories about children and because they are simultaneously the corporeal, ethical, and intellectual subjects of their own universes. What's odd then about living in fact and fiction or reality and poetry as if these categories were truly separate? Right now the mother's son is driving around with two professors: one is a philosopher of history and the other is his father, a scholar, and a poet. Are they talking about Kant and Habermas? And categories of value that must be kept separate? What happens if there has never been a positive category of value assigned to the mother that can be aligned with rationality/economics/aesthetics or pleasure/doing good/disinterest. The mother is a mess in the universe of classifications because she is not assigned a role that can his birth, and the interruptions in the text performed and designated a relationship to time I enacted as writer and mother in my work. Now we are much more engaged in a body of overlapping work. Right now he is practicing the piano with great attention.

Clicking with civil disobedience.

But I was talking about questions of power. My power would only diminish if he were not also powerful, if he did not have in a very real sense his own life. The life that he and I live is alongside, with, and between each other as it has been for a long time.

Nipples in a vortex.

These questions of power are still interesting: when they address issues of female sexuality, female aggression, female ambition, and the relationship of women to their own motherhood in respect to the way motherhood in bourgeois society has been represented historically by men and the way the artist confronts them in her work when she is also a mother. For what she always experiences is a discrepancy between the representation, her own experience, and her art practice—all three. The event of motherhood only magnifies the discrepancies that have always been present.

Love to present themselves as first blood.

represent a category of value that can be kept separate. Aesthetics and ethics are not that far apart. Childbirth and sexuality are not that far apart. The fatal attraction of the man to her is not that far away. It is separated from the child who separates from her. Thus, the mother shadows the child, catalogs his activities, keeps track of his arrangements. She is dressed to kill and calls him on the phone to get an account of his plans for making dinner and to suggest he try the onion soup with the Vidalia onions. So this is the life of our dear detective, what is she trying to find? Who is the murdered? And when the mother and the femme fatale *become the detective, isn't she rather like all the great male* noire *detectives that precede her? She is a mess because she is alone, responsible for something outside herself which is intimately connected to her own private nature, a small fish in a big pond. But no matter how small she makes herself, her shadow is too large.*

NOTES

1. Jacques Lacan, *The Seminar of Jacques Lacan: Book I Freud's Papers on Technique 1953–1954*, ed. Jacques-Alain Miller, trans. John Forrester. New York: W.W. Norton & Company, 1988, p. 172.

2. Nathalie Sarraute, *Childhood*, trans. Barbara Wright in consultation with the author. London: John Calder, 1984, p. 36.

3. Carla Harryman, "There Never Was a Rose Without a Thorn," anthologized in *Poems for the Millennium*, Volume II, ed. Jerome Rothenberg and Pierre Joris. Berkeley, California: University of California Press, 1998, p. 677.

4. Thanks to my student Jesse Deneaux for this concept based on his experience of a poetry reading he attended.

5. Sarraute, *Childhood*, p. 38.

6. Mark Poster, *Critical Theory of the Family*. New York: Seabury, 1978, p. 96.

◊

CARLA HARRYMAN is the author of eleven books, including two experimental novels, *Gardener of Stars* (Atelos, 2001) and *The Words After Carl Sandburg's Rootabaga Stories and Jean-Paul Sartre* (O Books, 1999); two volumes of selected writing, *There Never Was a Rose Without a Thorn* (City Lights, 1995) and *Animal Instincts: poetry, prose, and plays* (This, 1989); and a book-length dramatic work, *Memory Play* (O Books, 1994). Her works for performance have been staged nationally and internationally. Harryman's most recent production was the staging of her play *Performing Objects Stationed in the Sub World* at the Zeitgeist Theater in Detroit and at Oxford Brookes University in England. She teaches creative writing, women's studies, and literature at Wayne State University. Her son, Asa Watten, was born in 1984.

Part Three

Signals Given:
Language Paradigms

Doublings

ALICE NOTLEY | PARIS, FEBRUARY 1997

I became a poet somewhat coincidentally to becoming a mother. I wrote my first "good poems" in early '71 and bore my elder son in '72. My first "good poems" weren't numerous, and, being sonnets, weren't in the unprecedented forms I felt destined for. So though happy enough to be pregnant (I didn't plan my pregnancies, I am an experimentalist), I felt at times desperate about my poetry. How could I become the poet now? Ted once suggested early in my first pregnancy that I might have to put off becoming the poet for a while, but that, he said, would be in the American tradition of late-blooming: Look at Whitman…"Song of Myself" at age 36. I was 26 and didn't want to wait ten more years, resolved quietly and like steel not to. So, then, what to write? How to write? The same questions I still always face, with much the same urgency: Where is the form for this as yet unidentified meaning growing inside me? In 1972 it seemed obvious that my subject was what I was carrying, because he signified enormous change and because, most especially, there was little poetry that dealt with this change.

> IT
>
> It lies curled up all around is dark
> warm water, we did too but can't
> remember, or envision such aquatic
> shelter
>   right side up it sits one day
> the next stands on head, awake or
> sleeping   swallows   hiccups, even
> opens eyes. Too dark for sight
> too dark to read its mother's mind[1]

I've kept very little of what I wrote during my first pregnancy. I remember an infatuation with the word "quickening," which I finally managed to use to my satisfaction, after Anselm's birth, in the poem "Dear Dark Continent." I think that during the pregnancy I must have been doing apprenticeship work, work in forms. Certainly I was writing, I always have since then, and maybe the urgency of my feeling that I Must write Every Day because All is Against me and will Stop me Soon, stems from that time. But I didn't have my subject, in 1972, until the baby was born. I enjoyed two months of calm, a sort of calm shock, and then was hit by a painful, lengthy, inscrutable postpartum depression. It was so difficult for me to read that experience (I'm still not sure I can) that it had to become the center of my poetry for several years, generating form, feeling, and wisdom. I was two people, the one I had always been and the new one who was suffering. The strangeness of being one suffering, being one so other, coexisted alongside a happiness with and a fascination with my son. How could being be so double? Giving birth was about doubling, and marriage was, and poetry was:

> She combs a form of the senses
> the principle of destruction the double hook
> closes into the figure S for she or
> healthy shame or shanty or shaggy
>
> the body body rings the mind mind
> gestures the body mind spreads
> with sight the speaker addresses audience
> and they are each other[2]

The poetic forms I used were often either thick slablike shapes or swirlings, influenced by painting and designed to hold a lot of thoughts and feelings and observations in one suspension, just as the contradictions in me were united in my selfhood. Which I have never for a minute disbelieved in. Social construct, sure, but that's surface, and there's a helluva lot more than surface, baby, or I wouldn't have been so knocked on my ass by this subterranean force. Or been capable of getting back up afterward. *I* did it not a social construct; not myriad selves and voices, not my friends, not obtuse society, not Ted. Did both the falling down and the getting up. It wasn't the chemicals—hormonal imbalance—and it wasn't a syndrome; it wasn't "postpartum depression" it was a self facing the poetry, violent and contrary, of this world for the first time. It was how I got to be the poet, got to be born too.

When in April of '73 Ted, baby Anselm, and I moved to England for a while, I got to take my dark depressed double first to London, then to the English countryside, Wivenhoe in Essex. I got pregnant again there. But first I remember sitting in a room of my own (we still lived in houses then) thinking about Sylvia Plath going mad in a similar English scene. I wrote in a now-discarded poem the line: "But Poetess X was a shit; she killed herself." I suppose that was a little harsh—I had to survive, didn't I? I still hate people's fascination with her, their dangerous uses of her. This house where I sometimes thought about her, rented from a man named the Reverend Lovelace, had an immense English garden in back with three—was it more?—apple trees, a sepulchre-shaped compost heap, lots of rose bushes, herbs, new flowers blooming monthly, a shed, and a bomb shelter. Ted had lied to the estate agents and told them I was an enthusiastic practiced gardener; being a poet he figured it was almost true since I knew the names of flowers. So it was against a conventional symbol of fertility, this spectacular stage for manifold flower appearances, that I wrote *Songs For The Unborn Second Baby* during my second pregnancy. This was a 46-page poem in a wide-open form, which used my emotions positive and negative as flowerlike colors and shapes:

> We cannot burn the witch she is
> shot throughout the splendor
> of the thoughts of the spirits
> circumvolving
>   round the jacinth glint
>   green stem

"jacinth"…
I keep inventing these sunsets
                    Actual twilight
is hard, fleetingly
            then night the fleece
                    the flesh around and it is
known morning
            will be sound
                    bitter
                    ardent
                    mustard
                    faith
                    object
                    sun
                    letter

Anselm is in large part the muse of the work:

I showed him rain
                glass making spreadout
                            its true pitch which
        space and strength was a pet-name
                        which I could only name then
        now and then
                    pungent aromatic voracious American in
        eclipse is not his name
                    it is something like
                                sweet motive[3]

The ending of the poem includes passages from Dante's *Paradiso*, but the final line is "Not too bad for a"; I wasn't sure of the precise name for anything everyone else was sure of, though the poem is full of its own precisions.

I gave birth to Edmund in Colchester Maternity Hospital in August '74, and then we returned to the United States, to Chicago for a year. Chicago is a cold hell sometimes; I spent an interesting time inside in '74 and '75, watching *Sesame Street* and *The Electric Company* with Anselm. I examined words as they were stripped down to the letter on those shows, while Anselm himself learned to read early. I also finally got to take some pills for my depression, having gotten a "diagnosis" of it in England, but having been told that I couldn't take the pills until after the pregnancy. The medication seemed to render me highly color-sensitive: I studied art and made a lot of collages. I continued to observe my changes, always interested in what I was "going through." The poet is that observer of her own experience, even if it's presented in poems as observation of others or of things, and if she can hold on to just a thread of the artist's detachment during pregnancy and motherhood, will manage to discharge the double function of being a person and a poet. And there's further the double function of being poet and parent. Children don't need money spent on them, they need to have their parents around; poets can work at home making hardly any money and being good parents.

I began while still in Chicago to write works incorporating my sons' voices. I was working in collage-like forms influenced by the literal collages I had been making, and so at first whatever Anselm said seemed object-like to me, something to be laid next to something else:

> Chicago summer
> dressed in flak
> silver buttons
> down her back
> "The wind bumped me!"[4]

I also liked to imagine what he was thinking, before he could talk well, and write that down. After we moved to New York in '76 I became fascinated by the sound of talk. As I do keep saying, we lived in the tiniest of doorless apartments under salon conditions so I was constantly bathed in conversation, including that of my sons. I invented forms which included all this talking as much to keep writing as for any other reason: I had to write while people were around. And in the midst of active mothering. I invented

conversational poetic narratives and diaries spun out of outer talk and inner mental nar-
ration in prose-like verse and verse-like prose separate and mixed. I wrote down what
people said, but also improvised sayings for them and also turned visually apprehended
events like dreams into conversation; everyone and everything seemed to be talking. My
children were people too and they were talking, all the time. They were as inventive in conversation as all the poets who visited were, they made themselves just as high talking,
were less melodramatic and intense; their feelings were cleaner and there was a pure clean
light around their talk which I liked to be near and which I liked to include in my work.
I don't believe I intruded on their privacy; though in our apartment there was no privacy,
only manners, and I think we had good manners. Anyway, I was mostly interested in the
quality of their thought and speech:

> Where'd you get this thing?
> I didn't get it from anyone, it's mine. I got it from my grandpa.
> You mean my grandpa.
> Yeah.
> What are the names of your grandpa?
> Shut up.
> Spareribs and Dingbat? Spareribs and Nobody? Heathcliff and Dingbat?
> Shut up.
> My very words to Bernice.
> That's Fish.
> No that's my very words to Bernice...[5]

I think I must have stopped using my sons' spoken words around 1982, '83, because
they were growing up and their talk was evolving somewhat away from playfulness and
more toward considerations of personal character. Also my own poetic forms needed
transformation again. I remember referring to a conversation with Anselm, in a work
called "Jimmy Valentine," summarizing it rather than repeating it, about who our favorite
characters were in the *Iliad*. He chose Patroclus, I chose Cassandra, whom I never would
have thought to choose before so I must have been changing. He saw himself as a true
friend and hero, I saw myself as unheeded female foreteller of doom, maybe at this point
because Ted was dying, and my poems were foretelling it though my consciousness
wasn't. I haven't said much about Edmund yet: he was weird though also normal. He had
believed Ted one day when Ted said God wore a red dress; then Ted had later footnoted
that locution with the observation that that didn't mean God was a woman. Edmund
therefore obsessively referred to God as "she/he/or it." He was some sort of new human

in the making, and Anselm and I watched him a lot and tried to get him to tell us funny things, about for instance what a "cran" was, an insect he'd imagined in his room one night though it might have been a bedbug or a roach. Or it might have been a dream. "I saw a cran," he'd said with conviction. From the age of six Edmund in fact wrote his own poems, and I early on become a voice in *his* poems, since I collaborated with him on poems that appeared in *his* books:

> ROBOT WORLD
> Fake robots don't count in
> the Real Robot World---
> Blade-Runner blow up Robot,
> Robot punch Blade-Runner---
> But the Doctor doesn't care.[6]

The year after Ted died, 1984, Anselm, Edmund, and I made some list works together which appear in my book *At Night The States*, e.g., "The Ten Best Issues Of Comic Books," "The World's 21 Greatest Animals: A Play." This is the first poetic activity of Anselm's that I recall. I continued to collaborate with Edmund sometimes, and then he began to bring me more and more of his poetry to react to, and also he would show his poems to Doug (the British poet Douglas Oliver) after Doug and I were married. Later, around 1990 I think, Anselm, too, mysteriously began to write poems. I don't think he expected that to happen, it just did one day. We are now all practicing poets, and are liable equally to be present in each other's works, as in these lines of Anselm's from a recent poem, "In The Paintings Of Will":

> What colors February inhales
> between birth & death
> are greys & pink outlines of fallen leaves
> pasted to paper
> Brother slumped in chair
> Mother hands on lap
> seated in front of foliage flaring up
> as molten lava tearing thru' wood[7]

Thus mothering's culminating effect on my poetics has involved the emergence of new poetry colleagues for me to interact with and to be influenced by. I've produced a "double" generation, persons and poets, and am as a good poetry mother, real mother, and older poet, interested in the work of my sons' poet friends as well as their own.

NOTES

1. Alice Notley, "IT" in *Incidentals in the Day World*. New York: Angel Hair Books, 1973, unpaginated.

2. Alice Notley, "1985" in *For Frank O'Hara's Birthday*. Cambridge, England: Street Editions, 1976, unpaginated.

3. Alice Notley, *Songs For The Unborn Second Baby*. Lenox, Massachusetts: United Artists, 1979, unpaginated.

4. Alice Notley, "Pure Weather" in *Alice Ordered Me To Be Made*. Chicago: The Yellow Press, 1976, p. 33.

5. Alice Notley, "My Bodyguard" in *Waltzing Matilda*. New York: The Kulchur Foundation, 1981, p. 56.

6. Edmund Berrigan, "ROBOT WORLD" in *Dinosaur*. New York: Archipelago Books, 1982, unpaginated.

7. Anselm Berrigan, "In The Paintings Of Will," published in *GAS 8*, ed. Kevin Opstedal, Winter 1996/7.

◊

ALICE NOTLEY was married to Ted Berrigan and then to Douglas Oliver, both noted poets, both deceased. She has two sons by Ted Berrigan, Anselm Berrigan, born in 1972, and Edmund Berrigan, born in 1974, both poets. She now lives in Paris, France.

To book as in to foal. To son.

Kathleen Fraser

1. monologue

Catching two words. Pulling apart and rePasting a paragraph on the same night spiders crowd and come pushing out from the closet door at the actual child.

Working in the next room without knowing this, to hear him tell of it years later and to hold this. Nights of long fear.

To sorrow the poem, to sorrow and tear at its lines, to open its vein. Looking for blue. Expecting it.

Instead, to find red. Scar tissue. Long hollow empty place. Quill of a feather.

Writing lines, watching lines elasticize and tatter, not knowing how to solace the dark, child's eyes open/eyes awake, with mind yet struck in infant night-terror. An otherness you know nothing of. Can you write this? Can you hold it quietly?

Deferral. To other's book.

To work at night to work when child is sleeping is drawing. Each chore that wants you. Assignments marked. To unplug the phone on Sunday when the child is with his father, to not answer a knock, to put away the folders of others, other's book, put away feeding. To sit in the chair in silence. To place suddenly urgent books on the cleared oak table, to touch the new notebook, to open it at the blank page; lines on the page that mark emptiness. To feel the lines recovering one, into them. Falling into the page. Away from every other.

To book as in to foal. To son. Those first wobbly legs. To have this actual child. To try to show him how to stand up. The two of them now, instead of the three of them, yet not deleting the father.

The father at the door on Saturday,

or the father with the actual child between them, swinging him along, and then… then the actual child comes home. The poem comes home. She is home.

Through necessity's trap door. To be with other poets (mothers, among them) sitting in a basement room, ones who can barely speak yet must write. Can sometimes reach into their own and private horde. But some cannot speak because cannot lift out the sleek word into this sudden formal classroom air. Broken thoughtline chatter and humility. Interrupted minute. Someone's daughter is zipped shut but writing inside of that. You hear her trying. Trying to put it right. Tight squeeze through these neat and tidy lines. Lanes. Starting gate's official gun. The poem leaning forward. Taut. Not to swing away. To allay fear.

Look at her. In arrears. Delayed.

Taught to frustration.

To wake up and know the body is dead. To notice the air is bright but the body is not. To substitute little trays of food with cut animal shapes of sandwich, baked cookies and mother cake with mother chocolate, stories before sleep, "this little piggy went to market," hands rubbing his feet. To sing: *A grasshopper hopped on a redbud tree/and said "Come away, come away with me. Come awaaayyy, come awaaayyy."* To lower the light.

Then to fall into the saved book, her own bed and again to be called back into the dark. Hark, the spider's interruption.

Book gone, song again. The mother is singing as her mother sang, putting the sound in her. Now she rocks him or is a bird and does not know who is who.

Then remembers the weight of the first little book her father gave her, with a father's silly drawing inside it, bird named ODAROLOC standing on one foot, leg long, head hidden under wing. Now the bird appears again, in sleep. In its beak an empty book. She opens it.

To book again, to son. To teach him *al dente* pasta and first-pressed oil, the garlic and parsley tossed in. Not to be helpless, yet to weep helplessly in front of him, not to dissemble. To choose this particular quill for making shapes and marks. To give him that dropped feather. A crayon, a brush and paint, a wall of paper endlessly unrolling. To give him red and blue jars of thick paste color. His hands in it and the brushes making their mark.

To admire and want. To want to say, but feel chagrin for obvious saying, but to be urgent, defying, pinning together and sewing, to be ripping apart and wiping, to be cooking soup and typing, often to be starting and not finishing, but to be planting in the garden with him, watering and digging, watching for the spider, but to be edited out, but "to submit" and to be "rejected," but to choose a desk and a chair and to feel the singleness of it, the actual child of it coming home.

The child howling with hunger of her, anger at her going out the door, not wanting the others to take her, but pushing her away from him (her coming in the door for him). Himself unto himself. More himself.

Then her feet shod with shoes of red to be danced, coming and going, saying "Look how we work beside each other," she with her hollow door desk and he with his solid child desk. They make pictures and cross out words and everything is in pieces all over the desk and the floor and scribbled over pages drawn to their edges with Spiderman moon-walks, weaponry inventories...whatever is needed.

To have this actual son in this child. To try to explain absence, the two of them now, or often a different three of them. Flying out of his sightlines. The book of her and the foal of him without deferring to one of them. To find this peculiar path and follow its constant changing. To sit alone at the table. To revise a passive construction. To choose the ticking body parts and the knocking poem unable to speak. To talk to it. To mother it.

Violets from the ever-so-lightly lover the woman in her wants and is given...and the child is also given plastic models and metal toys whose hooks and claws soon break. But he glues together parts of monsters that don't fit the cheaply printed instructions. He unfolds hybrids. Nobody tells him how, his being a child and curious. And used to gluing.

To get lost, then to look for the true pact between them, teaching herself the motherpart, how to think and to learn that grammar of his lengthening. To revise. To leave him alone. To worry. To give him a push. To book, to foal, to write partial sentences. Hiding her worrying. To glue each sentence together with parts of its making. To have written the sentence's smooth beauty and, later, to break it apart.

To let the poem pour from the closet, long erratic music-tugging lines and word horde of the broken-in-on nightlight.

To tango.

To monster.

To let the lover into the mother world.

And that boy, what a boy, what a gorgeous boy, what a soul in that boy, what a poem in that boy.

INTERVAL

The pen runs along the page like a seismograph, its motion alternately evoking large, ominous crags and thin, immaterial crests which run, uphill and down, across an otherwise white page like notes on some monumental orchestral score.[1]

2. dialogue

A: So what do you think?

B: About what?

A: About the monologue.

B: I was glad for the last line.

A: What do you mean?

B: Your story was sad, otherwise.

A: Sad? Maybe sometimes…but mostly we were just trying to figure out how to find what we needed, being two strong individuals and such a tiny family. We were in the car a lot, in the summers. I remember the red rock canyons; he took pictures of the dinosaur statuary. Sacred Indian places, country music on the radio, dust storms. We always had a cat or two, wherever we lived. He would name them for how they looked—Gum-camel, Witchy, Watermelon. And then Maynard kept coming from over the back fence and finally stayed.

He liked to wander loose in malls, I preferred friends' kitchens. We both liked museums and Chinese food, camping-out for awhile and then, after a few nights, thick white towels and TV. Once we woke up to a bear prowling in the next campsite…

B: Hmmm…

A: Why hmmm? Do you mean I shouldn't talk about those times?

B: I just don't see the point of writing about it.

A: But it's part of how we grew up. Side by side. Looking back, I think it was a pretty good model—showing him how to "work," by stealing time to do my own. I was close by. That wasn't sad. What was sad was each of us losing someone out of our daily lives, someone we loved and needed. One way or another it happens, but ideally not so soon in a person's life. But he didn't lose me and I didn't lose him. He helped me to pay close attention. I learned to let him grow up. We both had our own long journeys going on inside us. Whenever we hung out together—especially in the car, when the motion seemed to loosen us up—we had some great talks. And laugh! Sometimes I had to stop the car. But when he was drawing he was often in planetary space, whereas when I was writing I was attaching myself to the page as if I were driving or drawing all over it.

B: But in the story, the child seems to be an obstacle...

A: You mean, to the writing? Everything was an obstacle. That was part of the perceived problem of trying to write *outside* of a vacuum—that is, to have always imagined the poem as something that could be written only *inside* perfect, uninterrupted time, an air-tight vacuum: quiet. Waiting for the day when this moment would finally arrive. But everything kept breaking in on continuity; everyone wanted your attention, if you were a mother. Each person imagined he or she was the only one. Apparently the maternal image is in there, pulsing pure neon. You could be carrying a dozen other lives inside you waiting to unfold. But it seems unavoidable, this leaning toward motherlove. This wanting to be held and listened to. This continuous presence of expectation.

B: You mean signed and sealed in the genes?

A: Or the years of someone before you, showing you... I don't know.

B: I never had trouble like that. I could just sit in the front room and write, with the kids playing and their friends tearing in and out.

A: Not me. I wanted a door. I had to get completely closed off from someone else's waiting and needing. It kept hovering. The phone was always ringing. You wanted to be available, to be a generous person. Especially to your actual child. But the milk kept running out, so it was off to Safeway again, instead of to the desk. I'd hear something starting up inside my brain, trying to get out—even just the *desire* to think *anything*, to find words for it, move them around on the page...and I'd run for a pen and begin, but it was mostly disruption and intervention, arguments and pardons, hugs and little cups of custard meant to last a few days in the fridge.

Time kept running out. You could either stop and cook or point at the refrigerator and fight the guilt. And always there was something new to track down, to keep that child's mind open and flexible and muscular, to honor its curiosity and persistence... (but oh, the tedium of playgrounds and birthday parties...my god, the chat could drive you to the edge!). I used to wince when I heard men—usually writer types—talking about "the abyss," as if it were an immense set of cosmic jaws lying in wait, in some abstract future oblivion. Whereas, I felt that darkness hovering around the corner, almost every normal day. And I *knew* what it was. It was the bleakness and frustration of no time alone, no free path into the forest, no access.

It was the problem of feeling trapped with no way out, feeling one had lost one's hold on an authentic self. I mean, if a writer can't find time to make notes and shape the perceptions and voices unraveling inside her, she can get very crazy. Much of the time, it was just the two of us and somehow that made for more interruptions than less. And of course there were the problems of earning a living—doctor and dentist bills, the car, the mortgage payment—thinking ahead, before sleep, about the next morning, the order of what must be done to get us both to school on time: his day, my day, his night, my night.

Meanwhile, art supplies, guitar strings, Star Trek uniform...only one certain color and fabric would do. The riding boots were researched for weeks. The kid's mind was avid. He loved beautiful things, quite particular things, and TV junk-hype and the terrifying, invented stuff he made up in his drawing books. Food and objects gave him a safety zone, proof of having enough of his own...that I would be there, through any question and every sorrow, to help him figure out his turf.

B: You didn't *have* to do all that...

A: But I *wanted* to. Except for writing, I was probably most directly connected in those moments, helping him feel taken care of and safe…yet, later, torn with guilt anyway, worrying I'd never done enough for him…or for me.

B: If you were enjoying it so much, why the grief? Why couldn't you just accept being a mother, since that's what you'd chosen. I mean, how many books do you need to write to make you feel okay?

A: It's not a question of numbers, some abstract measurement of accomplishment. It's really about survival…how one stays alive to one's private art, one's particular connection to being and making something new out of—well—the life you've chosen, but also what is choosing you. How do you stay alive to that? By working. Alone in your workspace. If you are a writer, you *must* write. To only think about it, and wish for it, without sitting down to do it, is to deny your gift, to damp it down. Either way, the muscle of the mind atrophies and the intimacy of one's relation to one's work (the *pleasure* of doing it) diminishes proportionately. Self-diminishment is painful. Poor mother, poor child— they both feel its effects.

But I *had* to find a way to write. Writing was different than loving him or working for us or all the big and little shifts of fiction and passing romance which kept going on above and below the life of me and him and of writing. Loving and writing and earning a living were the priorities. I had to find time enough for all three or I felt I would not survive. Bottom line. Still, my students kept arriving for conferences. Their manuscripts and midterms piled up on my writing desk. The weekends were entirely eaten up by being useful and resourceful. Necessity. Consolation. Transportation. One day it hit me. It wasn't going to stop. There wasn't going to be the perfect vacuum of silence and continuity. So I had to invent another way to capture the poems—a place I could walk into and back out of. Trust with a phrase or a sentence. Accretion of parts, maps of disruption.

B: But what about beauty and form?

A: Beauty, as I'd been taught to think of it, no longer interested me in the same way.

B: I really don't see…

A: ...how you can write a poem without it, right?

B: Right.

A: I had to keep my eye on things. I had to remember for two. The old idea of "beauty" no longer served—neither the question, nor the answer. My thoughts were blips and scrolls and departures. The task was to catch them just as they came up to the surface. Unexpectedness, chaos, pressures and breaks. Everything seemed to tilt, to barely maintain itself. In spite of all effort. I thought, why not write that way? While the beautiful, seamless poem stopped being relevant to my own way of working, the open field of the page became more and more compelling. That mark of a seismograph across an empty score.

INTERVAL

Gestation: (1) the act of carrying young in the womb from conception to delivery.
(2) the development of a plan in the mind.
—*Webster's Unabridged Dictionary*, second edition, 1976

3. pedagogy

Catching two words...pulling apart and rePasting...to tear at its lines, to open... watching lines elasticize...recovering one...often to be starting and not finishing... and scribbled over pages drawn to their edges...to find this peculiar path and follow its constant changing...to choose the ticking body parts and the knocking poem unable to speak...to talk to it...to glue each sentence together with parts of its making...to have written the sentence's smooth beauty and, later, to break it apart...to let the poem pour from the closet, long erratic music-tugging lines and word horde of the broken-in-on nightlight.

—for David, 5/30/1997

Notes

1. Michael Gibson, "The Landscapes of Raffi Kaiser," *International Herald Tribune*, May 1997.

◊

KATHLEEN FRASER has published fourteen books of poems, most recently *20th Century* (a+bend Press, 2000), *il cuore: the heart, Selected Poems 1970–1995* (Wesleyan University Press, 1997), and *WING* (Em Press, 1995). Her collected essays, *Translating the Unspeakable, Poetry and the Innovative Necessity,* were published by the University of Alabama Press (2000) in their Modern and Contemporary Poetics Series. Fraser is a Guggenheim Fellow in Poetry and has won two N.E.A. writing fellowships, as well as the Frank O'Hara Award (for innovative achievement in poetry). She lives for five months of each year in Rome with her husband, philosopher A.K. Bierman, and lectures on American contemporary and modernist poetry in Italian universities. She has one son, David Marshall, born in 1967, who is a writer, visual artist, and self-defense/martial arts instructor.

Notes on "Listen"

ALICIA OSTRIKER | PRINCETON, 1997

I: Notebook, San Diego–Denver Flight, April 1985

The desire of language, the language of desire

The famous masculinity of language that women writers take to be axiomatic: and upon this axiom theory builds its intimidating edifice

How impatient it makes me, how I wish to growl shout curse bellow, and how I also wish to reason argue prove demonstrate exhort

We were in Marilyn Farwell's car driving somewhere around the University of Oregon after my reading, and her undergraduate student was talking with us about French feminism. She was reading Kristeva. Or she was reading Homans. She was dead certain that language was masculine. She was dead! certain! that language! language! was masculine! I was dead tired. I was rude. I said: a premise can be a lie. You do not have to believe it. Language is not monolithic (etc.). Then it struck me—

Language is female. Wanted to tell her, the undergraduate. Wanted to harangue her: You learned how to speak from a female. As soon as you were born, a female began talking to you. Sweetie, she said. Hi, sweetie. The female held her face above your face so you could focus on her. She spoke intimately. Hello, you funnyface. Maybe it was more than one female. They held you while they spoke. They were feeding you, undressing and dressing you, washing you. They were wiping yellow milky smelling shit from your posterior creases, invisible to you. Rhythms were involved. While they did these things they talked. At times they sang. At times they mixed nonsense and sense for the fun of it. Oh yes, they were semiotic, semiautomatic, somatic. Probably you would not be alive if this were not so. Often it is not so and the child dies. The child dies, for example, in orphanages in China and Thailand—you can read about this today because it did not happen to you. With you, they were being playful. Their hands were caressing you, squeezing you, petting you so their arms pressed you to their body. There was a lot of rhythm and a lot of repetition. Language is female. Their arms pressed you to their body. Language is food, clothing, information, immersion in water which frightens you the first time then you enjoy it and a towel. You were crying. You were at the top of your own lungs crying. They were angry. Language is anger. Language is screaming. Language is she hits you. There isn't food. You throw up. Language is she says the things she says again and again. She says shut up. Shut up. Shut up. She says that.

She talks and talks. Do you remember her face when she is talking? She slaps you. She shakes you. You brat, you stupid brat, will you shut up will you stop screaming. Will you eat this. Will you hold still. Will you stop wiggling. Will you get over here. She kisses you, she laughs and makes you laugh. She tells you a story once upon a time. Language is female. Language is female. A bunny rabbit a fairy a funny cat. Come sit on my lap, come cuddle, give us a hug. Are you embarrassed? Do you remember her face when she is talking? Language is female. Are you embarrassed? Are you afraid?

Are you afraid if he hears us. Are you afraid to think:
LANGUAGE IS FEMALE.

Silence is masculine. Masculinity is silence. He isn't there. He buttons his lip. He keeps a stiff upper lip which makes it difficult to talk. Silence is golden.

He gives orders. Does that make him like her, but more so? He gives her orders (according to the story). He reads the bedtime story. (Like her?) When he talks it is more important (it says in the story). "But not in *my* family," yells somebody. "Not in *mine*," yells somebody else. (But they don't count, they're ethnic.) She teaches you how to read. She teaches you to write. She teaches you arithmetic. And social studies. Language is female. Often you are mad at her. You despise her. She disgusts you. She embarrasses you. Language is female. The mother tongue. The mother. The mother. The tongue. Are you embarrassed?

Logic is male. Theology is male. Philosophy is male. Business is male. Grammar is male. Law is male. Medicine is male. (Healing is female, and women who do it get paid less.) The university is male. The church is priests. Where have all the priestesses gone. Why can't a woman be a manager, she asked her boss and the boss said A woman can't be a manager because God is a man. Also the *shul* is male. Talmud is male. They uprooted her groves. History is male. Mathematics is male. The university is male. The pentagon is male magic. War is male. Science is male. Weapons systems are male. "Discourse" is male. If you can draw a line around it, it is male. If you can beat somebody with it then it is a symbolic phallus and male and it is might and right.

First of all language is spoken. Then it is written. Then it is printed. Then it is printed-out. The more dis-embodied the words, the higher their status. If it is in a library, it must be true. Then it is object-ive. And then it is dead. The living language is speech, which is constantly regenerated at the core, like the pith of a tree. The dead language is exhibited on library shelves. Burn the libraries, says William Carlos Williams, who of all the male modernists is the most embodied in matter and the least threatened by women.

Discourse attempts to make you forget a human woman ever held you in her arms and was God. It eliminates agency and responsibility and is abstract as all hell—

It is sans teeth, sans eyes—
it is without gesture
it is without facial expression
it is without odor there is no milk spilling from it
it intimidates
it is not necessarily trying to kill you but it does not care if you live or die

When we write, we mean to communicate so we try to incorporate in the printed language the *equivalent*
of a face, a body, gestures, a smile, frown, screams, an
angry blow—intimacies—

Are you embarrassed?
Are you afraid?

II: The Theory and the Practice

That is all very well. That is all very well and very true theoretically, but now I have to connect *language is female* and its seed *the mother tongue* with my own practice. I who have written maternally for thirty-three years, the age of my oldest daughter. In book after book. My first two pregnancies combined in my first long poem *Once More Out of Darkness*.[1] Ten years of family life and the question of maternity and violence in *The Mother/Child Papers*.[2] The mother-daughter poems in *Imaginary Lover*.[3] More mother-daughter poems in *Green Age*.[4] An essay on poetry and maternity in *Writing Like a Woman*, which dozens of women tell me has changed their lives.[5] But what was I thinking of technically? What does motherhood mean to the molecules of language in my writing?

That the language of the poem will produce an illusion of speech. That the speech will be personal. That it will not be remote, it will not be "discourse," it will not be bloodless. The body will be behind it, and inside that body, swaying like a tide full of kelp and sea turtles, bearing booming whalesong, all the desire fear anger power pride helplessness and so forth of my motherhood. The potion of emotion, the horrible awesome need to squeeze life out of oneself and to have it grow into all its potential energy, the need to train it and explain the facts to it, the need to wind its little DNA up and let it dance, the hope that if you water and feed it the thing will develop into whatever it was intended to be, sweet pea or spreading chestnut tree or burdened with enormous apples, and the stumbling piteousness of one's failures. It ought to all be inside the poem.

That the poem exists to reflect and support life. That it wants life to sail beyond itself, and wants to have helped lift it on its way. That the life of the poem is erotic.

That the poem must take one risk after another. In honor of all the millennia in which childbirth routinely swept mothers away down the river of pain, and so often over the ledge of death. That the poem must hold nothing back. That the poem must not be ashamed of itself. That the poet must care for the poem, not herself, and that the poem must care for the ongoing lives of its audience. Give them an opportunity to laugh and cry, to extend their lifespans in each direction.

That the poem will go from the feeling the poet already knows and understands, inward and downward to the feeling she does not understand, the feeling she fears.

III: Notes on "Listen"

The beloved oldest daughter had been in San Francisco on leave of absence from college, living with the boyfriend, working at the Tower Records, learning to play the bass guitar, having a good time. The mama was tangled, clotted up, hogtied by her own confusion. There was the distress stemming from the daughter's personal coolness to her, which had been creeping along like a mist for—what was it, a year or three. Or was she inventing it. An equal and opposite distress was the anxiety that the daughter was in fact still too attached to the mama, appearing to drift but actually tethered, unable to set her own course, though the mama had thought she was raising the girl toward freedom and autonomy. The mama had thought she was unpossessive. She wondered exactly how self-deluded she might be. Racked by fear, she was uncertain what she feared. If everything was going just as it should, the daughter properly freeing herself and finding a path, or if everything was going all wrong, the daughter wasting herself, how would the mother, knotted in good intentions and greedy need, how would she know. The mama considered the daughter's boyfriend unworthy, and was not crazy about some of the daughter's activities (dear reader, you fill in the blank here with whatever would disturb you), but so what.

I had already, in back pages of notebooks, begun several poems that never lifted off the ground. I had attempted angry epistles, pleading ones, love poems. I cannot begin a poem with forethought. Words or lines appear in the mind, and the hand writes them until they stop appearing. Sometimes the words are worthless, or too skimpy ever to become a poem. Sometimes I find I have something substantial to which I can return. Then I can add and subtract, revise and pursue. The poem becomes a problem I hope to solve, and in so doing, to discover what I mean. Clarify a confusion. Understand, make sense of, a turbulence. What *is* the truth? I will revise endlessly in the hope of finding out. On this occasion in the late fall of 1983, I received thirteen lines, beginning "Having lost you, I try to attract substitutes." When I returned to that scrap I deleted "try to," for compression and candor. The thirteen lines described, with what I hoped was some vivacity and wit, my warm relations with my students. *They* like me even if you don't, was the gist. To that scrap I added, under a cloudy doodle at the bottom, the words "Trying to Leave You the Fuck Alone," obviously a caption or summary of what I thought the poem was supposed to be about. That sentence never went into the poem. The rest arrived over a period of months in interpolated chunks. One chunk elaborated on the student/teacher description. A second developed the idea that the daughter's abandonment of the mother was healthy. Lastly came the chunk in which I say "I want."

The first finished draft was, in fact, chunky. I had been writing lately in unrhymed couplets and triplets whose elegance and coolness I liked. They had an interesting tempo, tended to turn corners sharply, the ghost of Wallace Stevens breathed in them and it pleased me to use these aesthete tricks to my own contrary purposes. Here, in contrast, was something lumplike, heavy, unrefined. I tried putting it in triplets for distance and coolness. Wrong. I returned to the original form, and when I did so, a final piece formed. The poem did not wish to be elegant, it wished to push past the censor, it wanted to make me say more and more of the unsaid, the unsayable, and it wanted to retain a sense of the difficulty of coming at these truths.

> Having lost you, I attract substitutes.
> The student poets visit, think me wise,
> Think me generous, confide in me.
> Earnestly they sit in my office
> Showing me their stigmata
> Under the Judy Chicago poster
> Of her half-opened writhing-petalled
> Clitoris that appears to wheel
> Slowly clockwise when you gaze at it,
> And I sympathize. Then they try on their ambitions
> Like stiff new hiking boots, and I laugh
> And approve, telling them where to climb.
> They bring me tiny plastic bags
> Of healthy seeds and nuts, they bring me wine,
> We huddle by the electric heater
> When it is snowing,
> We watch the sparrows dash
> And when they leave we hug.[6]

Opening straightforward: I boast and am grateful that my desire to mother people through sympathy and support seems needed and used by students. It is ironic that they confide in me more than my own children do, but I am convinced I successfully strengthen them. There is some light sense of erotic connection here. It remains light. The poet's voice is not uncomfortable.

> *Oh silly mother,* I can hear you mock.
> Listen, loveliest, I am not unaware
> This is as it must be.
> Do daughters mock their mothers? is Paris
> A city? Do your pouring hormones
> Cause you to do the slam
> And other Dionysiac dances,
> And did not even Sappho tear her hair
> And act undignified, when the maiden
> She wanted, the girl with the soft lips,
> The one who could dance,
> Rejected/deserted her?

Second section: Daughter mocks mother; I "can hear" her = I am sure she does or would, that she no longer values what I value, if she ever did, and/or she dismisses my boast, thinks I fool myself. I submit to this hypothetical mockery as natural and proper; the daughter must separate from the mother just as she must obey her own body. I try to be good-humored about this, keep the levity afloat. Likewise it is natural for the mother to feel pain at this predictable event. Tone of slight exaggeration, slight self-mockery: tearing one's hair is a bit of a joke.

Mentioning Sappho as precedent, however, does several other things.

It invents. Who knows if Sappho was undignified in "real life?" The poems in which Sappho is being rejected are "art," but is it not undignified to reveal desire and pain? Does art purify humiliation, make it acceptable and unembarrassing? Apparently I am in this poem engaged in a parallel artistic act, although if Sappho is my precedent I will have to cut the comedy, the hijinks, such as they are, which constitute armor, and let the poem go deeper, find what is at the core and say it, which I will try to do in the rest of the poem. But to invent, and to make the Sappho comparison, is already to take the self more seriously, to begin to make claims and seize space. Now the erotic element is stronger. It implies that I "want" my daughter as Sappho wanted her favorite girls. This is pushing rather far and is in fact an exaggeration, but there is a core assertion of eros here, and I am also, not incidentally, implying that Sappho, that any mother, wants the same.

I am unsure of the word "rejected." It is the accurate word but has that awful aura of psychobabble about it. A soap opera word. A *Psychology Today* word. A word my own mother solemnly likes to use. Ah well, then. I reject "rejected." "Deserted" alliterates nicely with "dance." What next?

In its third section, the poem pushes yet further into the reality of maternal desire. It is not that the mother wants the daughter to "succeed" or be "happy." No, what she wants is far more aggressive, more willful, more laden. She wants the daughter to excel her, specifically. She wants to have launched the daughter, to have sent her forth, further than she herself hopes to go.

This longing is deeper than sex. I have felt it for ages and was never before able to articulate it. The sequence of metaphors, *apparently* hyperbolic, *apparently* comic, says precisely what I mean. And there is a sweetness to these wishes, there has to be a sweetness. I recognize them with a smile when Anne Sexton says to her daughter "You've picked my pocket and left me empty" or "I'm an old tree in the background." But there is also all that pushing (to launch is to push), the will to direct and control, that unconscious seeing of the daughter as an extension of the mother's self instead of another being whose direction will not be tied to the mother's direction. And so the poem descends to its final section, to its dreads. There are two of these. First, that I cannot seem to stop myself from begging my daughter to excel me, and that far from having successfully escaped me she is still beneath the shadow of my monster hand, shrinking from my wishes, trying to protect herself from me and becoming smaller instead of larger! Weaker instead of stronger! And all because I cannot quit *desiring* her to grow and strengthen. And the other dread, at which the poem can only hint: that the daughter's life depends on the mother's death. That if the mother were suddenly removed, the daughter would become immediately stronger. Would suffer of course because of the love between them—and would burst into fleur.

In the closing ten lines, the poem abandons its leavening levity, then grammar yields to run-on blur, and lastly the question mark which would imply the possibility of an answer is eschewed in favor of an abrupt and numb full stop. The emotional cause and poetic effect is a sense of exhaustion, of having reached the end of one's rope, or having passed through door after door and arrived at a blank wall.

> Do I suffer? of course I do,
> I am supposed to, but listen, loveliest.
> I want to be a shrub, you a tree.
> I hum inaudibly and want you
> To sing arias. I want to lie down
> At the foot of your mountain
> And rub the two dimes in my pocket
> Together, while you dispense treasure
> to the needy. I want the gods
> Who have eluded me
> All my life, or whom I have eluded,
> To invite you regularly
> To their lunches and jazz recitals.
> Moreover I wish to stand on the dock
> All by myself waving a handkerchief,
> And you to be the flagship
> Sailing from the midnight harbor,
> A blue moon leading you outward,
> So huge, so public, so disappearing—
> I beg and beg, loveliest, I can't
> Seem to help myself,
> While you quiver and pull
> Back, and try to hide, try to be
> Invisible, like a sensitive
> irritated sea animal

Caught in a tide pool, caught
Under my hand, can I
Cut off my hand for you,
Cut off my life.

IV: The Mother as Speaking Subject

I remember attending a panel on Psychoanalysis and Feminism at the Modern Language Association meeting in Chicago. The topic of all three panelists was the failure of feminist theory to include the mother as speaking subject. Most of their references, since they were psychoanalytic critics, were to various branches of psychoanalytic thought and the position, present or potential, of the maternal in them. Mostly of course the maternal is absent or is ideally passive, but they all felt it (she) could be present if we pursued the right theoretical lines.

Susan Friedman protested: Why aren't you reading the women who write as mothers?

Why aren't they? Why are they worrying about the right theoretical lines (discourse is male), instead of noticing what is in front of their noses (language is female)? As Susan tirelessly points out, we already have not just a few exceptions but a large and continually growing body of poetry by women who write as mothers and who are making clear, if anyone would care to notice, that our culture's sanitized idea of what "mother" signifies is absurdly reductive, and that to rethink the meaning of "mother" would mean rethinking everything else we suppose we know, from the meaning of sex to the meaning of history. Adrienne Rich pointed this out decades ago in *Of Woman Born,* and the data keeps pouring in. No, "mother" is not single or simple, nor is she dual, nor is she "good enough": she is ineluctably plural, layered, tangled. Here is a short list of women poets who have written extensively from a maternal perspective and have changed *my* life. It is alphabetical for convenience: Alta, Margaret Atwood, Eavan Boland, Lucille Clifton, Patricia Dienstfrey, Toi Derricotte, Sharon Doubiago, Rachel Blau DuPlessis, Carolyn Forché, Susan Griffin, H.D., Marilyn Hacker, Rachel Hadas, Shirley Kaufman, Marilyn Krysl, Maxine Kumin, Audre Lorde, Sharon Olds, Marie Ponsot, Minnie Bruce Pratt, Adrienne Rich, Muriel Rukeyser, Ntozake Shange, Anne Sexton, Ruth Stone.

A short list. Some of these poets are black, some white, some heterosexual, some lesbian, some middle-class, some working-class. They/we write lyrically, angrily, comically, intimately, politically, tragically, mythically. Most of us have written both as daughters and as mothers. A difficult transition, for we begin by writing as daughters, the oppressed ones who are preoccupied with breaking our chains, the powerless who must recognize the sources of power above and beyond—while to write as a mother is inevitably to recognize both power and the limitations of power, not only outside but within the self. We engage in a struggle which possibly exemplifies the struggle of any woman, whether she is biologically a mother or not, when she tries to discover and use her array of forces. We mother, or try to, our writing, our work, our students, our friends, our own mothers, our own selves, our world into which we have been thrown—and whatever we try to mother will fight back. Will fight free of us, and we can never know, can we, if we have actually helped them be alive. And we will keep on finding other ways to try. Listen, we say. Loveliest, listen.

NOTES

1. Alicia Ostriker, *Once More Out of Darkness and Other Poems*. Berkeley, California: Berkeley Poets' Press, 1974; reprinted 1976.

2. Alicia Ostriker, *The Mother/Child Papers*. Los Angeles: Momentum Press, 1980; reprinted, Beacon Press, 1986.

3. Alicia Ostriker, *The Imaginary Lover*. Pittsburgh: University of Pittsburgh Press, 1986.

4. Alicia Ostriker, *Green Age*. Pittsburgh: University of Pittsburgh Press, 1989.

5. Alicia Ostriker, *Writing Like a Woman*. Ann Arbor: University of Michigan Press, 1982.

6. Ostriker, "Listen" in *The Imaginary Lover*, pp. 30–31. Reprinted in *The Little Space: Poems Selected and New, 1968–1998*, University of Pittsburgh Press, 1998, pp. 88–89.

◊

ALICIA OSTRIKER is the author of ten volumes of poetry, including *The Imaginary Lover* (University of Pittsburgh Press, 1986), which won the 1986 William Carlos Williams Award from the Poetry Society of America, and *The Crack in Everything* (University of Pittsburgh Press, 1996), which was a National Book Award finalist and won both the Paterson Poetry Prize and the San Francisco State Poetry Center Award. Her volume of selected and new poems, *The Little Space* (University of Pittsburgh Press, 1998), was a national book award finalist and a finalist for the Lenore Marshall Award of the Academy of American Poets. Ostriker's most recent book is *The Volcano Sequence* (University of Pittsburgh Press, 2002). She lives with her husband J.P. Ostriker in Princeton, New Jersey, and is mother of Rebecca, born in 1963, Eve, born in 1965, Gabriel, born in 1970, and grandmother of Abigail and Naomi. Ostriker teaches English and creative writing at Rutgers University.

Beyond Impatience:
On Motherhood and Poetry

Pam Rehm | New York City, 1996

The Simple Truth

Somewhere between childhood and adulthood, I lost my patience.

I sometimes think my poems are merely apologies for my impatience. Impatience doesn't have a care about it. It leads nowhere. Having a child has helped me break down my impatience to find a "pace in time"; a pace, stretching between yesterday and tomorrow. A pace that is set by those who are closest to me and that gives me the confidence to keep going.

Finding a pace in time, beyond impatience, is what I am trying to do as a mother as well as a poet.

However, it's hardly that simple.

A Coper or a Cop-out

> *Women have been the doers of life-sustaining things, the "copers," those who have understood that the reception of the gift of life is no inert thing, that to receive this gift is to be engaged in its tending, constantly.*
> —Beverly Wildung Harrison[1]

> *...a woman must have an amazing genius if she is still a poet after childbirth.*
> —Mary Webb[2]

I wanted *at least* five children; I'm 29 and have one. I'm sure we'll have another, but five doesn't now seem possible. How many poems do I want to write? How many poems could my body possibly produce? This was never a question. But now that I think about it, I believe that the factors that have limited my capability of having more children—no money and living at a distance from both of my immediate families—are similar to those that have often left me bitter in the face of a lack of time for myself, for reading and writing; for obtaining that "amazing genius" status.

But if I were given a year of time to just sit at my desk and write, I doubt that I would write a word. I can't wait for a poem as one would wait for a lover.

Yet, I feel caught, wrought up, tripped up by Time. Time is that yoke I'm always straining to get out from under. And so the idea of the poem must wait. It must somehow endure the seemingly endless echoes of my own anger at not having any time to create, an anger out of fright that there's only so much time left.

My grandmother always says "here today and gone tomorrow." This has been so ingrained into my thinking that if I *want* time alone, away from my son, I immediately feel guilty; I feel like I'm being a bad mother.

It's the biggest contradiction because all I complain about is not having any time to myself, and yet if my husband says, "Okay, now's your free time," I can't manage to do anything in it. So I've learned to take a day and run it into the night. I cope with time in that way. But I've also learned how to take a day and curse it the whole way to bed.

This past summer, my father said, "I've been working my *whole* life. When am I going to have time to enjoy it?" He's 55.

If I had a gun I'd shoot all the clocks and then go for a walk.

Emily Dickinson wrote, "They say that 'time assuages,'—/Time never did assuage."[3]

Is this My Body, Is this My Blood?

Approximately eight months of each year, today's dairy cow is both pregnant and lactating. During each tenmonth lactation period, machines drain her of ten times the milk her calf would suckle.

—Joan Dunayer[4]

Is it any wonder that most women are fatigued by life!
—Beverly Wildung Harrison[5]

I never thought of myself as a woman until I was pregnant. I certainly did all of the things a "woman" does—worried about dirt, made the bed, washed the clothes, moved furniture to every possible location in the house, viewed my own body as an object—all the things that are a sign of a "misspent" life. But how or why would I not do these things?

My mother and grandmother do everything without a word of complaint. Not once have they devalued the domestic, not once have they made themselves into victims. (Although my grandmother always manages to slip in the "You girls don't know what work is" line to my sisters and me as a reminder of how "easy" we've got it.) This is the example I've been given, and one that I don't know how to give up. But this doesn't mean I continue to do domestic chores in a passive or unaware way. I am bound to do them because they have to be done. I don't have the sense that these things should be done for me, that I should be tended to. But I do think that women tend to assume more of the domestic responsibilities because we know that if we chose not to do them they simply would not get done.

Now I get my son involved in helping out. At two and a half he is actually asking if he can help me make dinner. Sharing in this way makes me feel equal and I think my son can feel it too. In her essay, "Caring for Animals," Rita Manning writes,

> ...caring does not mean that we simply accede to the wishes of the one cared for. Rather, we should respond in the interest of the one cared for, insofar as furthering that interest is compatible with our abilities and where this response sustains the network of care that connects us.[6]

We sustain one another so that our care is not only "for" but "about."

The more our lives become intertwined in this way, instead of me acting as the powerful mother in control over the helpless child, the easier it becomes to make our own pace. We are both preceptors.

I often read my son poems, after his usual slew of bedtime stories. Niedecker and Dickinson are the funniest to him. He prefers Creeley to Blake and Hopkins. And although I know that he begs for them, most nights, just so that he can fall asleep with me in the room, I feel thankful that he allows me to hear poems out loud after a day totally lacking in anything close to poetry's magic.

Her Own Life

> *For a time I used to think I should not write anything*
> *about myself because I couldn't express it, and because*
> *of that, I would only be annoyed about it afterward.*
> —Annemarie Arnold[7]

Ninety-nine percent of my poems have been written "for" someone. When I'm writing a poem, I have to hold every word as if I were holding another person's body.

I haven't written poems *about* motherhood or baby poems per se, but I think the fact that I am a mother comes into the work indirectly. My own seeking has been enriched. Having a child has made me approach the question, not only of what, but whom *do* I live/write for?

I never hide my feelings from my son. I think women have always had to swallow what they feel out of a fear of being self-indulgent. Because my own mother swallows so much I have always felt ashamed to talk about my feelings with another person. A poem, for me, has always been what I do with what I feel, but not in a sentimental way. What I've come to realize is that when all else stops making sense, my own writing understands me; without it I lose part of my definition.

I've always used words, on the page, to speak for me. Finally, with the birth of my son, I'm discovering my speaking voice. The great thing about living with a child is that life becomes lived fully in the present. The language develops out of the living. From the rhyming of folk songs to the Englishness of Dr. Dolittle, we are building our own network of communication. Language development is inextricable from the life lived, which also means that it's inextricable from the spirit the life creates as it's lived. Being able to communicate with a two-and-a-half year old is very energizing, but I've never felt compelled to "use" his words to create a poem, although the poem is also created out of the same spirit, or lack thereof, that the life is creating.

So I'm discovering the orality of language. From the mundane, everyday "what's for lunch" language to the challenge of creating stories when the situation calls for it, I'm hearing language develop. For a long time I actually thought about not having children because I'm not a good storyteller. Sometimes, at suppertime, my father would tell us stories, very funny ones, about his youth, and to me, storytelling became a requirement for being a parent. So how could I, "has-the-cat-got-your-tongue" girl that I was, manage this requirement?

One day I said to my husband, in a child's voice, "Papa, tell me the story again about how you sailed to Byzantium?" And he did. To this day, I am completely in awe of that story and completely crushed by it.

What is it that has given men the stories and the ability to tell them? While, on the other hand, the women in my family have always used talents—talents with a use value: canning, baking, sewing, gardening—to represent themselves, never words.

Growing up, my house was usually silent. I never knew what my mother was feeling or thinking, and that has always made me afraid of my own voice.

The text from the book of Mark, "There is nothing from without a man, that entering into him can defile him: but the things which come out of him, those are they that defile him" has always haunted me.

I think my poems are full of words that I'm afraid of saying.

Home

> *Our knowledge of God is in and through each other. Our*
> *knowledge of each other is in and through God.*
> —Beverly Wildung Harrison[8]

I've always written poetry, so I'm not afraid that raising a family is somehow going to take this away from me; the one does not betray the other. However, it's the endeavor to keep a balance of time for nurturing each that often brings my mind to a standstill.

It leaves me standing still. How could I want to be sitting at my desk when my son is asking me to play with him?

I believe that the love one has for other people is a greater affliction, to steal Simone Weil's language, than the love one has for God. The love for other people is an immediate, face to face confrontation. It is a daily call to action. It is through the intimacy, the questioning and arguing, the development of trust, and the silence of familiarity that one becomes present in the other's eyes. Is this not more afflicting than the thought of the love of God?

My poetry wrestles with this.

Books, words, letters, what I call potency, are all I have to try to pierce through, or into, how I define Love, God, and World.

Trudge language behind sleep. Sweet shadow dress. Frantic feet.

For me, writing, and reading for that matter, are not ways of escaping, but are ways into what's real. They are the pathways I use to find a home amongst the dirty laundry and the small face asking for one more story, for one more word.

NOTES

1. Beverly Wildung Harrison, *Making the Connections: Essays in Feminist Social Ethics*. Boston: Beacon Press, 1985, p. 10.

2. Mary Webb, *Gone to Earth*. New York: The Dial Press, 1979, p. 205.

3. Emily Dickinson, *The Complete Poems of Emily Dickinson*, ed. Thomas H. Johnson. Boston: Little, Brown, 1960, p. 339.

4. Joan Dunayer, "Sexist Words, Speciesist Roots" in *Animals and Women: Feminist Theoretical Explorations*, ed. Carol J. Adams and Josephine Donovan. London: Duke University Press, 1995, pp. 13–14.

5. Harrison, *Making the Connections*, p. 33.

6. Rita Manning, "Caring for Animals" in *Beyond Animal Rights: A Feminist Caring Ethic for the Treatment of Animals*, ed. Josephine Donovan and Carol J. Adams. New York: Continuum, 1996, p. 105.

7. Annemarie Arnold, *Youth Movement to Bruderhof: Letters and Diaries of Annemarie Arnold (née Wachter) 1926–1932*, ed. Woodcrest Bruderhof and the Hutterian Brethren. Rifton, New York: Plough Publishing House, 1986, p. 98.

8. Harrison, *Making the Connections*, p. 41.

◊

PAM REHM is wife to Lew Daly and mother to Nathaniel, born in 1994, and Cora, born in 1999. Her first book was *Piecework* (oblek editions, 1992). Other books include *The Garment in Which No One Had Slept* (Burning Deck Books, 1993), *To Give It Up* (Sun & Moon Press, 1995), and *Gone to Earth* (Flood Editions, 2001).

Allowance:
A Poetics of Motherhood

Frances N. Phillips

I. Baby

First I was the mother of a baby, and all of my body changed for her making and feeding. I was taken up by effort.

Before her I was a writer, but felt like a different person. I went through childhood casting off dolls, lace, posture. I would not be fussed over, dressed up, straightened. I was not a grubby child, but independent. By the time I was ten, I had a docile horse and could ride long distances alone. In that time was my great happiness.

My writing was always filled with the casual story, the overheard conversation. Strangers on the bus would attach themselves to me. Sometimes, listening, the full force of their random sorrows would enter me, or I would catch sight of my reflection in the chrome around the window and it would be dark—seem to shrink from the foreground. What if they were to enter my darkness and I could not control it?

After the child was conceived, I was less hospitable to these strangers. I was happier, but I cried easily. I was afraid to write of my infatuation.

My own mother was small and soft. If you were whimpering and crawled into her lap, her sentimentality flowed over you. I didn't want her tears in my hair. To most, her warmth was her greatest quality. I thought it would drown me.

Then I was the mother, drowning in sentimentality. After years in rock 'n' roll clubs, at performance art, and poetry readings, I was a woman in a flowered blouse. When your head fills with words of baby culture—layette, humidifier, coverlet, bonnet—does it empty of other things? Could I still discern, criticize?

I had been happy alone, adrift, on horseback. The next time I was that happy, I was pregnant. I wrote poems about pregnancy that contained bowls of water, fish, and moons. Every one was set in the dark and used the word "little." Like my body, they were beyond my control. I couldn't avoid clichés. In the years that followed, I had to get used to them. If I tried to subvert them, I would not be writing at all.

We turned my study into her bedroom. That night I had a dream that I went to work and they had given my desk to somebody else. The other person taught night classes and would not be there when I was there, but still I was upset that I had no place for my work. It was a portentous dream. I have never been able to recreate a workable study since then.

The baby was born early and too small, so she fed slowly and all the time. She nursed for at least half an hour every hour and a half. Asleep, awake, asleep. The nursing makes such peace, it draws a halo about you. You are in love, fuzzy minded, and inarticulate. When you put her down, she smells of milk and she is you, full of you. Your boundaries have expanded through her. She also is a kind of screen. When you walk down the street, everyone is pleasant, but they look into the stroller, not at you.

First the baby looks, looks hard at the black and white mobile. Then at a postcard of a painting called "Nellie." You sing and the singing comes out warm and clear:

> Sleep baby, sleep
> Thy father guards the sheep
> Thy mother shakes the dreamwood tree
> To shake down tender leaves on thee
> Sleep baby sleep.

Is that the way it goes? Did you know those words or did you make them up?

It's a pleasure that your body is needed. Every day is made of smells, dampness, physicality. The baby nurses and you are full, then empty. This is a wonderful feeling, sensual and intoxicating, you could nurse all the time. You feel a little guilty about how pleasant it is, how it consumes you.

Without sleep, you become instinctive. *Pear, plum, Tom Thumb, little crumb.* It slurs together in nonsense and sense, in things you might have heard long ago. At the border of what you know. Rhyming is in there, bits of old stories. *Inside the house, /find the mouse/lock the door/away, away!* I talked to her all the time, but not to make sense. Could I write in that language?

Having milk took over my life. One night my husband, who was tired and trying to watch TV, blew up because I was using a breast pump to save milk for the baby while she was at the sitter's. He was tired of the milking, nursing, seeping. This sensation, this faint odor was all through our lives, and I was singular in my purpose to provide milk, as if it would make me the perfect mother.

In front of my class one afternoon, I made a provocative point to rouse them. At that moment, when I'd opened myself, set up my authority against their disagreement, I glanced down and noticed dried baby spit-up on my shoulder.

In all my dealings I felt like a charlatan, except with the baby. With her I was authentic, but scared. So much could go wrong. Who can cut the baby's fingernails without pinching her? All the baby—soul to toe—trembles, simmers.

At certain times of day, there is nothing you can do but let her cry.

"Sleep, baby, sleep/Thy father guards the sheep…." Who is guarding us? I'm balancing the sack of groceries against a knee, unlocking the door. Walking down the long hallway of our apartment, I think about sheep, their patient dumb presence bumping slowly against my knees, and I strive to keep my balance.

Because of the slowness of readying the baby to take her out into the world, when I was not holding the baby I had to do two things at once, or hold the baby and do two other things. Outside of this practice there were automobiles, deadlines, calculators. I worked outside time in a slow marathon of striving. Like my earliest days of cooking when each part of dinner was finished at a different time, sequence and order were out of my control. The boundaries of the poem must be vast and interruptible or narrow and efficient to tell the story of this imbalance. And that's one way the poems came forward: confounding, fine knotted chain.

There is a rhythm in rocking, walking, burping. That rhythm could come into the poem. Its pace is a kind of strumming. Change, burp, walk, hum. This must be like playing a stringed instrument—a harp, a bass, or a cello vibrating through your chest.

II. Toddler

She is busy. She moves in a quick, rocking, intent manner, leaning into her movements. She is the mistress of little stuff—pennies, ribbons, jacks—and they are everywhere. I compose short, stocky sentences:

> Here we go.
> Up we go.
> No more.
> All gone.
> Round and round.
> Bye-bye.

I make a leash of my attention. How far do you let her run away from you toward the shore? I'm the tether and poems circle, containing the same ideas, working them out over and over again. And then the spondees, squat lines, pronouncements, carry the poem like a slow climb up a spiral staircase.

If a day is the time it takes to do something, then day is never done.

She is angry, always in the business to buy something, have something, take something—*my, me, mine.*

First the chaos was captured in receiving blankets, plastic lining. Now it's dry, but harder to contain. I find she's unpacked every book I had just put in the moving box, taken the plugs out of all of the banks, removed all the tissues, unrolled the toilet paper, taken the caps from t he tops of the pens. I stop her just as she is pouring a glass of water into the drawer of the bedside stand.

Once there is walking, there is the playground. Then sand seeps and slips in every cuff and crease, through every shoelace hole. Sand penetrates the sheets, the floor, the rug. She is damp, spreading this grit over all she encounters.

When she stopped napping, time became the crisis. No time, no space. She still woke up in the middle of the night, and sometimes I stayed up, used that time from two to four to be in my own world. I could open the blind and write under the illumination of street lights. The room would waver and breathe as headlights caught the corner and slipped down the wall. That was a time my husband was working long hours. When he got home, we were still so new at being her parents we liked to stand over her bed together, taking easy, slow breaths of adoration. If only she would sleep more.

What was writing out of that particular blur? There was mess and there was will. Raised in a house that was scrubbed and guarded and radiantly clean, I now lived in a house of sand and stickiness. It was hard to think. I have never been able to write a chiseled, clean, directive poem, although I admire such poems. My writing has always come from a broad casting, accidental connections. My mind had to be very open to an uncorrected world. Then I could cut and move and reconnect the words. During this shaping, I had to be in the poem all day, solving its little problems in the shower, in the car. When one lives, then, in an open field of chaos, it is hard to cut and shape. The world keeps coming in anew. Before the poem is made, a new poem begins with its own questions. And it's hard to be receptive in a hurry, hard to allow the accident to resonate.

When the child is an infant, she cannot be bad. She can be exasperating, but the forming instinct is beyond criticism. This is a wonderful period of grace. Then the decades of discipline begin and all the voices of my childhood about clarity and firmness, about children who are spoiled, about the selfishness of only children, enter my head. By this, the world will judge you. It is hard to sort such judgment out of the harder threads of making the child confident, inquisitive, happy, moral. As you correct the child, the world of adulthood looms over your shoulder, shouting contradictory instructions.

The *right, wrong, yes, no* you bring is met on the child's side by a fierce repetitiveness. With one hand, she's spinning around every parking meter on the block. "No! No! No!" and the ubiquitous "Why? Why? Why?"

So I make a distraction. I am over here, no, over there. I am picking you up, spinning you. The spoon heading into your mouth is an airplane. I am in constant improvisation.

She is learning the lists: alphabet, numbers, parts of the body, colors, cries of animals, wheels on the bus. If you have never employed consonance before, it will come to you through a brush with preschool. On her first day she makes the paper puppet who sings:

> I'm Poka Pig
> And I'm playing the piano.
> I'm Poka Pig
> And I'm peeling a po-ta-to.

You may, indeed, write in this time, but how will you exert your will over the text no less unruly or arbitrary than she seems to be? "No, no, no. Why? Why? Why?" You have to stop stopping yourself.

I become less patient with students who are needy and late. All my patience and compassion are fully used up every day at home. How could I give the poem my tenderness, cut it the slack it needs to come into being? There are so many reasons not to write—time, work, tiredness, deadlines, husband, child. What makes it to the page has to be the poem or there is no poem. If I discard the weak beginnings, I may have nothing.

And I was so in love with the child. Why make something less perfect, less complex?

III. Daughter

When my book of poems, *Up at Two*—which is about my daughter's infancy—came out, she was six. For a few years she was honored to be in the photo on the back cover, and to be in all of the poems. She called it "our book." Then she became my critic. She told me she didn't want me to come into her school and lead a poetry workshop because the kids might think that I'm "not a real poet."

As we get closer to her school in the morning, she walks a few paces ahead of me.

For her sake, her privacy, I try to strip her out of my poems, but this is hard. Often I get to write on Saturdays while she is in ballet class, and the rooms full of willful, ordered young girls come into the work. I am trying to let her hide, to make her own light. Losing her as a subject saddens me. Like watching her step away as a toddler, this new distancing is a shaky process. We adjust in small steps, allowing her time alone in the house, to order her own soda at the counter, to have her own money, which is called "an allowance."

I forgive my own mother for her sorrow, her need to hold us.

With the baby I was steeped in being. As she grows, both of us are more conscious, critical, complicated, the thread of our connection stretches. You must measure your writing against this new position. For her sake you must be responsible and present, reassuring and calm. This is the "good mother," reverence turned to sense. You begin to attend to how algebra is being taught.

Now I do not dress or undress her, and in this new effort to hold back from shaping her to my vision, I am lonely for her. No one will be so close, so inside my boundaries, ever again. I must be fluidly available to her world, but able to let her drift out beyond my comprehension. And then I am here, by myself—where I always wanted to be when I was a child, but sad now, my love tested by her acceleration.

◊

FRANCES PHILLIPS is the author of three collections of poetry: *The Celebrated Running Horse Messenger* (Kelsey St. Press, 1979), *For a Living* (Hanging Loose, 1981), and *Up at Two* (Hanging Loose, 1991). She works as a Program Officer for Arts and Humanities at the Walter and Elise Haas Fund in San Francisco and as an instructor of creative and technical writing at San Francisco State University. Her daughter, Alice Hutton, was born in 1985.

The One Absolutely Beautiful Thing:
My Relationship to Poetry and Motherhood Through the Voices of Women Poets

JILL BIALOSKY

I.

After I finished my first book of poems, I embarked on an awkward and self-conscious journey most poets travel as they begin to find their way into new material. Two years passed before I began to find the thread into the subject matter for my second book, which would become the poems in *Subterranean*. Part of my hesitation had to do with permission to allow myself to explore an area in my life that had been particularly difficult, and wondering whether poetry was the appropriate form. When I sat down to write, the early fragments that were most vital and urgent were those about the losses I had suffered in my thirties when I wanted to have a child. Reflecting back, after completing the cycle of poems about loss and motherhood, I wondered why I needed permission to write about the loss of children in poetry when the experience was so profound and altering. Did my insecurities reside in the feeling that the poems would be regulated to that mushy and uncomfortable category called "women's poetry"? Was the need for permission something inherent in my gender? Would the poems be thought sentimental, or too full of feeling? Were they too dark? Once I realized that I would have to explore the losses in my poetry, regardless, I began to look to other women poets for counsel. In this essay I will explore both the reluctance and need to write about the loss of children in verse and to reflect on the tradition of poetry of motherhood and loss.

◊

I was the middle child in our family. While my oldest sister talked on her princess telephone and my younger sister climbed the huge oak tree at the end of our block with the neighborhood boys, I was in my pink and white bedroom creating an imaginary family with my collection of stuffed animals, toy soldiers, and dolls. I discovered a universe where I orchestrated when it was time to go to bed, what to prepare for supper, the stories I would pass on to my child.

As far as I can remember I was drawn to the idea of recreating a family and a home, and children were always part of the equation. In the dawn of a July morning, when the fourth sister in my family was born, I was ten years old. I diapered my sister—I can still remember the chill of her scream when I accidentally stabbed her with a diaper pin—warmed her bottle and read to her. When she cried out in the middle of the night I rocked her back to sleep. The reciprocal and circular nature of love and dependency fundamental to mothering was part of my character. I never questioned its place in my life, but I knew that when my sister quieted down in my arms, when I looked at my reflection in the black glass of her window, I felt I existed.

My first child was conceived in the twilight between midnight and dawn on New Year's day. There was no angst or worry or fear surrounding it. I had no reason to question whether I could carry a child to term, but I never took the miracle of a child's conception for granted either. A child drawing nutrients and sustenance from my body and breath from my lungs was the most powerful experience I had known. Four months later that pregnancy was complicated by hospitalizations and medications to prevent early labor. The thirty-two weeks I carried my child are frozen in my memory, like essential water underneath an arctic lake. Those weeks experiencing my child in utero and the few minutes I held her would be the only tangible memory to mark my daughter's life. Her lungs were too premature to survive outside the womb, and she died shortly after birth.

Though the pregnancy was fraught with physical discomfort and anxiety, I never expected to lose that child. Loss of a child was unfathomable. In the poem "Child Burial," Paula Meehan describes the surreal experience of burying a child:

> Your coffin looked unreal,
> fancy as a wedding cake.[1]

Giving birth to a child represents a new passage for a woman. It marks the journey into adulthood and selflessness. When a baby dies, her mother is thrust back into a netherworld of darkness. Like Demeter, who loses her child to the underworld, she is in a state of perpetual winter. A sense of unreality characterizes the experience, caused, in part, by the confluence between the expectation of a future with a new child, and the sudden reality of death.

Two years after my daughter died, my son was conceived. I went into premature labor at twenty-seven weeks, and he was delivered by emergency cesarean section. He weighed under a pound, and died of kidney failure in the ICU three days later. As if she could bargain her child back, Meehan writes:

> I'd cancel the love feast
> the hot night of your making.[2]

Grief over the death of a child lessens over time, but the loss is eternal. When Niobe's children are slaughtered, she continues to weep, even as she is turned to stone. The relationship between a mother and child commences long before the sperm and egg collide. Mine began in the bedroom of my childhood, in the historic longing to form connection between one life and another. I had yearned for that white-space ever since I can remember. After the losses, the slate of my future and all that I had imagined prior was wiped clean. I questioned who I would become without the possibility of being a mother. My losses were a result of having been exposed to DES, a powerful synthetic hormone, in utero. Exposure to DES damaged my uterus, cervix, and uterine lining and made it difficult to carry a child to term. I was unwilling to risk another pregnancy, but I was not willing to relinquish the need and desire to raise a child. Two years later we adopted a healthy newborn son.

Part of the art and mystery of poetry is its ability to capture the suspended and unfixed moments of experience and time. The years when I was pregnant and lost my children changed my worldview, in the same way that losing a parent, or experiencing a divorce, changes us. Experiencing motherhood was equally as profound. And yet, as a poet, I questioned whether those experiences were just subjects for poetry. What was it about those experiences that terrified me? Was it the fear that I wouldn't be capable of giving appropriate voice to the power of those experiences? Was it because I questioned whether I would be able to express the meaning (and miracle) of my son's existence in my life without sentimentality? Was it because I was reluctant to allow myself the full range of emotion in order to enter that state of incantation where the conscious and subconscious collide into language because the losses were so painful? Was I afraid that through the power of bringing experiences to words I would also have to see anew, as I walked my son to school each morning, and read to him before bed, the moments lost with the two babies who died? As a poet, I felt protective of my reader, wondering if the difficult subject matter would be too unbearable. Nevertheless, I felt compelled to turn the painful and life transforming experiences into art.

◊

While my losses were private, I knew I was not the only woman to have lost children. Women have mourned children and have been thwarted in childbearing, in the silence of their homes, throughout history. The biblical story of Sarah and Hagar is one of the earliest narratives about the sorrow and devastation of infertility, and the first story of surrogacy.

God commands Abraham: That he "shall surely become a great and mighty nation, and all the nations of the earth shall be blessed through him. For I have singled him out, that he may instruct his children and his posterity..." The burden upon Sarah, who could not bear Abraham a child, is unimaginable in this light. Not only did she defy and disappoint Abraham, she betrayed a nation. Sarah's story is representative of the grave burden of history that women who want a child also bear when they cannot conceive. To have desired a child and failed is a formidable human story. Eavan Boland writes in "The Lost Land":

> I have two daughters.
> They are all I ever wanted from the earth.[3]

II.

If the desire for a child is such a powerful human story, why throughout history had so few poems about the experience survived? And why are poems about motherhood often considered too sentimental, personal, and private? Part of my hesitation about documenting the experience of loss and motherhood in poetry was that themes of motherhood, the desire for a child, even the loss of a child, I feared, were subjects still relegated by the patriarch to the realm of domesticity. As if private lives, birth, the dialogue of human suffering were less important than poems of war and meditations of nationhood, they were "outside history," as Eavan Boland termed it. And yet, some of the most powerful poems of human experience are poems about love and death, themes inherent in the relationship between a mother and a child.

Regardless of how transforming and consuming the experience of conception, the event of pregnancy, and the shock of loss, as I began to mine the territory of motherhood and loss in my new work, I struggled with the agonizing voices of self-censure. In exploring motherhood in poetics, would I be considered a domestic poet, and hence a lesser poet of more narrow range? This coincided with a debate happening in poetry about the nature of autobiography and the move toward more language oriented and fragmented poetics. When I discussed the quandary with another poet who was flirting with the genderless poem, she suggested I write about the experience less autobiographically. But autobiography wasn't really the issue. Poems I admire always come from a powerful interior world that transcends the limitations of the self. And what is the responsibility of the poet if not to write about the experiences of her time? If I did not document the experiences of loss, wasn't I annihilating a part of my history and the necessary record of the natural history of human nature? In spite of my hesitations, my poems kept circling back to the themes of grief, loss, and desire for a child. I realized that my challenge as a poet was to experiment with language and style to find the appropriate form for such emotionally charged content.

III.

As I was wrestling with the inner debate between my reluctance to explore the loss of children and motherhood in my poems and the powerful compulsion to do so, I began to consider and trace the role of motherhood and loss in other poets' work. Emily Dickinson. Edna St. Vincent Millay. Marianne Moore. Elizabeth Bishop. Louise Bogan. As a young poet, many of the women poets I read were childless. These poets wrote primarily about loss and love, concerns of immortality, existential questions of the self in relation to the world. I was drawn to these poets because in my late teens and twenties the subjects I sought out in poetry were those that had bearing on my life: loss, love, sexuality, and selfhood. It wasn't that I didn't admire or find necessary other poets' work—for instance, I was passionately drawn to the poems of Wallace Stevens and Hart Crane—but it was imperative to read poets whose histories intersected with mine. (A friend of mine calls these poems the kind we clip onto our refrigerator door.)

But aside from Anne Bradstreet, who were the poets who wrote about motherhood and why hadn't more of these poems survived? Motherhood traditionally wasn't written into the larger story of poetry because domestic experiences were subjects not included in the canon. Adrienne Rich metaphorically captures the canon's exclusion of women's experiences in "Diving into the Wreck," as "a book of myths/in which/ our names do not appear."[4]

In Jane Cooper's remarkable and forward-thinking essay "Nothing Has Been Used in the Manufacture of This Poetry That Could Have Been Used in the Manufacture of Bread" she ponders, after two decades of teaching young gifted women, why so many of them stopped writing. "The commonest answer...Is that marriage along the old, accepted lines, and especially, childbearing and child-rearing can sap energy, privacy, a sense of the earned right to write."[5] I wondered whether that "earned right to write" also included writing about motherhood and the desire for a child—whether women, once they became mothers and were raising children, questioned whether the focus of their lives was meaningful enough to record in poetry.

Cooper explains that "this was one of the true problems of women writers at that time. The men's lives seemed more central than ours, almost more truthful. They had been shot down, or squirmed up the beaches. We had waited for their letters."[6]

In one of Adrienne Rich's early poems, "Ideal Landscape" from the collection *Diamond Cutters*, she writes poignantly about a mother's submissive place in society:

> We had to take the world as it was given:
> The nursemaid sitting passive in the park.[7]

In "Anger and Tenderness," one of the many path-breaking essays from *Of Woman Born* in which Rich politicizes the role of motherhood in society, she writes forthrightly about the less sentimental and more complex realities of being a mother. She boldly throws a wrench into societal assumptions about the maternal role: "First, that a 'natural' mother is a person without further identity, one who can find her chief gratification in being all day with small children, living at a pace tuned to theirs; that the isolation of mothers and children together in the home must be taken for granted; that maternal love is, and should be, quite literally selfless."[8] When asked "Don't you ever write poems about your children?" Rich responds: "The male poets of my generation did write poems about their children—especially their daughters. For me, poetry was where I lived as no-one's mother, where I existed as myself."[9]

Anne Sexton, a glamorous and sexy Fifties housewife who turned to poetry in mid-life, uses her personal life as the center of her poems. She was the poet of my mother's generation. Is there a poem in American poetry before her that records the particular history of a mother who also identified as a sexual being? Some of Sexton's poems about her children express ambivalence and inadequacy in relationship to the speaker's role of being a mother. In the following poem, the speaker witnesses her own daughter giving birth:

> Where a child would have cried *Mama!*
> Where a child would have believed *Mama!*
> she bit the towel and called on God
> and I saw her life stretch out...
> I saw her torn in childbirth,
> and I saw her, at that moment,
> in her own death and I knew that she
> knew.[10]

In these lines from "Pain for a Daughter" Sexton captures the awesome responsibility of realizing a daughter will also suffer; that a mother, in spite of her love, may not be able to assuage a child's distress.

Like Sexton, Sylvia Plath galvanizes the poem about motherhood to reflect the full scope of its experience. With haunting pathos, she locates the yearning to be a mother, and the joys and fears a mother interiorizes for her child.

> Remembering, even in sleep,
> Your crossed position.
> The blood blooms clean
> In you, ruby.
> The pain
> You wake to is not yours.[11]

Plath conveys the profound umbilical tie between mother and child, and also the despair of childlessness. In "Childless Woman," a woman who cannot bear children is a "moon discharged from a tree with nowhere to go." Her body becomes a graveyard filled with the corpses of unfertilized eggs:

> My funeral,
> And this hill and this
> Gleaming with the mouths of corpses.[12]

While Plath writes of the sadness of not being able to conceive, she also records the transformation a child brings into the life of a mother:

> Your clear eye is the one absolutely beautiful thing.
> I want to fill it with color and ducks,
> The zoo of the new

But also the anguish and sense of failure a mother experiences when depression and suicidal impulses bear in and threaten her health and the well-being of her children:

> Not this troublous
> Wringing of hands, this dark
> Ceiling without a star[13]

I never questioned whether I could be both a mother and a poet, though I did worry about the challenges involved in juggling personal ambition with the responsibilities of being a mother. Was it mere coincidence, I wondered, that Plath and Sexton, who wrote about motherhood in poetry, who were also mothers driven in their art, both committed suicide? Plath and Sexton wrote unabashedly and fearlessly about dark subjects: miscarriage, death, the erotic power of desire, maternal nature, the erotics of motherhood. In spite of critical derision from the patriarch, their poems opened the floodgates for poets in the generation that followed. Contemporary poets like Sharon Olds, Toi Derricotte, Joy Harjo, Louise Glück, and Jorie Graham, to name only a handful, have written poems about the complexities involved in the blinding desire to have a child and the awesome responsibility inherent in being a mother.

◊

None of the sentimentality associated with motherhood, nor the sense that the subject of the poems lacked importance was evident in Jorie Graham's poem "Wanting a Child," where the erosion of the shore becomes a metaphor for the desire to have a child:

> the living echo,
> says my book, of some great storm far out at sea, too far
> to be recalled by us
> but transferred
> whole onto this shore by waves, so that erosion
> is its very face.[14]

In Louise Glück's "The Garden," shrouded in the poem's signature mythic coolness, the fear of birth is twinned with the fear of loss. The poem about the fear of the body as a safe haven for the birth of a child ends with the chilling tercet:

> And then the losses,
> one after another,
> all supportable.[15]

In Lucille Clifton's poem about miscarriage, "The Lost Baby Poem," the speaker miscarries and flushes her "almost body" down the toilet to the sea underneath the city. The grief over the loss of a baby allows the speaker to understand what it means to drown or be drowned:

> The time I dropped your almost body down
> down to meet the waters under the city
> and run one with the sewage to the sea
> what did I know about waters rushing back
> what did I know about drowning
> or being drowned.[16]

Empowered by women poets before me who had written forcefully about the unexplainable yearning for a child, the powerful nature of motherhood, the tragedy of loss, and the need to explore my own obsessions in my work, I eventually discarded my former reservations and plunged ahead. The lost utterances of the children I lost, and the new ways the world presented itself manifest in the experience of raising my son, crept into the figurative landscapes of my poems. Would I find the words to express the inexplicable and mysterious power a child has over another human being in language and form that was fresh and universal while also being intimate? It wasn't until I began to trust the poem and the importance of the weight of those experiences within it that I was freed from self-censure. The reticence and the desire unavoidably created a natural tension and urgency in the line. In retrospect, I was sure that the inner argument I wrestled had also to do with not only my own self-consciousness in exposing an intimate story in poetry, but the movement in poetry away from the personal. Was this backlash against the personal in poetry also a backlash against women legitimately entering their experiences into the canon? Or as poets, did we need to experiment with new forms to find fresh ways of shaping and capturing experience?

◊

Contemporary women cope silently and in the privacy of their own homes with miscarriages and loss of children. Because women are pursuing careers and having children later in life, we are experiencing higher rates of infertility. Families are being made through high-tech medical intervention, donor sperm and egg, surrogacy arrangements, domestic and international adoption. These circumstances are changing the definition of motherhood and the nature of the modern soul. As the form of the poem changes to mirror the fragmentation of a culture, naturally so must its subjects and their forms to reflect it. If we turn to poetry to find a voice that speaks to the one within ourselves, our poems must continue to engage the narrative of human suffering and also the joys. And what more valid human story than the desire for a child? In Plath's "Wintering," she employs the metaphor of bees and their hives to write about the lives of women, who are "at the heart of the house."

> Will the hive survive, will the gladiolas
> Succeed in banking their fires
> To enter another year?[17]

NOTES

1. Paula Meehan, "Child Burial" in *The Man Who Was Marked by Winter*. Dublin, Ireland: The Gallery Press, 1991.

2. Ibid.

3. Eavan Boland, "The Lost Land" in *The Lost Land*. New York: W.W. Norton & Company, 1998, p. 40.

4. Adrienne Rich, "Diving into the Wreck" in *Diving into the Wreck*. New York: W.W. Norton & Company, 1973; reprint, 1994, p. 22.

5. Jane Cooper, "Nothing Has Been Used in the Manufacture of This Poetry That Could Have Been Used in the Manufacture of Bread" in *The Flashboat*. New York: W.W. Norton & Company, 1999, p. 95.

6. Ibid.

7. Adrienne Rich, "Ideal Landscape" in *Diamond Cutters*. New York: W.W. Norton & Company, 1955.

8. Adrienne Rich, "Anger and Tenderness" in *Of Woman Born*. New York: W.W. Norton & Company, 1986; reprint, 1999, p. 21.

9. Ibid.

10. Anne Sexton, "Pain for a Daughter" in *Selected Poems of Anne Sexton*. Boston: Houghton Mifflin, 2000, p. 112.

11. Sylvia Plath, "Nick and the Candlestick" in *The Collected Poems*, ed. Ted Hughes. New York: HarperPerennial, 1960; reprint, 1986, p. 240.

12. Plath, "Childless Woman" in *The Collected Poems*, p. 259.

13. Plath, "Child" in *The Collected Poems*, p. 265.

14. Jorie Graham, "Wanting a Child" in *Erosion*. Princeton, New Jersey: Princeton University Press, 1983.

15. Louise Glück, "The Garden" in *Descending Figure*. Hopewell, New Jersey: The Ecco Press, 1976.

16. Lucille Clifton, "The Lost Baby Poem" in *good woman: poems and a memoir 1969–1980*. Rochester, New York: Boa Editions, 1987, p. 60.

17. Plath, "Wintering" in *The Collected Poems*, p. 217.

◊

JILL BIALOSKY is the author of *The End of Desire* (Knopf, 1997) and *Subterranean* (Knopf, 2001), and a novel, *House Under Snow* (Harcourt, 2002), and co-editor with Helen Schulman of the anthology *Wanting a Child* (Farrar, Straus & Giroux, 1998). She is an editor at W.W. Norton & Company and lives in New York with her husband and son.

Heart Murmur

Carol Muske-Dukes

My poetics, in which I include my sense of prosody, derive from the sound of my mother's voice. If poetics can be defined (in a loose sense) as the science of any mimetic activity that produces a poem—and prosody broadly defined as elements involved in the rhythmic or dynamic aspects of speech—then my ideas about what is beautiful, what is a poem, remain pretty much inseparable from my earliest sense of language, the sounds of that language. And this earliest sense of language has to do with my mother and unpredictability.

I used to read authoritative essays by Harvey Gross or Paul Fussell or I.A. Richards on the subject of verse, its rhythm and meter—and meditate on the heartbeat, the oarstroke, the iambic of inhalation and exhalation—as the fundamental rhythms that undergird our sense of poetry's sonic inevitability. In an essay on the techniques of scansion, Fussell implies that order is resident in a poem's line or group of lines, urging the neophyte scanner to mark the stresses not according to any preconceived pattern, but "according to the degree of rhetorical emphasis residing in syllables." This discovered rhetorical emphasis had to do with the "relative force of its various syllables in projecting its meaning and emphasis...."

Robert Hass, in an essay in *Twentieth Century Pleasures*, remarks that "...we are pattern-discerning animals, for whatever reason in our evolutionary history. We attend to a rhythm almost instinctively."[1] What I have to say doesn't necessarily contradict this, but considers the possibility of the offbeat, the odd stress, the unpredictable inflection, and how the psyche responds to the "unpattern" or a kind of scansion.

My first sense of language was that it had rhythm, but startlingly, elusive rhythm. I was aware, as Fussell points out, of the "rhetorical emphasis" of syllables, but this emphasis kept changing. It seemed to adhere to no pattern. As to the profound evidence of precognitive order—that is, the totemic iambic of the heartbeat (heard amplified by the unborn in the mother's womb)—my own prebirth chamber was otherwise sound-equipped.

My mother had a heart murmur. A random murmur. I didn't hear (I suppose) the reassuring regularity of lub DUB lub DUB, rather, lub DUB-DUB—or sometimes, LUB dub-dub. If rhythm is itself a kind of meaning, then this was meaning's absence.

To this day I crave rhythms that accrue and alternate the "meaning" of the heart "murmur" with the regular heartbeat.

I suppose I grew comfortable in her world of free-association, non sequitur, displacement, dispositif, and ellipsis. My mother married at twenty-four. She was emotionally immature, haunted by her mother's death, a loss that more or less stopped time for her at her sixteenth birthday. Her ongoing grief kept her in a state of permanent distraction. She was childlike, mercurial, furious. She bore six children, who alternately annoyed and engaged her. She sang mindless songs to them, raged excessively at them, spoke nonsense to them, recited poetry, and subverted their sense of the authority of the plodding rational, the dubious logical, at every turn. She was spectacularly impatient. She moved fast, thought fast, spoke fast, sped through a range of emotions in a second. At times I felt vertigo: sick with a mixture of admiration and terror of her. She was in love with justice, yet she had no sense of its fair distribution. She was deeply compassionate (her finest quality), yet she had trouble expressing love to her children. She rarely touched us or embraced us, yet the force of her language bore down on us, swept us up, nursed us, ran in our veins, left us exhilarated.

She interrupted herself in the middle of speaking as new thoughts presented themselves. To follow her required a tracker's ingenuity, which I early acquired. I could decode (and still can) her most tenuous connections, her most elusive referents—there was always hidden logic to her linguistic peregrinations. Years later, reading Joyce's *Finnegans Wake* for my master's thesis, I felt entirely at home. Gertrude Stein or Jacque Lacan might have found her natural capacity for neologisms amazing as she teased out the warring forces of signification. My mother prefigured the Language Poets. To people outside our family, she was almost, but not quite, intelligible.

One of her sentences: "Schooop now, kids, schoop! What is this (dumb dedoshek!) they tell me don't come?" It wasn't the influence of a foreign language—or perhaps not entirely. She had grown up hearing Czech spoken as regularly as English at home, and her older siblings spoke Czech exclusively before they went to school, but English was her language from the beginning. Czech words like "dedoshek" (grandfather or old man) were used humorously by her, poked fun at as "bohunk" (her family's embarrassing Slavic tongue), interspersed with her made-up words ("Splink that faucet off! Pook that door shut!") and her mock-synergistic profundity ("He thinks too loud, big butter-and-egg man! Do you hear how deaf he left behind?"). There were jokes, insults, implicit in her syntactical anarchy. "Throw the cow over the fence some hay!" she'd shout, and laugh. I never knew if she laughed at the funny inversion and its satire on expectation or at her own similar construction. I knew that she loved language, but seemed to have lost control of it. I couldn't tell how aware she was of this loss. She would hoot with laughter, one hand on her hip, the other held delicately away from her body, flapping wildly, unconsciously, like a wren's broken wing. "Uff da, Mrs. Nelson!" she'd crow, mocking my father's Norwegian mother. "Haumfloowitz der snergowten Schnaut!" she would roar, saluting my father's German father. She made dismissive noises which sounded like words, "Fsssk—get away! Fsssk-it!" or real words or names that sounded like nonsense: "Ishkabibble!"

She had a smattering of French and some church Latin. And she had a deeply passionate recall of pages of poetry, learned by rote in school and interspersed freely within her linguistic impressionism, in sudden asides to her large brood. I grew to love the sound of poetry very early on. I sense that I somehow inherited the order that I craved in language, struggling to emerge from the fiery shipwreck of words.

"When I consider how my light—PUT THAT DOWN!!—is spent...."
"Sunset and evening star and one clear call—ARE YOU DEAF??—for me...."

I still hear those "splices," her swift dizzy marginal comments, when I read Milton or Tennyson (or Wordsworth, Shelley, Keats, Shakespeare, or Dickinson, for that matter). First I hear the words recited in a mock-portentous, reverent, "mindless" tone, then the interruptions an octave above, sudden red interjections of anger or surprise. These interjections are authentic feminist commentary, some might say. Why did I struggle to hear some connection over the volume of her frustration? She ransacked, she rewrote: I reinterpret.

I witnessed her inflecting the lines of memorized poetry arbitrarily, paying absolutely no attention to the governing structures of meter, end stops, or sense itself. She spurred her strange skittish horse of usurpation over the eloquent, paved terrain.

Thus, "The world is too much with us" became "The world is too *much-with-us*." Or "I sing of arms and the man...." became "I sing of *men in arms*...." Or "O Wild West Wind, when wilt thou blow?" became "O Wild, West Wind: when wilt thou blow?"

I still hear her voice reciting, rising, as she stands in the kitchen in an apron covered with flour—her eyes flashing, her index finger pointed straight up, then held to her temple as if she was receiving divine dictation at some inaudible-to-ordinary-mortals decibel level. The dog stares at her, occasionally barks. Her riptide parataxis derived from some unquestioned internal voice, like her heart murmur. Ultimately, I suppose this blood-deep eccentricity had an unsettling but finally fair-minded effect on me. I learned justice and compassion from her along with word-passion. Her diversions were indeed commentary on her unfair life. She never had a quiet moment, an undistracted spell. My father, a businessman, arrived home late, expected dinner on the table, did not assist in household chores. They fought, but again, she was an anarchist guerrilla—she bombarded him with words, blind-sided him, but refused to face him.

I lived in a kind of benign fugue-state myself. I listened to recorded music and turned in circles, faster and faster, and made up stories and poems in my head. I hated being treated "like a girl," I hated it when she wouldn't stand up to my father. I stood up to him. I learned about confrontation and pretension in speech, its power. About terror at word-collision, word-war and follow-through in the enactment of language.

I couldn't decide how I felt about her. Some of the time her erratic, inexplicable behavior shamed me, yet I knew instinctively that she was a poet, that the words that flowed through and around her could save my life. She was the source of everything emerging in my soul—and my little wit—as poetry.

That voice internalizing, subverting, claiming the poetic line of towering authority, became my own voice, irreverent, echoing. "Tyger! Tyger! burning bright... how'd you catch on fire tonight?" or "Captain, my captain... wake up and die right!"

I was a hit-and-run smartass. I smarted off without warning. Most of the time I was a well-behaved, shy child, the pride of the nuns at school. But I would suddenly rebel, as they put it—I began to realize slowly that I was, like my mother, funny. And furious. I had, of course, also inherited her madcap syntax. I had to be very careful to try and "pass" in language. When I tried to put sentences together in school or on the playground, I often made no sense. Context, meaning, slipped away from me in speech. People stared at me, mystified. I felt as if she ran in my blood, that when I opened my mouth, she spoke. Only when I wrote things on paper did I discover freedom from her—and freedom and order in language: I could harness the great betrayer. I could approximate symmetry. I could make "sense."

I could recreate lines of beauty, I could write down music. Was this her oddly given gift? Was she pushing me to write words on paper against those huge clouds of words swarming in the air, taking my breath away? Much later I realized that I could "write" her too. I could give her life symmetry.

◊

The birth of my daughter, years later, allowed this symmetry—as if the solar system had shifted and there was now a new sun. I felt I'd been handed a clear slate, though of course I hadn't. Still, memory seemed to vanish when I looked into her infant face.

> The pure amnesia of her face,
> newborn. I looked so far
> into her that for a while,
>
> the visual held no memory.
> Little by little, I returned
> to myself, waking to nurse....[2]

I wrote poem after poem to her, looking for the exact words, her epitome—impossible! I could not find the time to concentrate. Her extraordinary energy and bright questioning woke me and put me to sleep at night.

I wrote a bit in her infant and toddler years, but my poems grew shorter, the lines broken abruptly.

I remember listening to Fay Weldon on the BBC the summer Annie was four and we were in London. We were in London where my husband was acting in a BBC film of Eugene O'Neill's *Strange Interlude*. Weldon's interviewer had noticed that when she first began publishing her sentences were long, then they'd grown shorter and shorter. Now, he noted, surprised, they were long again. Fay Weldon laughed. "I have kids," she said. "They interrupted me every second when I was trying to write. I could hardly finish a sentence. That's why they grew short."

The rather slow-witted interviewer tried again, "But why are they longer now?"

Weldon sighed, "My kids grew up."

◊

My poems began to reflect interruption, lack of sleep—distraction. (Recently a critic, a former editor, male, said that my early work was "tighter" than what I'm writing now. This is unfortunately true.)

I found the one quiet time I could work was late at night. I stayed up till 2:00 or 2:30—in these hours, I found a place to "hear" myself in my writing.

Unlike my mother's riptide effect, my daughter, a calm centered child, inspired connections for me.

> By day she's not so sick. She hits
> the hound, then kisses him: nice dog.
> He cringes, then his wolfish face lights up.
> To me, she does the same. At two, her love
> of power's in two parts: love and power.[3]

Around 1990, when my daughter was seven, I began researching cosmology and biochemistry for a novel called *Saving St. Germ*. The novel is a mother-daughter story, set in the context of contemporary science theory.

Just as in poetry, my daughter inspired me—my sense of her unusual nature helped form character—and my sense of her "correctedness" to some thing I could not articulate informed my readings of science. I discovered, for example, that proteins in the brain when making thought connections literally reach out to each other. This image of protein reach, which I did not wish to sentimentalize or trivialize, nevertheless moved me and reminded me of the mother-daughter bond. That reaching out to the "like" or what is perceived as "like," though it is unknown, is bound up with the writing of poetry for me, bound up with love.

◊

Out there on the North Dakota prairie, my mother's high school English teacher, Miss Byars, taught the class from the Harvard Classics volume of 1931 or '32. She read Tennyson and Wordsworth to upturned faces: farm children, skinny offspring of immigrants, Depression generation, children of the Red River Valley. The valley was blasted that year by a drought so deadly the crops dried up and flew away in the winds. My mother remembers writing her name in the dust on her desktop: ELSIE KUCHERA. The poems Miss Byars read to them circled in the air like a sea breeze, fresh, steady, revivifying. That spring, my mother's mother, beautiful and strong, died. That same spring, my mother graduated and was named salutatorian—she stood at the grave inconsolable, weeping. Someone from the city, from the hospital, had brought irises, placed them on the grave. They were the only flowers anyone had seen that blighted spring. Miss Byars stood beside her suddenly, speaking poetry.

"Weep for Adonais..."
"All my life's bliss is in the grave with thee..."
Then: "After great pain, a formal feeling comes..."

My mother wept some more, then she tried to speak. Her inflection, her rhythm was sprung, heartbroken, idiosyncratically alive.

◊

In my own poetics, I am bereft, dumb to convention. I do not hear the drumbeat, the downstroke: harp, anvil, oar. I don't find meter or rhyme inevitable or authoritative. Though the sonics, the music—that means something.

The rhythms of poetry that saved my mother are not the rhythms that saved me, though poetry has been as specifically a salvation in my life. That I have a daughter, that has taught me about steadfastness and deep love, that the line of my poems has grown longer and stranger finally because of the ways she's altered my life is a given.

After great pain and great love, a formal feeling comes that is new. The particularity and intensity of the mother-daughter relationship, the mother-child relationship, configures how we hear and to what, in language, we are sensitive. In this way, I've been instructed in the powerful, tender anarchy of voice—that a poem, altered and differently mimetic, can be a new kind of poem.

NOTES

1. Robert Hass, *Twentieth Century Pleasures*. Hopewell, New Jersey: The Ecco Press, 1984.
2. Carol Muske-Dukes, "August, Los Angeles, Lullaby" in *An Octave Above Thunder*. New York: Penguin, 1997.
3. Muske-Dukes, "Summer Cold" in *An Octave Above Thunder*.

◊

CAROL MUSKE-DUKES has published six books of poems (the seventh, *Sparrow*, due out from Random House in 2003), three novels (the most recent, *Life After Death*, Random House, 2001), and two collections of essays (the most recent, *Married to the Icepick Killer: A Poet in Hollywood*, Random House, 2002). She is founder and director of the graduate writing program in Creative Writing/Literature at the University of Southern California and Professor of Creative Writing and English. She lives in Los Angeles, California, and has a daughter, Annie, born in 1983, and a stepson, Shawn, born in 1967. Her husband, actor David Dukes, died in October 2000.

In a Ring of Cows Is the Signal Given:
Ruminations on Mothering and Writing

C.D. WRIGHT | SEPTEMBER 21, 1998

For the first thirteen months He did not sleep. Four hundred nights is a long time for hard-bitten adults to negotiate daylight, meals, jobs, and all the rest without REM. I managed to write: "What No One Could Have Told Them" and "Detail from What No One Could Have Told Them," related to this unendearing phenomenon. When my husband and I met other couples with a baby, we joined heads and bored into their glowing faces to ask in abrupt, strained unison if "it" slept. And if "it" did, we shunned those people. When our fatigue turned pointedly stressful one was wary of relieving the other, of leaving the other either behind or alone with the baby. One could not describe what one was wearing or eating or saying. "Go comb your face." "What did you say? Did you say something? Were you talking to me?" Thinking was prohibitive. Writing ceased to come up. A friend told us having a baby was like having a bowling alley installed in your brain. That sounded close.

He liked motion. We rocked. We cranked the swing. We rocked. We drove through the carjacking ruins of Providence in the hours when even the slickest car thieves were in their cribs dreaming. We rocked. We cranked. We drove. He did not like the Jolly Jumper. He thought it was a trap. He liked to stand in His back carrier putting a little friendly pressure on the coccyx. He liked to push His carriage clearing the sidewalk of all other pedestrians. There was a passing concern about homicidal leanings when from the bicycle seat at my rear came the mantra "buy me a toy gun mama buy me a toy gun buymeatoygun..." When we got His first wheels our thoughtful, paranoid, racist neighbor precipitately relieved us of the tricycle so that no one else would take it, failing to mention, until he noticed that we were moving away, the trike was in his safekeeping.

There were the unmentionable concerns about brain damage due to medications I took during mid-pregnancy hospitalizations for degenerating fibroids and premature contractions. There were the chronic ear infections, the nonstop antibiotics, and finally tubes inserted into the miniature animate ears. He was croupy, so there were the steamed-bathroom nights, all-weather-all-hour drives with the windows down to break up the cough, and stoplight-running dashes to the hospital when neither worked.

Not to be forgotten was the near-death experience of childbearing itself. Ten units of blood swiftly down the drain. Listening to my body rattle on the metal table as my temperature plunged. Watching the anesthesiologist's eyebrows bush into alarm. Noticing the room fill with uniforms and empty of husband. The edema. The bruising. The belated milk. A younger homeopathic friend had suggested I have the baby in a room at Women & Infants appointed to resemble a real bedroom, and then be released after a rapturous recuperative nap. I was thirty-seven and I really did not have anything else scheduled for the baby's birthday. I told her I thought I would pack my little bag and stay overnight in the hospital. Not meaning a week. "Was I in a really bad wreck or did I just have a live human baby?" I made an attempt to make a charged explicit record of what I considered an experience that did not bear repeating book-long. It is not a poem I would press upon pregnant friends.

There was the unmentionable concern about brain damage due to a fall from a chair against a stucco wall in Bonaire, three months old.

The dumb questions: Will He always have cradle cap? Will His plates close? Will He get VD if we don't circumcise Him? The schnattering bourgeois concerns about every aspect of development: Will He walk? Will He talk? Will He count? Will He read? Will He make friends? Will He find love? Will He have to have a stupid job?

Not to mention the threats and bribes that became the *modus operandi* for getting through the day. Adult: I'm calling Santa Claus. No, I'm calling the police. Do you want to go to the electric chair or do you want a pony? I'm sending you to military school. Child: That's just for serial killers. Adult: I'm not ruling it out. And the shame my stormy reactions to His provocative behavior rained on me. "You broke my little blue chair," the whispered reproach from the rear of the car.

There were two blessed naps a day, then one blessed nap, then no nap. He liked motion.

He liked the three pigs. He liked to tell it:

> There was Red Riding Hood. Then Snow White came and the wolf said, "With these big eyes." And then the pigs blew and blew. And Snow White said, "Oh no, Mr. Oink."

He liked "Beauty and the Beast." Every night the beast implored Beauty to marry him, every night Beauty refused, the beast turned away moaning. Every night the boy cried, "I will marry the beast!"

There was the ludicrous concern about brain damage when it was discovered He had eaten a few of the Absolut-filled candies intended for the adults.

Not that writing comes any more naturally. I just never feared the failure in writing as much as in mothering. Not that I fully believe they nurture each other. Time being crucial to each, they are in a rudimentary, practical sense exclusive. Factor in time for husband, employment, house, pet, car, and literary press. And sleep. All that B-S about quality time is B-S. In post-modern living, Time, as it is designed to be experienced, is not extant. There is just limited time under ever-increasing degrees of heedless pressure. That *anything* worthwhile comes of this busyness is the real wonder. The Mayan prophecy says the final and fifth apocalypse will be motion.

The other major exclusionary quality between writing and mothering is the nonstop siphoning of your mental operations. One cannot get beyond the bovine levels of ruminating when there is no room left up there for any entity but the son. When He is not invading my breathing space, His broth fills my brain pan. I can talk about Him until the room empties, as it surely will once I begin. I comfort myself with comments such as Larry Rivers made to Frank O'Hara—that so much of art is energy, the ceaseless insistence upon making decisions in spite of continuous physical and mental interruptions. But I regularly slam into my limitations, energy being one, and I guard my desk like an attack dog. Snarl turns to whimper only when I know I am licked. Life intervenes, and so it should. Nothing I or anybody else can commit to the page will ever be a match.

There is the all but intolerable concern about failure. As a writer, one assumes bouts of failure. It is in truth the preferred goad for a number of us. For those of us who take the view that the downward slide is greased and waiting; for those of us who have an uneasy to miserable association with competition, failure is *the* base even if *a* base stimulus. My most recent book came from the teeth-gritting will to live down the one before. Failure in writing is not necessarily a sorry mother. But as an actual mother, one worries less productively. Is this the error that will sear Him, uglify Him. Is this the mother of all child-rearing mistakes? Where is the outer margin of error; what is the quota?

Poetry and mothering are symbiotic—the relationship is close, protracted, and not necessarily of benefit one to the other. They are different organisms, different species. There are certainly periods when they fill each other up, and there are just as certainly periods when they drain each other's cup. It is not my choice to forego one for the other. I was asked by a poet who reluctantly chose not to have children what conditions I would require to become the best poet I could. And I had to allow, I had them, though I struggle for the opportunities to enter that clearing where I am alone and afraid and humbled and pregnant only with the anticipation of thinking, dreaming, creating, writing without interruption. I had to allow, I require the distraction, that I require the attachment, and that unencumbered I merely dissipate; I come undone. I admit, I require the struggle though it brings me to my knees when I most long to be standing free.

And then, there is the gift of tongues, *homo loquens*. The arrival of language is one of the unbeatable pleasures to attend, and one of the rejuvenating moments in an adult's linguistically bromidic society. First word: *huh oh*. The initial disconnected strand: *go, ear, no, nobody, car, money, mama, mine*. How supersonically we were transported from, "Will He ever talk?" to "Please, please, shut up for five heaven-sent minutes. We will pay you." Early unadulterated language, that is the hardcore seduction of having one underfoot, and I had just enough presence to keep a quasi-legible notebook.

His imaginary friend very briefly shared the bed, the car seat, the stroller. I have forgotten his name, some mature-sounding name, Henry or Arthur or Theodore. I thought him harmlessly creepy and did not regret His disappearance. We were simply informed that Henry or Arthur or Theodore left. Poof.

And, oh, the things He did to the long-suffering dog, our three-legged beagle Karl Barx. Everything from feeding him a bottle of aspirin, which Karl quietly upchucked in a perfect white chain of peaks under my desk, to trying to plug a forty-watt bulb into Karl's behind.

His nicknames: Angel Brains, Hairball, Muffin, Glowworm, Whistle Pig.

The names we didn't give Him: Audie Hart, Sawyer, Harper, Agee, Warren, Ryder, Shelby, Jamie Forrest, Asa Gray...

The names He instructed us to call Him: Muscleman, Musashi, Zorro, Captain Planet, Super Hero; all appended with the order: "Don't tell anyone my secret name."

The marvelous questions:

> Can girls have beards?
> Are there any blue hairs on my back?
> Is ice made out of glass?
> How many feet do a duck have?
> Do police sleep?
> Why don't the Three Stooges ever go to the bathroom?
> Why is that camel always smoking?
> The true color of Santa's beard is a mystery, right?
> Can girls wear hats?
> Is it illegal for men to shave their legs?
> Who invented talking?
> What is black and white and doesn't smell?
> How did the letter Y get its name?
> What has four wheels and doesn't feel?
> If god made people who made god?
> If one of an earthworm's hearts stop, do all five stop?
> What is yellow?
> How do you shrink things?
> How do you make skin?
> How can I write a Bobbsey Twins book, I'm not even Italian?
> How many things are there on earth?
> Who invented money?
> Why don't rich people talk at the table?
> Do giraffes have mohawks?
> What are balls for? Are they to hold medicine?
> How many days are there in a life?

Then the marvelous answers: "Brecht, do you know what an outhouse is?" "Yes, it's when the rich have their servants and when they come back in the summer they say, repair for my return."

"Protect me!" He hollered from His room at bedtime, even to the babysitter, frightening her.

He is grafted to the heart as soon as He issues from the body. He is. Therefore and nevertheless, I poetry. We will not know whether He is good for anything sitting or walking for a couple of decades yet. He is a major reason for going on and exactly how that is applied to writing is a mystery, right?

THE ORACLE'S RESPONSE

in a ring of cows is the signal given
that is the true beginning of all things
the fog would soon rise as if on cue
and the grasses would begin to sweeten
inside their elaborate stomachs
that is always the true start of things
it happens in the morning
when the crows wake up to attack the corn
and the boy turns over in his bed to shield the light
from the face and the face from the light
this is the true beginning of all things

to the frog the sign has already come
and it has come to this animal
with more power than it will ever come again
to the frog it has come as a heavy gavel
to symbolize judgment
which we so quickly failed to dodge
to the root it came as the leaf
which we so happily brought to green
as the door opens to a wedge of day
to the crow and the frog of the day
this is the beginning

of all things
and we the sparrow kings will not let you by
if your markings are not right

—Brecht Wright Gander, 1996

◊

C.D. WRIGHT has published ten collections of poetry, including *Steal Away, Selected and New Poems* (Copper Canyon, 2002); the book-length poem *Deepstep Come Shining* (Copper Canyon, 1998); *Tremble* (The Ecco Press, 1996); and *Just Whistle*, another book-length poem (Kelsey St. Press, 1993). Her poems and essays have appeared in *American Letters & Commentary*, *Arshile*, BRICK, CONJUNCTIONS, *sulfur*, and other magazines. With photographer Deborah Luster, she won the Dorothea Lange-Paul Taylor Prize from the Center for Documentary Studies at Duke University for a collaborative project concerning prisoners in Louisiana. Wright is Israel J. Kapstein Professor of English at Brown University in Providence, Rhode Island. Her son, Brecht Wright Gander, was born in 1986.

Part Four

A Third Space:
Temporal and Other Crossings

Language and the Gaze at the Other—
A Poetics of Birth

GILLIAN CONOLEY

Surely to write at all, to use language at all, is to glimpse a heightened sense of "the other." Reading is the same: so is viewing. To experience extreme unity followed by extreme separation. To experience one's identity merging, then dividing, separating. I have a friend who after seeing a film says she "goes around for the next couple of hours wearing the actress's face."

When I was in my mid-twenties I read a novel that was very important to me, *Nadja*, by André Breton. The novel is constructed around a female character who is the central force from which all events and concerns spin, yet she never completely materializes. Nadja is a woman of both presence and absence, someone who was just seen at a street corner or a café—a trace of her is left wherever she goes, marking her existence, though we never fully see her. She is erotic, mysterious, haunted, powerful, all the things I wanted to be. She is, above all, free to change, mercurial though revolutionary. Simone de Beauvoir describes Nadja as being "so wonderfully free from all regard for appearance that she scorns reason and law alike."[1]

The novel was important to me because in it I recognized my own free-floating sense of identity. I have never felt like I had a particularly set-in-stone identity, like I could say, "Yes, there I am in the photograph, that's *me*, and I am the same person." This was particularly troublesome during adolescence, for while my sense of self was by nature porous and procreant, some part of "me" was quite concerned with erecting a much more consistent, solid self, one whom I could never quite get to remain. At the same time, I wanted to be able to change at any moment, or, at least, to think I could. Gradually I got older, read philosophy, feminist thought and theory, and sought out the work of like-minded women and men. At some point I began to experience this floating identity as something pleasurable, even comfortable. I discovered that I could live this way.

What I was not prepared for was the heightened experience of this floating identity after I had given birth. Nor could I imagine how much I loved being pregnant. The corporeal reality of there being two present in my body—two intelligences, two biologies, four ears that could hear, four eyes that were open, two souls—this was a beautiful evidence of the multiplicity I had felt all my life. For the first time in my life I was *physically* not "myself."

And once my daughter was born, a third collective identity was born—this was the third that she and I became together in the space of all that passed and was to pass between us. In her early infancy and first year, I could particularly and quite keenly sense this space as a kind of third world, one that was palpable, that was pre-language. And because this space was pre-language, or unlanguaged, it was one where identity seemed to matter less and less, whose was whose. This was for me, as I suspect for many mothers, a time of great enchantment and joy. This sense of the two of us composing a third has never completely gone away, nor do I suspect it ever will.

I remember experiencing something quite strong once at a playground when I was pushing my daughter on a swing. The ropes of the swing, the back and forth momentum—the flying, giggling, singing child, the standing, laughing, singing mother—and the visual presence of a rope that went away from me and came back—this spurred a very distinct, palpable memory of the umbilical cord that felt like a phantom limb. We were outside of each other, we could fly away from one another, and we could fly back.

As I write this I realize that this third identity is finding expression from my point of view, so perhaps there is a fourth from my daughter's point of view; the divisions continue and continue. In the writing yet others are produced on the page, the fifth, the sixth, more multiplicity, more reproduction. And on the page, I recognize how this process is akin to the ever-trailing chain of associations in language. Then I couple my own associations with language's being overpopulated with the intentions of yet other "others." I am reminded of Dorothy Richardson's phrase: "a shapeless shapeliness."[2] And of Julia Kristeva on motherhood, "I cannot realize it, but it goes on."[3]

Lately I have been turning over and over in my head a paragraph by Madeleine Gagnon and Hélène Cixous:

> We have never been the masters of others or of ourselves. We don't have to confront ourselves in order to free ourselves. We don't have to keep watch on ourselves, or to set up some other erected self in order to understand ourselves. All we have to do is let the body flow, from the inside; all we have to do is erase... whatever may hinder or harm the new forms of writing; we retain whatever fits, whatever suits us. Whereas man confronts himself constantly. He pits himself against and stumbles over his erected self.[4]

I both agree and disagree with this passage. I have never been the master of myself, though I have certainly tried, and I have also tried to master others. I feel that earlier in my life, and now, I did and do "erect selves." And I confront myself, endlessly. What motherhood is teaching me in relation to identity is the rapidity with which these selves can come and go, and how fiercely they are erected and erased. For me, one of the least understood and discussed aspects of motherhood has been the extent to which our own children shape and alter our identities, and we, theirs, each of us demanding of the other a constant shifting of reality. With my daughter's own temper tantrums as model, I can shift, must shift, as she shifts, from rage to joy without a trace, from Medea to madonna in a matter of seconds.

At this writing, I am four years into motherhood. There is no doubt in my mind the extreme extent to which motherhood *acts* on identity. The formulation of identity, the slip and slide of language in bespeaking identity, the narratives "identity" constructs, the presence of spirit, of grand mystery, the way all of this can come together in a single phrase—these are consistent concerns in the writing. To understand how motherhood affects the writing is like trying to glimpse the impossible (which is perhaps what all writing attempts?) Julia Kristeva says, "A mother is a continuous separation, a division of the very flesh. And consequently a division of language—and it has always been so."[5]

And so, the impossible. To be a mother is to know a love like no other. It is to be in contact with an "other" in a way previously impossible, unavailable, and unknown. Kristeva writes of the complexity of this experience very lucidly:

> Pregnancy seems to be experienced as the radical ordeal of the splitting of the subject: redoubling up of the body, separation and coexistence of the self and of an other, of nature and consciousness, of physiology and speech. This fundamental challenge to identity is then accompanied by a fantasy of totality—narcissistic completeness—a sort of instituted, socialized, natural psychosis. The arrival of the child, on the other hand, leads the mother into the labyrinths of an experience that, without the child, she would only rarely encounter: love for an other. Not for herself, nor for an identical being, and still less for another person with whom "I" fuse (love or sexual passion). But the slow, difficult and delightful apprenticeship in attentiveness, gentleness, forgetting oneself. The ability to succeed in this path without masochism and without annihilating one's affective, intellectual and professional personality—such would seem to be the stakes to be won through guiltless maternity. It then becomes a creation in the strong sense of the term.[6]

It's interesting to think of William Carlos Williams at this point, despite the fact that he, obviously, was "only" a constant observer of birth. Williams left us a poetics highly influenced by his own experience as a doctor. His principal activity was obstetrics. He witnessed countless beings taking their first breath, *seeing* for the first time. He called himself not a "repeater of things second-hand."[7] He insisted, as Marianne Moore wrote, on seeing like a child, "contemplating with new eyes, old things, shabby things."[8]

Williams's ideas on the imagination also appear to be influenced by his continual witnessing of birth. It seems that what Williams wanted was to have what he called reality, "the thing he never knows and never dares to know... what he is at the exact moment that he *is*" find equal growth with an imagination "not 'like' anything but transfused with the same forces which transfuse the earth."[9]

This strikes me as about as close to a poetics of birth as we have. Still, it's uncomplicated by the split of the body, by what one could call participation in a maternal space—and it's written from the viewpoint of an observer, Williams's classic stance. His language, his grammar, goes through a similar equation/formula:

> The word is not liberated, therefore able to communicate release from the fixities which destroy it until it is accurately tuned to the fact which giving it reality, by its own reality, establishes its own freedom from the necessity of a word, thus freeing it and dynamizing it at the same time.[10]

Actuality. Contact. These are the domains he witnessed. The domains of birth and of the mother, of one body leaving another. And the clouding of identity that happens when the imagination is called into play:

> In the imagination, we are from henceforth (so long as you read) locked in a fraternal embrace, the classic caress of author and reader. We are one. Whenever I say "I" I mean also "you." And so, together, as one, we shall begin.[11]

For the mother, this embrace, the blur where "I" end and "you" begin, would be maternal: this "blur" becomes an actuality, a physical, psychological, and spiritual actuality of extreme unity, followed by extreme separation. Williams's "together, as one" I also depart from, thinking more of a splitting off, molecule by molecule; something more like a "together, as many" suits me better.

For every birth is also a death, is also many deaths. The death of the pregnancy, the two-bodied body. The death of the woman before she was a mother. The death of the fetus adrift in amniotic currents as the new body encounters air. The presence of death in birth, a presence our mass marketers do their best to disguise with pastels, with images of joy, warmth, and completeness, was, for me, a very strong presence. Being pregnant was magnificent and frightening. One was carrying a life that could die at any moment. One could die. My labor was horrendous—six days of contractions, four days of intensive labor—back labor, predromal labor, a cervix that preferred to stay clinched like a fist rather than, as the midwives softly and irritatingly urged, "opening like a rose." I am certain that without modern medicine, had I been a frontier woman crossing the West, or holed up somewhere in a shack, I would have died. A new ferocity entered my life. To have my daughter, today, I would, without hesitation, perhaps even with joy, step right back into that fire. Hélène Cixous writes, "Hell returns us to something mysterious and enchanted that we know nothing about but that is deep inside us: our genesis."[12]

In her wonderful book *Three Steps on the Ladder of Writing*, Cixous dedicates a whole section, the first "step," to what she calls "The School of the Dead." Being pregnant, giving birth, I experienced a distinct feeling in my psyche, in my writing, in my life as an artist, that there had been a great deepening. Whether peers or critics or reviewers thought so was and remains immaterial to me, and it is not something I can qualify or want qualified in terms of becoming "better" or there being an "improvement." I can only acknowledge the feeling of what I experienced as a great psychic deepening. And I attribute this to the presence of death. I love this passage from Cixous:

> To begin (writing, living) we must have death. I like the dead, they are the doorkeepers who while closing one side "give" way to the other. We must have death, but young, present, ferocious, fresh death, the death of the day, today's death. The one that comes right up to us so suddenly we don't have time to avoid it, I mean to avoid feeling its breath touching us. Ha![13]

The truth is, I survived. My mother, who had experienced two such labors, survived, too. My daughter survived. We each survived the split of the body. The journey to the void, and back. The merged identities turning into one, divided, separated, forever, from one another. And then the attentive, life-long gaze at the other.

In writing about death, Cixous writes of the benefits of loss to the writer. She reminds us:

> Montaigne said philosophizing is learning to die. Writing is learning to die. It's learning not to be afraid, in other words to live at the extremity of life, which is what the dead, death, give us... So it gives us everything, it gives us the end of the world; to be human we need to experience the end of the world. We need to lose the world, to lose a world, and to discover that there is more than one world and that the world isn't what we think it is. Without that, we know nothing about the mortality and immortality we carry. We don't know we're alive as long as we haven't encountered death: these are banalities that have been erased. And it *is* an act of grace.[14]

Surely the mother experiences a heightened sense of other, for she has quite literally, physically, produced one. For the mother who is an artist, this other, this experience of the other, comes very much into play in one's aesthetics. I think one of the most interesting questions becomes the question of who *is* the "other" when an artist who is a mother creates. Who gets shut out? Who remains? This process, complicated for any working artist, seems to be multiple for the mother. Here is what Cixous says on the other and the artist:

> What do we do with the other when we create? What does the author do? What does the painter do? That is, what do we do? This is our portrait, the portrait of the artist done by himself or herself, the portrait of you by me: it is oval: the Egg of Evil. What do we do with the body of the other when we are in a state of creation—and with our own bodies too. We annihilate (ourselves) (Thomas Bernhard would say), we pine (ourselves) away (Edgar Allan Poe would say), we erase (ourselves) (Henry James would say). In short, we institute immurement. It all begins with walls. Those of the tower. Those of the chateau we enter as we follow a seriously wounded narrator.[15]

As a writer, I glimpse my experience of "other" as one that is well acquainted with mutability. With transformation. If I were in Cixous's sentence, I might say, we *multiply* (ourselves) away. Hence, perhaps my attraction to Nadja. She is both creator (since she is the central force in the novel, and she makes things happen) and creation (because she is very much a "made" thing, she appears somewhat as a collage does—piece by piece). Like truth, the moment we think we see her, she is gone. When she tells Breton's narrator her name, she says, "Nadja, because in Russian it's the beginning of the word hope, and because it's only the beginning." She is always about to be born, she is always about to vanish. Most importantly, she is somewhere between life and death. Breton writes:

> To distract her, I ask Nadja where she is having dinner. And suddenly that frivolity which is hers alone, perhaps, to put it precisely, that freedom, flashes out: "Where?" (pointing): "oh, over there, or there (the two nearest restaurants) wherever I happen to be, you know. It's always this way." About to leave her, I want to ask one question which sums up all the rest, a question which only I would ever ask, probably, but which has at least once found a reply worthy of it: "Who are you?" And she, without a moment's hesitation: "I am the soul in limbo".... She makes me promise to bring her some of my books, though I urge her not to read them. Life is other than what one writes.[16]

Nadja is both in the writing and outside of it. Breton makes a strong distinction between "life" and the writing. And yet, what goes on in the life also goes on in the writing, Nadja's identity drifting quite comfortably somewhere in between. This "in between" state, unlanguaged, deeply mysterious, this gaze at the other one can never truly know, and yet one *knows* more intimately than one could know anyone—this is the domain of the mother I most acutely experience when I write. Breton ends his novel with the following passage:

> There are sophisms infinitely more significant and far-reaching than the most indis-
> putable truths: to call them into question as sophism, it must be admitted that they
> have done more than anything else to make me hurl at myself or at anyone who comes
> to meet me, the forever pathetic cry of "Who goes there? Is it you, Nadja? Is it true that
> the beyond, that everything beyond is here in this life? I can't hear you. Who goes
> there? Is it only me? Is it myself?"[17]

Not "myself." Perhaps something more like "the seriously wounded narrator" Hélène Cixous favors over an erected self, and then, to quote Williams, "transfused with the same forces which transfuse the earth."[18] The presence of life and death in birth can bring such a condition about: the impossible, the impalpable, the unlanguaged. One body leaving another, then the lifelong gaze between. Life: Death: The immeasurable pathways back and forth. Who doesn't go there? How many times a day?

NOTES

1. Simone de Beauvoir, quoted on back jacket cover of *Nadja* by André Breton, trans. Richard Howard. New York: Grove Press, 1960.

2. Dorothy Richardson, *Oberland.* New York: Random House, 1928, p. 211.

3. Julia Kristeva, "Stabat Mater" in *The Kristeva Reader,* ed. Toril Moi. New York: Columbia University Press, 1986, p. 173.

4. Hélène Cixous and Madeleine Gagnon, *La Venue a l'Ecriture.* Paris: Union Generale d'Editions, 1977, p. 142.

5. Kristeva, "Women's Time" in *The Kristeva Reader,* p. 206.

6. Kristeva, "Stabat Mater" in *The Kristeva Reader,* p. 174.

7. William Carlos Williams, *Spring and All.* Dijon: Contact Publishing Company, 1923, p. 6.

8. Marianne Moore, "Three Essays on Williams" in *William Carlos Williams, A Collection of Critical Essays,* ed. J. Hillis Miller. Englewood Cliffs, New Jersey: Prentice Hall, 1966, p. 40.

9. Williams, *Spring and All,* p. 9.

10. Ibid., p. 22.

11. Ibid., p. 4.

12. Hélène Cixous, *Three Steps on the Ladder of Writing.* New York: Columbia University Press, 1993, p. 6.

13. Ibid., p. 7.

14. Ibid., p. 21.

15. Ibid., p. 27.

16. Breton, *Nadja*, p. 71.

17. Ibid., p. 144.

18. Williams, *Spring and All*, p. 9.

◊

GILLIAN CONOLEY's most recent collection of poetry, *Lovers in the Used World,* was published in January 2001 by Carnegie Mellon University Press. Her other books include *Beckon, Tall Stranger* (Carnegie Mellon University Press, 1996), nominated for the National Book Critics' Award, and *Some Gangster Pain* (Carnegie Mellon University Press, 1987). She is a recipient of the Jerome J. Shestack Poetry Prize from *The American Poetry Review* (1999), as well as the Pushcart Prize. Her work has been anthologized widely, most recently in *The Best American Poetry* (Scribner, 2002) and *The Body Electric: America's Best Poetry from The American Poetry Review* (W.W. Norton & Company, 2001). Associate professor and Poet-in-Residence at Sonoma State University, she is the founder and editor of *Volt.* She lives in the San Francisco Bay Area with her husband, the novelist Domenic Stansberry, and their daughter Gillis, born in 1992.

Eighty-Five Notes

MEI-MEI BERSSENBRUGGE

My thinking and writing addressed changes in my worldview and experience after our daughter's birth. What follows are some altered notes from this time.

Pregnancy

1. I think about the ideal, my relationship to it, and the relationship of change to the ideal.

2. There is a feeling of time focusing on itself, instead of time without direction, but this isn't easily perceived, because the time is changing.

3. A cohesion or surface tension of daily events starts to occur, a surface of contingency and necessity, distinct from any deep structure of cause and effect.

4. Reference is no longer a one-on-one relation to her, but a perceptual dimension.

5. Speaking can hold together what you say with a large unsaid or unmanifest, so your speaking can become very simple.

6. Change in meaning seems to be more like a change of knowledge than of experience, because your experience goes outside meaning.

7. Understanding includes the latent, meanings in translucent layers, esoteric forms.

8. The child could refer to a depth of meaning *and* exchange for meaning.

9. Then, exchange a transparent and allusive image for the opacity of presence.

10. She exceeds aesthetic form by an ecstatic form of metamorphosis. The speed is as if the speed of light could vary, with moments of stillness, when no image can reach me.

11. A feeling of being at sea level in the sea, of experiencing meaning without mediation of perception and interpretation.

12. Growth is coactive from many points, so there is not a linear memory.

13. Among fragments of time, the logic of a detail can lie next to a romantic fragment.

14. Laying my foundation on a mass of unknown materials and unknown solidity, floating, alive, at the edge of space: knowledge and meaning are pushed to extravagance, to retain this sphericity.

Birth: Events Become Things

15. The relationship of her fate to time and of phenomena to time. I want to move from fixity in time as an attribute of fate to fluidity in time as phenomena filling the events in.

16. What is the relation of her will to her fate?

17. Even though her image becomes the first fact of my consciousness, the objective world, the world as representation is external to it.

18. There is a template of feeling in me and a representation of a person to fill that feeling.

19. It is as if I put the need for a fate into its own shape and it fit her.

20. Relate concrete meaning to genetic meaning, decomposition, or mortal happiness.

21. You automatically make meaning out of her birth, but if you want to recall it, you have to use your body as a mnemonic device. Birth changes in the concentration of its image and of your empathy from disorder to emotion.

22. The emotion is without coordinates in the world, so I can rotate my experience of her on any plane.

23. The way light glints in sequence on her barrette, buttons, facets of a toy as I move, or the way light glints on something still and seems to contract, is moving from communicable thought to intuited thought.

Days

24. A day consists of ordinary, small, inter-animating contingencies within high-speed alterations of context.

25. The fragment consumes time and space. You cannot put an edge on the weave.

26. The sea of days is like a kinesthetic or a postural sensation and does not have degree of intensity or distinct qualities.

27. Time passing is like speaking, as if I had nothing in mind.

28. Like snow on peaks at the horizon, a line will merge with space here and there, and events lose their separation from space, during a day.

29. The time factor can fall outside my group of stimuli, but why not use that as a time?

30. Reject the infinite screen in favor of a viable internal structure of shifting weights and balances, the sense of a day being crucial to or inside itself.

31. Nothing is needed to go from here to there, because everything is immediate.

32. The edges of a context open out.

33. You try for a coherent tension between the accidental appearing and clearly organized passages within a day. Everything is a field or a maze you get through serially, from point to point. You follow, and you're left with a network of points, and these points may be able to become your thought.

34. To understand in what way a fragment contains the whole and is also an exploration of the edges.

Subjectivity

35. A sensitive empiricism makes itself inwardly identical with the object.

36. Empathy is a means of representation. Her subjectivity makes a relativity that unites the objective and subjective into her sensuous image.

37. Your actions are deeper than thought. There is no place outside to stand on.

38. You are an animal in the world like water in water.

39. Bringing elements of my nature onto her plane is precarious, but this relative precariousness matters less than the possibility of a viewpoint from which these elements are perceived as objects, in the attempt to perceive each appearance, self, animal, mind, from within and from without at the same time, as continuity between us.

40. The relation of your experience to your ground with respect to her.

41. Her body is an unexpected response I get from elsewhere, as if things began to tell my thoughts.

42. There's a freedom in my bias. Absolute value transforms into a subjectivity in the form of spirit.

43. How might the universe be constructed to allow the coherence of her intention to affect her perceived world?

44. Becoming a ghost limb of her unconscious, you acquire a potential for mercy toward your mother.

45. The mother is anonymous and social as language, but simultaneously concrete, filled with specific content, with many locations of identity and forces.

Value and Moral Content Become Explicit, Not Relative

46. Nature is full of causes that never enter experience.

47. The experience of having her is a leapfrog of knowing before seeing, or experiencing.

48. Experience is an experience of meaning.

49. Spirit is not subject to interpretation, because it is not a symbolic or mediated event.

50. Trust and confidence are not tainted by cause.

51. One wants generality, which is what I call a child.

52. I feel my responsibility is to unfold new life, but I understand it's not to compromise life as a whole.

53. I feel the energy of the whole, which is somehow bound with value.

54. The mechanism in her genes for maintenance of the individual organism seems saturated with value.

55. The appeal of narrative, subject-driven art.

56. Poetry is not an end in itself.

57. There's transference among art and its others, the moral, the political.

58. Evaluate the situation in regard to the beauty of its vulnerability.

59. The unassuming spirit of play and togetherness needs no further justification.

Presence

60. A boundary is that from which she begins her presencing.

61. The power of presence triggers innate meaning.

62. Presence is not opposed to distance. Her image insists at any point, near or far.

63. The voice is a value of presence.

64. Vocal calls are controlled by neural structures in the limbic system and brain stem that are older than the structures controlling language.

65. You are attached to a person who can both inhabit the other and cohabit with it, temporarily.

66. My body is self referential to her body. It cannot take the role of the other.

67. The nonphysical light in our relation. Her physical matter is the densest level of physical light.

68. Her flesh when it is suffering is formless, because of my emotion. When it has form, it provokes anxiety.

69. The difference between an other opposed to me, and a non-opposing other, not *my* other.

70. A Noh play in which the mother must eventually accept she will never know if her lost child is alive.

Form and Matter

71. Growing is at home with complexity and apparent disorder.

72. Interruption is a method of form-giving.

73. You understand cause as a gap, not a comprehension.

74. A web of myriad presuppositions is holistic and particularistic at the same time.

75. Trying to stabilize a day or self without a figure, to perceive her as in a field with no figure, with random distributions.

76. The form of the body by which the subject anticipates the maturation of her power is given to her as a gestalt.

77. How she stands in the world, the top is metaphorical. Then growing crosses into the real.

78. To find form in substance and in relation, at the same time.

79. Energy is continually dispersed along the web of the inter-relation.

80. Matter is alteration which occupies time.

81. She and I together are the other for matter.

82. Emotion is so direct, it becomes concrete.

83. An innate form of knowledge is solicited by matter.

84. You have to accept that each girl is transitory.

85. The rules do not form a system, and experienced people can apply them.

◊

MEI-MEI BERSSENBRUGGE's books include *Empathy* (Station Hill, 1989), *The Four Year Old Girl* (Kelsey St. Press, 1998), and *Nest* (Kelsey St. Press, 2003). She lives with artist Richard Tuttle and their daughter Martha in Abiquiu, New Mexico, and in New York City. Martha was born in 1989.

Resuscitations

SUSAN GEVIRTZ

arm leg kindling gather where water blankets sound take her
down again again quiet crown

was strong singing heart you swimming practicing breathing
stripmining the superfluous

to anything recalled ever to everything ever summoned the
former a project of the former

sea fence Sea Gate said promise of plenty said gather greens of
tomorrow mainland winds mountain up once every 4,200 seconds

from lucid sea like none ever witnessed abbreviation the
situation engineered a couldn't say (or far worse

and so tending to every and none seeing not saying bluntly a
management preoccupation in familiar waters

carefully considered beginning rests with the rest turning away
turns the turned

what is the meaning of the word *lagoon* what a tribute that you're
all still here sweet nothings

warm in flannel under the ground "here's what we'll do —
when you sleep I'll sleep, when you wake up I'll wake up"

a long way to Tipperary to the place by the ocean its fishermen
and fine sand see the crypt correcting herself

land owners want land boat owners want bones boats want
shortwave sound wants bait land lies in wait

someone was behind her also a man was near pointing "You're
still there" unable to name or swim panting

between finger and singer machine's refrain between teeth the
difference

crosshairs correcting the spiral of wandering attention's
gunscope once I arrived landscape's low status slow statues

of noise no promise longer than sea's sleep that never rests short
of words over over sent

stick figure swaddled in chain mail escape hatch unlocks picture
postcards finger's touch

by sea's preface before the world was faceless now her face take
swallows silence soon down

the word regret the word repent whiplash on halved horizon be-
headed by halves the almost left holds hope behind right's back

belies the way face belies fact an act to cover the desire for never
achieved or relation to idea as act

wound or sunken awoken profile proximity's imposition face on
face of

and at our last parting last words I promised enfolded routing in
the gulf offing

written in caterpillar scar constellation written in rain star launch
reserves literally last week's facsimile face used up

plenaria aria axis belief voids all attempts sent to preliminary
galaxy beyond belief's chair[1]

—For Clio
—For Helen

When the phone rings and no one is there I say to my grandmother, "Next time wait a little longer and we can speak." Absence of breath at the receiver. Because it conveys voice
the phone is an instrument of breath. But the poem is not an instrument, it's an inci-
dent. It occurs at the moment of picking up the silent phone. The moment when the
dead have just ceased to speak. And just begun to speak. And the newly born have not yet
resorted to the inadequacy of words—having just come from worlds of far more subtle
articulation. "For this moment, this death-in-life when our breath is taken away, yet turns
and re-turns, Celan coins the word *Atemwende*" (Waldrop).[2] The breath is clock. The
breath makes reading hearing. What time is it? Time to listen for your life, that is, to

write. "Sometimes we write… so as to name an age, the one that comes to us from our mother, sometimes to celebrate the natal event, and the author of the event, the mother" (Cixous).[3] Sometimes all authors fall away and writing writes the collision of events. Our breath is taken away.

It is true that Clio was born on April 6, 1997. And also true that my ninety-one-year-old grandmother died three weeks later. This three weeks was a "turning of breath"—a lathe—in which an encounter occurred, a shape was presented.

My grandmother never met Clio, but she saw pictures. I spoke to her on the phone a few hours after Clio was born. I called her often in the first weeks of Clio's life. In those weeks she was shuttling between many worlds, but whenever I called she immediately and clearly said, "How is she?"

The poem (as always) is about *about*. Which means that events were an environment of conversation, but the poem is not about events. The poem is about the impossibility of writing *about* events. In disguise as convoys for about, but actually serving only as decoys, since about is never actually possible, are the conventions of telling, of grammar, of reading from left to right, of story, etc. After the necessary abolishment of these decoys from the land of the poem, after *about* falls away, only about *about* is left (only the decoys of the decoys are left).

At the same time that my grandmother was going and coming, Clio was trying to stay. As with many babies, her breathing was erratic. She was kept an extra day in the hospital for observation as she had apnea—uneven breathing with alarmingly long pauses between breaths. I had sat at my grandmother's bedside for ten days in January when she seemed to be dying. Her breath was also ragged. Sometimes she sounded like someone running, then the parched lips and rasp of great thirst, then nothing, next a half-smothered inhale, a sudden deep breath and back again to an uneven rhythm.

The sound of the story, the shadow of the story on the ground, displaces its small body, high up in a sky, getting smaller and farther away each time the phone rings.

One evening during that January bedside vigil when I was seven months pregnant, my grandmother said she heard a baby crying. I was not in the room. My sister told me to come in. I had recently read that at this stage of fetal development babies can cry in utero. I found this disturbing—how can you hear the crying? How can you comfort a baby who is crying inside? When I arrived in my grandmother's room, she said, "Come here." She put one hand on my stomach and closed her eyes. Then the other hand too. "Oh, she's crying, but she will be okay," she said, her eyes still closed. Then she said, "Sweet baby..." and began to hum, then "You will be lucky, you will have a wonderful life, you will be healthy, all will be well..." humming to the baby, patting my stomach.

Are you there? Either of you? "I see my invisible... The thing that will come from us to us so as to escape us."[4]

After she died I dreamed of my grandmother wrapped in a black shroud laid out on a low table on a stage. I walked through the rooms of a house and found her there though I was looking for Clio. When I saw my grandmother instead I said "swaddle shroud"—I nursed Clio as my grandmother was lowered into the ground.

Each couplet in the poem requires a full breath and ends when the breath would run out.

NOTES

1. Susan Gevirtz, "Resuscitations" in *Hourglass Transcripts*. Providence, Rhode Island: Burning Deck Press, 2001, pp. 11–14.

2. Paul Celan, *Collected Prose*, trans. Rosmarie Waldrop. Riverdale-on-Hudson, New York: The Sheep Meadow Press, 1986, p. viii.

3. Hélène Cixous, *STIGMATA, Escaping Texts*. London and New York: Routledge, 1998, p. 64.

4. Ibid., p. 65.

◊

SUSAN GEVIRTZ lives in San Francisco with her daughter Clio, born in 1997. She was an assistant professor for ten years at Sonoma State University and now teaches in the Masters of Fine Arts in writing program at the University of San Francisco and in the Master's Program in Visual Criticism at California College of Arts and Crafts. Some of her books include *Hourglass Transcripts* (Burning Deck Press, 2001); *Spelt,* a collaboration with Myung Mi Kim (a+bend press, 1999); *Black Box Cutaway* (Kelsey St. Press, 1999); and *Narratives Journey: The Fiction and Film Writing of Dorothy Richardson* (Peter Lang, 1996). She received the New Langton Arts Bay Area Award in Literature in the spring of 2002.

Untitled (M)

NORMA COLE | SAN FRANCISCO, JUNE 1997

How soon this will happen
is another question.[1]

100% on the floor, pieces of paper or scraps of light. Birds, as though wanting it louder. Cartwheels, three volumes, so probably earlier. It shapes everything. There is in their existence a letter. A thing needing no explanation. 100% can't find the letter now, so must have dreamed it. At first there was a physical approval. Circumstances, the materials at hand. How often does any negotiation

Who could say—
"I have for the moment everything I need"?
all the time and in the while

Experience does not care, for it comprises a unified theory of the senses.

To verify the symptom of limbs

The territory and all its subterranean properties
underneath "Cartesia" the territory
in its entirety
all the while the territory
and its introduction. Its interruption

Having forgotten it too well[2]

thoughts, feelings and
decisions were accompanied
by fleas, lice and since
it was impossible to
get rid of them
except by burning
the cities, though often
that was done for
other reasons

["Momma what's this?" The little boy in the dream asking about the blood—on his finger, he touches my cheek with it. It's from his face, his nose has been bleeding. There is some blood around his nostrils. He has come to me, his "strategy" to call me or someone "momma" and see if she will be that.

notebook, 28.iv.97

"He touches his face then touches your cheek leaving a red mark. Momma what is that he says. Are their gestures not thoughts?"[3]]

> *For both were blinded. Of course,*
> *this is mere fancy; one can see such*
> *distant times only in fancy's light.*[4]

The measure of the field is everything you remember plus everything they remember. Language and the thoughts of people are inseparable. Take away where things merge as they do in life and in the mind substitute logic, the line with above and below. Remote from memory, the memory closing—how can such a state know memory? Evidence of the investigation. The future opens tomorrow, they said.

> *...the thought of it becomes*
> *unendurable, except in flashes.*[5]

Stanzas overlooking increased
seeing
          There were children
and then the children
were
          The children
are gods+there is no final
analysis=the double displacement
open-ended to thought+the effect
of the montage=something like if only
they could keep it up+people fear
what requires watching=the illusion
that presence could defer
the inevitable

Here is the falling down, or there? What was the first person? The clock? What it ate? Terror? Across gesture? When reading did you come across "strategies" that you could relate/connect to what we've been given? What if we'd been shaped to the contrary? Or finally worked in relation to the contrary?

Take a point accurate to it. Bring in questions, material. Deductible questions. Paraphasia: "language of the father." Pick her up today. That is why "thought are things—sometimes they are songs."[6] Wanting exercise. The address of same. Examine the linens to see what we owe. A Shakespeare collar helps.

[The generations were E, and J who was sleeping and not going to awake, there but gone; 100%; and W who fell out of the car when 100% opened the door from the outside, unexpectedly, since he had already gotten out and was going home. But he opened the door and W fell out, fell down on his face. 100% picked him up and quickly handed him to {}—he was alright, just a tiny spot of blood on his cheek, a scrape.

notebook 20.iv.97

"By design he fell out of the truck so I picked him up. There was one little spot of blood on his cheek. Someone had opened the door from without."[7]]

Out of phase—there (the only place) to go or to be. As the writers of these loves, they are the powers.

As for the warriors[8]

Everything comes true. This is only the story and not excluding others. So, you are reading the air. For some, it is like reeling in some film or other. That love and care are insufficiently theorized like the rest of experience. A bird was repeating the bell-like sound. Experience does not care about preparation. And so, although our contradictions differ, they feel, and it is an unusual engagement. The chips are down. We will need this and that. Falling off a log as acute sensation. Local effects among themselves. And to think "see the world with your eyes," a vividness.

Or blankness. Tiny pair of lungs. Attendance is the epitome of something. This is where it begins. "Did you ever drop the baby?" she asks, flinging it about. A gathering of membranous edging on each side. Now the heartbreak of the rational. One can always find another pen or pencil. One story keeps busting in on another.

Site of precipitation. That's not memory it's a picture as though it is still a possible action shaking like the idea of a leaf. The jump between light and the understanding of it. "But the Sybil, I saw her hanging there...." Or water and a few seeds. Can experience be a false bottom? Silence reports event, moment builder. Emergence, the beanstalk, the idea of "finding." And the firelight, flickering. Meaning like action takes soundings on positions. And down we go.

[Dream of T alive as form.]

The moments of grace are rare[9]

"I have sixpence in my heart, or at least a sliver of ice," she said. "A corkscrew, screwpull—PULL—an ashtray." Then he counted his money.

Experience contributes to the common fund. Silence unsettles the spoken things. Be good for nothing, be still. And not announce these numbers and not between and nothing here at all.

NOTES

1. Simone Weil, *The ILIAD or the Poem of Force*, trans. Mary McCarthy. Wallingford, Pennsylvania: Pendle Hill, 1956, p. 37.

2. Ibid.

3. Norma Cole, "My Operatives" in *Desire & Its Double*. Saratoga, California: Instress, 1998. Also in *Spinoza in Her Youth*, Richmond, California: Omnidawn Press, 2002, p. 104.

4. Weil, *The ILIAD or the Poem of Force*, p. 36.

5. Ibid., p.22.

6. H.D. (Hilda Doolittle), *Tribute to Freud*. New York: Pantheon Books, 1956, p. 137.

7. Cole, "My Operatives" in *Desire & Its Double*. Also in *Spinoza in Her Youth*, p. 105.

8. Weil, *The ILIAD or the Poem of Force*, p. 32.

9. Ibid., p. 29.

◊

NORMA COLE is a poet, painter, and translator. Her most recent poetry publications are *Spinoza in Her Youth* (Omnidawn Press, 2002) and *a little a & a* (Seeing Eye Books, 2002). *SCOUT*, a text/image work, is forthcoming from Krupskaya Editions in CD-ROM format. Among her poetry books are *MARS* (Listening Chamber, 1994), *MOIRA* (O Books, 1996), and *Contrafact* (Potes & Poets, 1996). Current translation work includes Danielle Collobert's *Journals* forthcoming from Litmus Press, Anne Portugal's *Nude* (Kelsey St. Press, 2001), and *Crosscut Universe: Writing on Writing from France* (Burning Deck, 2000). A Canadian, Cole moved to San Francisco in 1977 with her son, Jesse, born in 1971 in Cagnes-sur-mer, France.

Poetma

DALE GOING

I did not choose to be a mother. That is not to say that I did not want to have children—I always assumed I would, sometime. But sooner than that, at twenty-two, I fell in love with a family, a man and his eight-year-old daughter, and this daughter became mine. Became mine? No. We spent time together. Or: became mine: possession signifying an other. Mother signifying an other.

And stepmother, more so. Step-parenting thwarts the narcissistic impulse of parenting. There is no question that the child is her own self, not an extension. The child and I have not shared a body. Our connection is imaginative, not inherent.

Is it because of her that I am willing to let a poem be itself, even though I don't fully understand it?

I don't expect to understand it fully just as this daughter is a mystery who over time reveals herself more clearly and resolutely and strangely.

We are so different, my daughter and I! Despite our dailiness, our long history, the love I bear for her that matters more than birth-bearing.

My daughter and I commune through sounds more than words, and through silences as vocal as words or more so, a thickening between us like barometric pressure. Storm any moment, maybe. Between us all language is translation or untranslatable or sign language, physical and foreign, rudimentary and frustrating.

As though to emphasize that no true closeness, no understanding, is possible. It seems to me all hopeful, futile human effort is to chink that chasm. "Even this is a distance."[1]

This distance is my work space, my blank page. It enables and necessitates the kind of writing I've come to.

Wanting to be understood, writing to be understood—my daughter's (my stranger's) close and foreign presence complicates that quest, eradicates the possibility of a pragmatic, a programmatic writing.

I retreat, like deep sleep, into a world of words she wouldn't look up in a dictionary. Where our mutual lexicon is practically negligible. Where I am myself, not my role in relationship.

What the world calls clear communication—what is considered transparent—is fundamentally opaque—a blunt, flat surface. It is incomplete, abbreviation, code. It excludes and limits. Any real attempt at clarity and communication demands depth, not opacity. Depth is the true transparency—a dark, complex shimmering built up of multiple fluid layers. When I write I let in words, phrases, ideas and connections left out of the common language, the shorthand of parenting and other jargons, whose artificial, distancing stance is that of authority, of certitude.

>   (remember
> an earlier fight,
> when she lived with us, her shouting,
> "why do you always have to be right?"
> me shouting,
> "because I AM!")[2]

◊

Poetry is not primarily a communication. It is a communion. It is a selfish act, it is an intimacy.

If the writing is authoritative, how can I come close?

◊

To say that I did not choose to be a mother sounds resentful. Also, possibly untrue.

Conversation with a friend during a family-free Thanksgiving about the choices we make—my fretting over (what I perceive as) a limiting decision my daughter has made. My friend believes we make the choices that propel us toward the life our spirit requires. His dysfunctional family, for instance, was precisely functional in his becoming an artist: they offered little comfort and left him alone.

I remembered my husband telling our daughter, who in an adolescent fit had screamed that she wished we weren't her parents, "Some people believe you choose your parents." Without a pause, she replied, "If that were true, I'd be living in Beverly Hills with a Rolls Royce."

My daughter, through a series of choices she did or didn't make since she did or didn't choose her parents, is living a life that in no way resembles that fantasy, in the high desert of New Mexico with her husband, two preschool daughters, and a menagerie of dogs and cats she's rescued as an animal-rights activist.

I, through a series of choices I did or did not make, became a mother and raised a daughter, doing the kinds of service work that accommodate a mother's hours—waitressing, teaching—and delayed a writing life.

Registering the external world, categorizing, checking off the events—the facts of a life are not where the life takes place. Circumstances are inducements. My daughter's internal world—yes, it is stirring. At 31, she is forming a spiritual identity. I try to keep track by remembering my life at each of her ages. The circumstances so different. But the inner life—at 31, I too was just beginning to urge toward an expression—in poetry—of that inexpressible.

Living with my daughter may have delayed my writing, yet I expect it would have been delayed without her. As would having a child have been delayed. I was not, in either arena, "ready."

A feminine dilemma, this needing to get it down before doing it. Practice, practice, practice. The ritual sweeping before stepping across thresholds.

The practice, as in meditation, that leads to the opening.

That leads to the entering.

Having her in my life has also allowed my writing. "I had to act as if I knew more than I did."[3]

The practice.

There was no possible practice.

◊

I did not write until she was grown. In this regard I am like all the mothers who enter a second life when their children leave home. As though her leaving home meant I too was grown. In this regard I am no prodigy. I took twenty years to come seriously to writing after first writing poetry like so many teenage girls. Poetry was a sporadic obsession. Trying to write was like trying to diet.

During the bad poem years I did try writing short stories.

Because I couldn't imagine "the truth"—its authority—which is what I thought poetry was.

I thought fiction was invention and poetry was revelation. I might find time to make something up (being a mother was about making it up as you went along), but I certainly couldn't find uninterrupted time in which to be receptive to revelation.

I took solace and guidance from a parental statement by Raymond Carver. He said he wrote short stories because there was no time, raising a family, for anything longer.

He'd sit out in the cold in the car to write.

The last time my daughter and granddaughters came to visit, despite my now having "a room of one's own," it was impossible to write with them in the house. I took refuge in my car.

Five minutes later, my daughter was knocking on the window.

◊

My daughter appears among the windows and chairs in "The View They Arrange," a poem about composing one's world. In our different ways, we each tend toward spatial and temporal arrangement. I in the inner world, in art, the created object—easier (it seems to me) to control. She in the outer world, where she prefers being early, spatially isolate, comfortable in a thinnish wedge of temperature and tempo.

When I learned recently that our house was to be photographed for a design book, my response was to spend the weekend rearranging the pantry—a private space not on the list for the photo shoot. I found this juxtaposing of the beautiful hidden somehow a necessary prelude to the visible.

In "The View They Arrange," my daughter and I go to the movies and
> sit in the last row
> —she doesn't want anyone behind her—spatial
> boundary preemptive,
> compelling
> throughout the movie
> she tells latecomers the two seats beside her are taken.[4]

I arrange my view by moving my chair or looking in a different direction. Or by arranging small objects—dishes, or words.

My daughter's (often frustrated) wish is to arrange her view by making everyone else (or the view) move.

Reminding me of the child—it could have been she—I watched trying to glue a gerbil to her collage.

I talk to her about

imagining her aura[5]

...

      imagining her aura—huge and wide—
      so if someone sits near—it won't matter—
      she'll still have personal space—"I know, I know"—
      driving her Delta 88—and she squeezes my hand—[6]

◊

Nothing has challenged her instincts toward arrangement more than having her own two wonderfully willful daughters.

Recently, for the first time, I have heard her speak with satisfaction of "the dishes being done," that small, temporary victory in the claiming of space. She is correlating that order with an order in her mind. This makes me alert to the lost girl in her, the girl who defied valiantly, each night, doing the dishes, willing her ill temper to wear her parents down.

My small orderings. Perhaps there is no courage in composing still lifes. But I never move plates in the pantry without thinking (with interest) about the next earthquake. I precisely love poetry above all written forms for its resistance and movement. The poetry in my daughter's world—as a girl, she took her gerbil on a plane and tracked it through the cabin after it chewed its way out of a cardboard carton.

◊

"The hallmark of a decision in line with one's inner development/is a feeling of having laid down a burden/and picked up a more natural responsibility," the artist Anne Truitt wrote and I quoted in "House Dreams."[7]

What I'd lost, and have been able to retrieve since my daughter has grown and gone and is herself a mother, is my girlhood. That is my writing room.

To feel the freedom and power I felt at the age my daughter was when I first met her.

A few years ago, when my own mother died, my image of my mother shifted from a single image defined in time—how she looked at the age she then was—to a lifetime of images. I could think of my mother and see her as an infant, a girl, a young mother. (All this, following a grieving in which I could only picture her in the acutely alive instant of her death.) She was freed from time.

My daughter's becoming a mother similarly released me. The cycles of motherhood and daughterhood have become more fluid. I can be with her now and still contain my girlhood, not just hers. We can be several ages, several selves, at once.

The girls we were thought we could control our worlds.

My daughter's first appearance in a poem was in a narrative of a party where everyone has written fortunes and passed them around:

> The one who asks *What if you get your own?*
> is the one who does.[8]

She was young but growing older. She asked this anxiously. It is a question girls ask when they start doubting themselves—when pubescence sets in. What if you get your own future, the one you desire, the one you write?

I so wanted to tell myself what to do. Not to be told. The retrievable gift of my guideless girlhood—like my artist friend, I was allowed to wander. I was independent and not depended on. That makes a stretch of time and space, unbroken!

◊

I never figured out, as mothers who write must, how to act and reflect in the same time/space. How to live/how to write, without the slash.

Yet I was able to write finally because other feminist-mother-artists had done so.

Feminism entered my life like yogurt. I wasn't heating and straining my own culture. I noticed yogurt when it showed up in plastic cups at the supermarket.

Around the time my daughter was leaving home, I went on a reading jag (begun during a prolonged illness that left me with little energy but with an expanse of time—inducive to reading and thinking). I was reading mostly contemporary fiction, and—I came to notice—most of it was by women. Once I noticed this, my reading became deliberate. Eventually—propelled by a return to Kathleen Fraser, whose early work I'd loved at fifteen—I began to read experimental poetry by women—and this changed everything for me. "The authenticity (not authority) of others' visions."[9]

The sense that I'd had, that poetry was "the truth," became even stronger as I lost the sense of its being "revealed truth." This most artificed of written forms seemed far less artificial to me than the conclusive linearity of sentence, paragraph, beginning-middle-end. A trepidation I felt in writing fiction (and am having now, in this essay) is that as soon as I write something, it takes on an aura of authority that may not be real.

The "central" fiction is perhaps hers, yet is continually disrupted.

(This word whose connotations I don't entirely or exclusively intend or negate.)[10]

I want to offer alternative versions. It seems more honest. Often, I notice, an ending of a poem will be an opening in another direction, as though I had reached what I thought was a destination only to turn a corner. I don't feel pressed to be exclusive or conclusive.

Tempered by motherhood, I learned a way of coming to writing, a gathering as of laundry, as of laying things at the foot of the stairs to be carried up later. The work collects in moments, for months, in fragments. It doesn't know what it is, only that it is noticed. It accumulates until—like the laundry, the dishes—it can't be ignored. The pleasure, the palpable necessity of the task! I set out to write my world. I tell myself.

◊

And I notice now, in rereading, that my punctuation marks the tempos of a mother's time—parenthetical, full of dashes—interruptive, connective, hesitant, inclusive (making little pockets for one's overlapping lives). Syncopation—the unpredictable. Preverbal percussives—our first communications—nonsense and music and silence—continuing their work.

◊

I wonder if we meet most deeply in the silence—that space between—in the syncopated rhythms of the disparate. Is it that we reveal ourselves hopelessly, selves the other can barely glimpse?

An offering, as inexplicable as any. Motiveless, goalless, open. The threshold where we both step, for an instant, before moving into separate worlds.

Being my daughter's mother has been an exquisite, frightening, revelatory experience of trusting and attending to uncertainty, mystery, disruption, eruption, the absurdity of authority, the frailty and surprise of connection.

Which makes imaginative action possible.

Which makes the present possible. (Anything less is a repetition.)

Which makes a poem possible.

Broken writing

on a broken ground.[11]

In the age of illuminated manuscripts, that made the most beautiful page.

The natural connectors. I think of poets as being the natural connectors. I think of mothers as being the natural connectors. Despite and because of everything I've said, I think that. It is our paradoxical work.

NOTES

1. Dale Going, "Services for the Little Hours" in *The View They Arrange*. Berkeley, California: Kelsey St. Press, 1994, p. 64.

2. Going, "The View They Arrange" in *The View They Arrange*, p. 58.

3. Going, "Or Less" in *The View They Arrange*, p. 53.

4. Going, "The View They Arrange" in *The View They Arrange*, p. 60.

5. Ibid.

6. Ibid., p.62.

7. Anne Truitt, *Daybook: The Journal of an Artist*. New York: Pantheon Books, 1982, p. 66; quoted in Going, "House Dreams" in *As/Of the Whole*. San Francisco: San Francisco State University, 1990, p. 14.

8. Going, "House Dreams" in *As/Of the Whole*, p. 14.

9. Going, "The View They Arrange" in *The View They Arrange*, p. 59.

10. Going, "Services for the Little Hours" in *The View They Arrange*, p. 69.

11. Dale Going, "Heard" in *ROOMS 5*, Fall 1998.

◊

DALE GOING's books of poetry include *Leaves from a Gradual* (Potes & Poets, 2001), *The View They Arrange* (Kelsey St. Press, 1994), *She Pushes With Her Hands* (Em Press, 1994), *Or Less* (Em Press, 1991), and *As/Of the Whole* (San Francisco State University Poetry Chapbook Award, 1990). Going is the recipient of two fellowships from the Djerassi Resident Artists Program and a California Arts Council fellowship. She co-founded the periodical *ROOMS* and as the proprietor of Em Press publishes letterpress editions of poetry by women. She lives in Mill Valley, California, with her husband, Philip. Her daughter, Rebecca, born in 1967, is the mother of Tess, born in 1994, and Nadia, born in 1996.

FIRST THINGS FIRST:
notes toward a discovery of
BEING A MOTHER BEING A WRITER

Barbara Einzig

> *After all, ecstasy*
> *can't be constant*
> > —Lorine Niedecker, "Laundromat"[1]
>
> *I wanted to say something,*
> *That my heart had such a burden,*
> *or needed a burden in order to say something.*
> > —Robert Duncan, "Doves"[2]

1

Initially the subject of motherhood and writing appears personal and particular. The states of being a mother and being a writer are both passionate sites of identity that have at their source the involuntary, the given. The child arrives with its own face and person, and the words heard when the poem begins have their own life. Both states involve great labor and care, discipline and practice. We reach out to find where what is required by children and by the book we are writing stops; we are surprised when it goes on and on.

The writer follows the words into the poem or story or essay, and they lead somewhere—through them things are found out. Whenever I have completed a book something big has always happened in my life, as if the book divined and made the future.

Just as I write this I find myself in a garden with two kinds of flowers—the anemone and the rose. Whether I choose to include these apparitions in what I write as bright yellow or pink images or whether I keep them out, they are here. They flower in the mind; their real existence allows them to take up residence in the mind of all those who have beheld them.

Although I may describe them I do not capture them; the subject is more than personal. The intense and passionate state of motherhood requires so much to be well realized, and its results are so immediate and continuous—the whole world of human beings. Yet how is it that the imaginative reality of a woman's life as a mother has been so kept out of the world of letters?

The anemone and the rose arrived from two gardens that existed in the past—my own and that of my mother. The "windflower" began as a dry claw and turned into a swaying mass of iridescent petals; the roses were above my head, somewhere around my mother's waist, tight buds unfurling overnight into blossoms that lasted for less than a week. The mother is the queen of the world that disappears, the world that appears in angles of sunlight.

2

When I was pregnant, I told one of my friends that I needed to finish a book I was in the middle of (*Life Moves Outside*).

"Oh, my mother was working on her dissertation when she was pregnant with me. I was colicky and she never finished—that was as far as she got."

"Well, I'm going to finish."

Niedecker: "I've spent my life on nothing."[3] She repeats this line and then changes the "on" to an "in" in the last line: "I've spent my life in nothing."[4] And in her poem that begins with the name "Paul" she lets a name be the same as any other word:

Paul
     When the leaves
          fall

from their stems
     that lie thick
          on the walk

in the light
     of the full note
          the moon

playing
     to leaves
          when they leave

the little
     thin things
          Paul[5]

It is after all not a self-effacing poetry but one that stakes its claim among the things—"carpets, dishes/benches, fishes"—that do not last, in the daily round.[6] Emily Dickinson also wrote: "I'm nobody! Who are you?"[7]

Both of these writers asserted their freedom to not be "public, like a Frog,"[8] and the space they took in which to write and to publish informs the work, as the white space of a poem is a vital part.

3

With motherhood I discovered the hours between five and seven A.M., when my child—a night owl from the start—could be relied on to sleep. I was living in Piermont, a pretty village full of strangers by the Hudson. Writing in the darkness of early morning was not so different from writing in the darkness of midnight, as I had done before I had a child. Although less than an hour from New York, Piermont was dark enough for stars.

Black air turned dark blue and then light, night pulling away from it, drained, a secret vanishing. Early commuters drove down our winding, hilly street, and the sun came up on the river. For a moment, caught at the wrong angle, my previous self was blinded by the rays. That was only the first fierce moment of the day. Then a gentle, milky light diffused there, as if to keep us from stumbling.

The only distraction arrived with the dawn raccoons, intrepid and hungry. A particular anticipation, quadrangle, alphabet, muscular resistance. Inside the houses that I saw from the bay window overlooking the drive, there were people still sleeping, joined to sleep as I was to writing. They were about to stir, and my new daughter to wake up, sure to want something, now.

We took long, green, exploratory walks following abandoned railroad tracks, down a tunnel of trees that twisted and rose above the Palisades and the river. The baby twisted against my chest, and I saw her eyes looking at what was far away as if it were within reach.

I wondered at how she would put it all together; I attended to her constantly. Hers was no abstract ambition but a determined, physical drive to find things out, a reaching out of the hand to see where the world stops. She was surprised when nothing resisted her fingers, falling into what had looked like a picture.

There were hills and the rocks that had given the county its name, and because it was the East there were no fences among the old-timers in the town. We wandered among the cascading gardens and the rusty pickups, visiting an old mustard-colored house where a woman named Dotty did us a favor before we had a phone and took our messages. She still ran a switchboard for a local doctor out of the front room.

4

The painter Rothko said that he painted large pictures because he could not place himself outside his own experience and by making a painting big, he remained within it, subject to it.

Being a mother has enlarged the experience of writing so much, I am still reaching out my hand to see where it stops and am surprised when nothing resists me.

Still, I was attached to the worldly and heroic, the canon and the filigree, the auditorium and the admiring Bog.

If motherhood makes a place in the Bog harder (to a degree depending upon those Austean constants of money and husband), motherhood (if truly undertaken) deepens being "in" it—as in "in nothing" and "you are in it."

The mother-writer accompanies her child into a language that is first private and then used between "native speakers." A mother pushes a stroller and talks or sings back to her child, who makes sounds that sound only to the mother like words, the more familiar words she speaks back. To be so intimately, day to day, involved in the recognition of the world as words—"language acquisition"—brings to the mother who is a writer a permeability, an openness, willingness to live with what is first incomprehensible—gibberish, nonsense, the arrangement of words against each other, texture and sound making the word into a thing that keeps and asserts its own qualities, the sound of a word before we know what it means.

There are no labels on things, at the beginning, and using the voice to name is aimed at getting to know them. Stein:

> So as I say poetry is essentially the discovery, the love, the passion for the name of anything.[9]

I always wanted writing to be as large as life, to be entered into as life is, without explanation.

When one is very hard pressed as many a single mother may be, the writer may be cast by the mother as a shadow is, parted from the mother's life as a shadow is, yet held to it.

The light shifts, the child is on its own, the shadow of the writer returns to the mother, she is in full sun at high noon. The shadow is the soul of the mother, and children, who are not supposed to step on it or on cracks on the sidewalk, may in these games divine this.

5

When the writer is writing the mother may be outside but is not cast but floats close by the writer as an angel might float, listening for the sounds of the child or "keeping an eye on it."

If this is true, the real life of the writer must depend on someone else sometimes caring for the child. The muse of such a writer is a babysitter, or the muse may be a husband. Yet the existence of such a muse, such a babysitter, could not in itself effect a bringing into the world of letters the state of motherhood.

The experimental writer has an apt teacher in a child fully occupied in the serious aims of play: to lift up her head, yell for food, stand up and walk over to where she wants to be, to figure out what she can do and where she is.

To bring into the world of letters the state of motherhood, the mother must be the writer and not an angel, a mother who must share the world of children, as despised and ineffectual and bedrock-like as it is romantic. Furthermore, if the writer is a poet, the writer is already among what Duncan called "the despised orders." For a mother to be wholly a mother while being a writer and not an angel would create a new literature.

6

The thousand cares of the mother have been a hard refractory quartz, making a kind of pyramidal stone, like the "ship's window" in the old sailing ships, yellow or white stones set in the deck of the ship. They magnify the light within the somewhat claustrophobic but working hold below.

This process of refraction can be helpful to a writer who is a poet and must like Lorine Niedecker live within a condensery of words. Giving birth is the work of an animal and makes the writer aware of being a human animal. The thousand cares of the mother as human animal would, if set into the deck of past history, bring a different light to what is seen there.

Is being a writer and a mother hard? Is it the hardness of that stone, the focusing of the light?

7

The child brings the writer to the world of citizenry, a frayed and dizzy world whose vitality is a form of power. The child brings the writer to the garden where the anemones are fragile in the wind and a rose is a rose is a rose.

Certain peoples have believed that when children say a word for the first time, all of the word's powers are renewed. Children in the beginning cooing stage can make all of the sounds of all of the languages in the world, and as one language becomes the child's native language, that infinite capability is limited more and more as the child learns to speak. The child's first use of words and phrases is original—one can see a child looking for a word and finding it and discovering its sounds, playing with it, finding new uses for it, calling things that the child doesn't yet know the names of by invented, personal, and particular names.

If the language of the public arena is now exhausted (and it is), aren't mothers who are writers and privy to their children's first words close to an original language we are in need of? Holding to and getting down what is in those baby sounds must be admitted into the history of the adventure genre. Ladies, how do you get it all down, let it all in, while setting the recurring table?

8

William Carlos Williams wrote that our current despairs have come from the triumphs of philosophy and science, but that things might change if literature addressed truth at another (higher) level.

From time to time the snowball bushes, insidious sumac, sea-glass on the factory beach, felt whole. The largest rocks as big as tables held plaques commemorating battles from Revolutionary days.

That was the world my child and I began in, but it swiftly changed. I had come back to the north after a long journey to the Orinoco rainforest, and saw on the Hudson some of the birds I knew from that other river. I took their appearance as a sign that I should watch out for them, and in the library read the Environmental Impact report devoted to the development now underway on the pier. Piles were being driven right next to the marsh where they nested. One thing led to another, and with others in the town we realized the site had been a dumping ground for the factory's toxic wastes. The wastewater pools used in winter as an over-the-fence ice rink probably contained dioxin, a byproduct of the process for making paper and cardboard. The sludge from these pools had been spread on the ball field in an era innocent of consequence.

We were implicated, we had to follow the story we were in, it took all of our energies and resources. The truth laid open, fraying havoc, the upheaval of mythology, the science.

To comply with the court, the developer spent eight million dollars to clean up the site. Yet he drained the pools in the middle of the night and proposed suing for defamation of title.

"He will lose, but he'll make your life miserable for ten years," our lawyer said.

9

The neighborhood resembles a military zone: roofs of the classrooms are falling in. Tiles slide off the roofs and knock the students unconscious.

While we buy our groceries we park the children in the indoor playground where they cavort on the gymboree.

She expresses concern at the degree to which children are now separated from the daily cares of adults and live in a zone of entertainment.

To bring the proportion of consumption into check, the whole stanza must shift. "Cards with these symbols accepted here." The truth laid open, fraying havoc, the upheaval of mythology, the science.

The end rhyme faces a wall, and on the other side is a forest. The woods are deep, and my little daughter and I lie in bed and I tell her a story. The hero is a boy who discovers many jewels in a hole in the woods. He pulls them out, and they are green and blue and orange and red.

"Are there many of them?" she asks. "How many are there?"

10

The truth is, you can't do everything at once. This baby wants milk, and I need to see her follow my finger into space. When we go to the Statue of Liberty, she expresses surprise that it is so big, for from where we lived it appeared "no bigger than my thumb."

It seems a heavy price to pay for eating a pomegranate, but we are no longer innocent of consequences, nor do we write down everything that comes into our heads. It is time for bed, or time for the sun to rise, or time to rise and shine.

The children leave the house, which she has likened to a story. You will come in now and before you leave will occupy a sentence, word, or syllable, as the silver chain hesitates at her throat where the bone rises beneath the skin.

The children of the writers generally object to their parents' occupation, although some become writers themselves.

She suggests we regard it as seasonal, and it will only be a while before she comes back from Hades. Everything is just under the surface.

11

Stein:

> The only thing that is different from one time to another is what is seen and what is seen depends upon how everybody is doing everything. This makes the thing we are looking at very different and this makes what those who describe it make of it, it makes a composition, it confuses, it shows, it is, it looks, it likes as it is, and this makes what is seen as it is seen. Nothing changes from generation to generation except the thing seen and that makes a composition.[10]

There were all those words for snow in the Arctic, and a lot of words for water by the Orinoco, and here there are equities and annuities and hedge funds and racketeers.

Stein said that one cares for one's works in the world, to help them find their way, since they are our children.

She wheeled her wheelbarrow through sheets broad and narrow, crying—

She says the key is to view it as episodic. In this part of your life you do one thing and then it becomes necessary to do something else.

NOTES

1. Lorine Niedecker, *Blue Chicory*. New Rochelle, New York: The Elizabeth Press, 1976, unpaginated.

2. Robert Duncan, *Roots and Branches.* London: Jonathan Cape, 1964, p. 88.

3. Lorine Niedecker, "What horror" in *The Granite Pail: The Selected Poems of Lorine Niedecker*. San Francisco: North Point Press, 1985, p. 18.

4. Ibid.

5. Lorine Niedecker, "Paul" in *Collected Works*. Berkeley, California: University of California Press, 2002, p. 156.

6. Niedecker, "What horror" in *The Granite Pail*, p. 18.

7. Emily Dickinson, *Collected Poems of Emily Dickinson*. New York: Avenel Books, 1982, p. 4.

8. Ibid.

9. Gertrude Stein, "Poetry and Grammar" in *Gertrude Stein: Writings 1932–1946*, ed. Catharine Stimpson and Harriet Chessman. New York: The Library of America, 1998, p. 329.

10. Gertrude Stein, "Composition as Explanation" in *Gertrude Stein: Writings 1903–1932*, ed. Catharine Stimpson and Harriet Chessman. New York: The Library of America, 1998, p. 520.

◊

BARBARA EINZIG lived in New York City by the Hudson River, a site that along with her Orinoco adventures inspired her collaboration with visual artist Clair Joy, *The City and the River* (The Museum of...the River Thames, London, June 24–September 2, 2001). She is the author of numerous books, including *Distance without Distance* (Kelsey St. Press, 1994) and *Life Moves Outside* (Burning Deck, 1987). She is completing a satirical environmental musical, "Below the Level of Our Concern," which will be performed in New York in 2003. Her daughter, Chloe, was born in 1985.

Split, Spark, and Space:
A Poetics of Shared Custody

BRENDA HILLMAN

I. (a poem)

An example often used to show ?? is *x* falling feet first into a singularity with a
watch on. Fate is what happens backwards. With regard to Persephone,
the seasons don't change till something agrees to her sacrifice.

When a child is dropped off in front of the other parent's house she creates a
history of space and yellow, hurrying in the unopposed direction as we
learn to read by hurrying meaning.

She got out of the car. Smell-threads of Johnson's baby shampoo. Redolence exists
by itself as opportunity. The end of the Cold War had come. In Russia,
more oranges, lizard baskets of capitalism. I tried to talk to her father; he
tried to talk to me.

As *x* falls by prearrangement with the experimenters, yellow is unopposed. The
child, leaving the car, drops an alphabet on the path. y. e. l. Shaving of
yellow, central plaid, black from a fraction if she has been brave about
including the math.

She hated her little bag. A Thursday humming followed. My writing was falling
apart. She was learning to read.

A fate begins to be assembled when the linear is shared. All it does doesn't work.
Should dirt not praise her efforts? Little pointed

arrows swerve around the (from the mother's perspective) vanishing skirt. Flashes
of letters here. Here. Home is the fear of size. A word can fall apart. y. e.
We sat in the car. Tiny bats between Berkeley double-you'd the air.

The lip of a singularity is an event too far beyond, good corduroy with its highs
and lows as the star dissolves in the just-having-spun and you're not
supposed to ask how *x* feels as he falls in. Persephone practices her yes,
her no, her this that and the other; the child approaching the house of the
father in motion of minutes, free for twenty yards of both of them makes
a roof with her good-bye: // bye \\ mom. They'll have to invent new
seasons to explain it.

The daughter grows a horizon. Somehow a line by which a life could be pursued.

When she started to read, I no longer heard language, it heard me. I had the stupid idea that she should dress up to leave.

x should have checked with Persephone about the kicking and screaming. I should have checked with the mother but I was the mother. Backward should try to fix loss so it is not devastation but chronicle.

Panic plaid, almost at his door, *I cannot see what flowers are.* Daffodils. Dirt's birthday candles; California is medium old. *x* won't be very young when he gets to the center, nor will the child, testifying to cloth, dropped, sent back fractal, active as the buoys on the bay, nor is the child very young.

If you are time you think in terms of next. If you are Persephone you think in terms of dirt. If you're the metaphor you'll let the thing stand for it. On Monday the flash of a dove, your hoping frame. The child *can* look back, the myths don't apply here, if you think one joy was sacrificed it's because you said it. What choice did it have when the thing undid but to call her in broken colors.[1]

II. (an account)

In the mid-Eighties, my poetry and poetics began to evolve unexpectedly. By "poetics," I mean the theoretical aspects of poetic procedure inherent in, linked to, the poems them-selves. The sense of the single "voice" in poetry grew to include polyphonies, oddly col-lective dictations, and the process of writing itself. This happened in part because of a rediscovered interest in esoteric western traditions, and in part because I came to know a community of women who were writing in exploratory forms; also, I had gone through a divorce and was mothering a child under those conditions. For the purposes of this piece, I want to consider the metaphor of shared custody—of children, of traditions, of poetic space—knowing this account is only a fraction of a story.

My daughter's father and I had a weekly shared custody arrangement. He lived nearby in a house at the end of a long walkway. Our daughter walked up a set of stairs in the twi-light to get to his door. Dropping a child off at the other parent's house is as strange a fact of life as it is common in California households. I had come to accept it as normal because my stepsons had also traveled between two residences. But it was with my daughter's odyssey that the new geography seemed metaphoric.

Realizing that a mysterious quadrant of my daughter's week would take place apart from me, I began to perceive phenomena differently. During this time, we all suffered in ways specific to our own lives. I cannot represent my child's experience of this time, only my own. One coping mechanism was to study each perception as it formed at the site of her disappearance and the moment of her return. This led to a new epistemology. It seemed crucial to pay attention to the micromovements of the thought-language-space-shape continuum so that such a reality might become bearable. A new set of *betweennesses* happened in language as her body came and went through time and distance. Individual words fell apart. Colors became letters. Yellow was plural, was daughters of yellow. Red was too much. Words like "see" "you" "soon" grated themselves into the air. A poetic method, which had heretofore been based on waiting for insight, suddenly had to accommodate process, an indeterminate physics, a philosophy that combined spiritual searching with detached looking. In this procedure of baffled decenteredness, my daughter and I shared a method of *across*.

To love metaphor is to exist in a state of becoming, and also paradoxically, to render the heart lucky and indistinct. To live in metaphor is to be eternally hopeful in relation to a missing term. It is to acknowledge that the element is missing because of the world's need, and the mind's, because one has entered into a permanent contract with the unknown. The acceptance of incompleteness is energy.

My daughter's courage and occasional defiance gave me courage as a mother and as an artist. Thursday nights I watched her walk away through the Berkeley evening with the bag that she had mostly packed herself. Dusk trapped colors of her clothing for chips of seconds as she walked off as cheerfully as possible. I sat in the car an extra ten minutes in the parking lot, hoping precreated words would rise in me. I began to hate "events," began to appreciate acts of mind. Closure became unlikely. An interior-sounding language formed, more separately and in a more detached way, as she came and went in an unowned territory between her father's house and mine.

These perceptions didn't cause an evolution in my poetry; they accompanied it. In the previous decade, I had been writing in the confluence of realism, abstract meditations, and within surrealist imagery. The interest in realism accompanied my working life: I had a job in a bookstore near Telegraph Avenue that would accommodate my family's schedule. As customers entered, there were rings of spiked light around their bodies. It seemed right to layer the personal and the impersonal in poetry, to render details of working life in the quotidian for those who were finding their way through aftermaths of drugged paisley war protest years. Both realism and irrational methods were needed to express the many possibilities of language, and straight description of anything was impossible. The condition of things in a generation quite ambivalent about physical possessions was like the territory of hallucination. Even the furniture of the late Seventies was comic and terrifying—those plaid, square couches with the fuzzy texture. Such physical realities might provoke gnostic inquiry into the nature of matter. During this time, there were many literary energies in the Bay Area, and among other things, an excitement about experimental women's writing which drew my interest. Working in the store and raising children, I felt the swirl of poetic possibilities, as if paradoxical imaginings were needed to capture both the dream and the waking in daily life. I had always written at the seam or site of a tearing, a rending, which the experience of the divorce then enacted.

In the shared arrangement, there was an intense perilousness in the connection to my daughter; life seemed on loan very briefly. These times defined themselves in a type of synesthesia, as the fragments that fell from her going also made sounds and shapes, even flintlike vowels when she had reached her father's door. In my writing process, "extra" language began to appear in very light marks outside the margins at the edge of the white page, or it would drop down, to the bottom of the page, like alchemists' ash. Language came apart in phrase-packets.

In a way, the word and the sentence share custody of the phrase. The start of a poem is a constellation of ideas, of perceived experience, of figurative language and phrases of abstract concepts that jumpstart more language. Like the child, the phrase travels between the word and the sentence. The word is one kind of home, the sentence is another. Each lurches, reforms its expectations caught in a shadowy motion. In a time of great cultural or personal change, the work of linear narrative, driven by plot or dramatic event, can be supplemented by a percussive zigzag of patterns. Uncertainty is to be preferred. In those years, many of us found we could reinvent the lyric, however shattered it might be. Though my main poetic companionship was provided by a wonderful new man in my life, I sought models of mythic women who had observed breaks in creation and had leapt across.

◊

Three images of the maternal presided over these changes. Demeter, the originator of shared custody, is one who both lets go and plants things. Ritual practices attached to this figure seem to have been as much about retrieval as about loss, as much about enacting a series of steps in order as about forwarding information. Her daughter goes off fifty percent of the time, carrying her booty of good weather. My daughter didn't go to an underworld, but when she went to the other home, she was unavailable to me. In shared custody, an imagination of an *other* across the chasm is forced on us.

Gnosticism, rife with images of anxious searching and of absurd retrievals, provided another image of the mediating mother. A particularly engaging form of cosmogonic mythmaking is found in the figure of Wisdom, or First Thought (she's sometimes called by the clumsy name of Trimorphic Protenoia), who springs full-blown from the primal deity's head like Athena. She creates the cosmos by having sex with her consort without permission and produces everything we see around us, while everything we don't see gets quickly out of control. This messy, sexy, boyish figure has descended from the fixed stars, from an unscheduled world of destruction, to manifest herself in the lower earthly realms so she can preside over a limitless order.

Alchemical texts provide the image of the alternative myth-mother cooking over her art. Sometimes considered the mother of alchemy, Maria Prophetessa is said to have invented the containers and the methods for the alchemical processes. This legendary Jewish alchemist of the second century is presumed to have invented the *bain marie*, the method of letting substances cook slowly in pans of liquid. Things boil away and get increasingly chaotic, so this artist makes recipes that are in keeping with, not against, principles of chaos. The requirements of alchemy are similar to those of any literary art and most aspects of mothering: to know the elements, to work at the transformation, to have patience.

These three figures share characteristics of cunning, even deviousness, that can save their creations. Often they interfere ineptly, or regard their new worlds with a mixture of detachment and irony but also with a wise inventiveness. They aren't experts at the job; they accomplish it by fumbling, they are mediators, working between heaven and the underworld, not to be worshipped but acknowledged for their power.

III. (a minifesto)

= A poem is the rescue of a vanishing body.

= Poems embodying original technique make units smaller than the sentence serve both the sentence and the line. They help rethink the relationship between word, phrase, or sentence every time they make one of those things.

= Fresh writing manifests consciousness; its ancient innovative tools include juxtaposition, repetition, interruption, and fragmentation. It could be said that these qualities are qualities of a mother's day. Or they could be seen as columns holding up a building if the building were not falling apart.

= The leaping irony of internal reference came to dominate postmodernism as a phenomenon both of the material and the sign. When a child begins to notice herself playing, she becomes a different kind of player.

= Juxtaposition of words/ phrases/sentences, including but not limited to non sequitur give each unit more identity

Repetition which has to do with absolute loss and qualifying humor

Interruption, which comes in two flavors, regular, like some phone calls, and mystical, like other phone calls

Fragmentation, which is to say, the partial is complete and never is

A mixture of the high and low tones in the day, as the best art mixes high things and low

= Original writing holds a new hope for the phrase or the sentence; it maintains the nature of a brain wave, and like a busy day, there is less and less drive toward coherence as time passes through it. It has a relation to nature that is strange.

IV. ((a physics))

Childhood is the building of a survival kit, a consciousness near a struggling populace. I was raised in a haunted sunny world. My own mother, an intense person with a fervent and philosophically inward nature, married something of an opposite: a tall, practical caretaker with a passionate American imagination. They produced three children; I'm between an older brother, an intense person with a fervent and philosophically inward nature, and a younger brother, a tall, practical caretaker with a passionate American imagination.

In the desert near our home, the horned toad had a collar of spikes. Plants talked back. Dust waved. Ordinary things were inhabited by a liquid fire that was simultaneously viscous and particulate, not an easy thing to manage, for a substance. This *ichor* was associated with extreme longing, melancholy joy, an erotic feeling in my gawky body; distributable magic had traveled between the known world and the beyond, with which I craved contact. This talking fluid fire, a transitive substance, was the secret between the child and nothing. It had been reinvented often by orthodoxies and heterodoxies from Heraclitus to the present: first and second century Gnostics, neo-Platonists, medieval alchemists, and Protestants of all inner light varieties. Nevertheless, as a brand of spiritual currency for the non-country in the middle of a small self, it did not fail.

The spiritual features of poetry are held in shared custody in this world and the unknown one, previous, ceded, invisible. Some of the ideas in western Gnostic and mystery traditions correspond to features of late twentieth century existentialism: the verb as spirit, the centerless search for a meaning as a byproduct of creation in a land where good and mischief are magical. In such myths, light, like the flexible childhood fire, speaks in a fractured way. This corresponded to the observation of my daughter's colors falling in her fierce journey at dusk; there is a shimmery principle that involves itself with meaning but is not trapped by it. It is the same as "dark" in some form.

The shepherd who found the scrolls in the caves at Nag Hammadi gave them to his mother while he fetched the sheep.[2] By mistake, she used some of the papyri to start the fire for dinner, which may account for the physical gaps in many of the passages. Perhaps the odd form of a text is caused by someone making food. A family eats the words.

V. (a method)

The main method is metaphor. The equipment for metaphor is space. Space is a metaphor.

Metaphor-making, the form of shared custody that starts earliest, doesn't involve loss. The child at play and the artist-mother can participate in this rescue operation. Has the artist-mother originally learned to play in solitude, under her mother's gaze? Probably not, or why would our play seem so daunting? Winnicott writes of the "potential space" in which the sense of the other is formed, juxtaposing this with the purely inner and outer worlds.[3] When we watch someone learn to play, we can understand the creation of metaphor. The space allowed by the mother gives room for the foreign cry. If the mother is absent, a cry is forced; if she is too present, what's forced is silence.

A child at play has made a great leap from the mother as surely as if she intended it. As soon as she has language, she plays within it. For the literary artist, as for the child at play, language and experience become intertwined almost immediately. The child tells the mother that the monster potato is breathing fire on the inside. The name for it is its design. After my child began to talk, we were both usefully disrupted.

The storytelling traditions in contemporary poetry, based on the metonymic functions of language, come from a Wordsworthian romanticism; a piece of story stands for the whole, a piece of family drama represents the condition of the species. Metaphoric traditions, especially symbolist ones that invoke mood, and surrealist ones that call the untamed association from the depths, come more from Keatsian romanticism. Metaphor goes back and forth in realms of lack. Jakobson discusses the metaphoric and metonymic linguistic functions in the studies he makes of their breakdown in aphasia, that failure of the metaphoric function is a failure of substitution, and failure of the metonymic is a failure of contiguity, failure to be "beside."[4] In making poems or a life with a child, we need both functions. When letting a child go, metaphor is useful because the emptiness has become animate.

The metaphor called "I," unhinged from its autobiographical story or used as a swinging door between the visible and the invisible, doesn't have to be an ego-bound instrument. Vanished conditions come in; an interrupting questioner arrives from the margins to prod. The alchemists knew that the fallen thing can be retrieved: so the marginal voices exist at the side, apart from the lyric, with a lot of white in between. Seemingly trivial detail offers itself easily to metaphoric space. The *between* is left blank and fertile.

Though rejoicing in community, we speak to the agonizing questions as individual artists: how it is possible for language to represent and not to represent, to be the deepest solitude and the most social thing we have. How the first love of meaning can stay when the helpless surface reflects not merely but absolutely a stream of phenomena that posits no center, no sureness that will be held by one thing. Some urge toward life in the world keeps seeping under the door, as if an appliance had overflowed. If deep tensions split my poetic practice, more poems will forge a new one. Like a child traveling back and forth, each poem is based on a reverberation between magic and suffering.

When my daughter was three and four, she made huge figures from buttons on the yellow rug. Her version of the Easter Island statues, these imposing female beings had bell-shaped skirts, wildly waving arms, no legs. Outlined in buttons from many decades, their interior fields were pure space. No one was home in the middle. It was a field in which only imagination would occur. In the void between two terms of a metaphor as in the space between the parent and the child at play, relationship is as a vibration of realities, like a body's unbearable vanishing and hopeful reappearing.

NOTES

1. Brenda Hillman, *Cascadia*. Middletown, Connecticut: Wesleyan University Press, 2001, pp. 19–20.

2. James Robinson, *The Nag Hammadi Library*. New York: HarperCollins, 1990, p. 24.

3. D.W. Winnicott, *Playing and Reality*. New York: Routledge, 1989, p. 41.

4. Roman Jakobson, *Child Language, Aphasia, and Phonological Universals*. The Hague, Paris: Mouton, 1968, pp. 13–45.

◊

BRENDA HILLMAN's six collections of poetry, *White Dress* (1985), *Fortress* (1989), *Death Tractates* (1992), *Bright Existence* (1993), *Loose Sugar* (1997), and *Cascadia* (2001), are all published by Wesleyan University Press. She has also written three chapbooks, *Coffee, 3 A.M.* (Penumbra Press, 1982), *Autumn Sojourn* (Em Press, 1995), and *The Firecage* (a+bend press, 2000). She serves on the faculty of St. Mary's College in Moraga, California, where she teaches in the undergraduate and graduate programs. She lives in Kensington, California, and is married to poet Robert Hass. Her daughter, Louisa Michaels, was born in 1979. She has five stepchildren: Ethan and Jesse Michaels and Leif, Kristin, and Luke Hass.

Gaps, Overflow, and Linkage:
A Synesthesiac Look at Motherhood and Writing[1]

Elizabeth Robinson

My son, Wilson, will be two in May of 1997. In the past several weeks, he has been dis-covering, with particular vigor, the wonders of language. One of his favorite words of late is "knock." "Knock, knock," he says, and this utterance is always followed by a rap-ping gesture. At first, it was an important part of the process that he find a proper door to knock on and that a body stand behind it, ready to emerge and greet him. That response is becoming quickly less relevant. Now he will rap on any stable, resonant object: table, door, wall, floor, and say, "Knock, knock." Occasionally, he will comment, "Door!" after doing this, whether or not he is connecting with a literal door. I imagine that he is, in a broad sense, sounding out a sense of solidity and presence in his universe. And of doors, entryways.

Now I will backtrack because sequence is nothing and everything with regard to writing and children.

When I was pregnant with Wilson, my primary fantasy lay in reading to him as my father had read to me. Long before I felt audacious enough to buy clothing for this supposed baby, I felt comfortable beginning to amass a library for him. The books I sought relegated color and illustration to second place. The words, the rhythms, so clearly, were more important.

I was recalling how my father had read to me. Starting from early grade school through to the beginning of my adolescence, he read to me a little bit almost every night. Not that the things he chose to read necessarily had the mellifluous aural quality that I wanted in books for Wilson: he read all of the Sherlock Holmes mysteries, translations of Gogol short stories, the Victorian novels of Wilkie Collins. Perhaps it was my father's fluency as a reader that brought such palpability and tactility to the texts he read aloud. In any case, I remember distinctly *hearing* words and speech that became perceptible in other modes: *taste, touch*. Certain books or characters in stories took on flavors. One character, I recall, caused me to taste a rich vanilla each time my father spoke in his voice. Or single words could inhabit my mouth whether or not I actually uttered them. Like a secret, unmelting morsel, or marble, I could roll around on my tongue, hold in my cheek.

I grew up to learn that the sensory crossover I had experienced (and still do) has a name: synesthesia. Synesthesiac terms are, in fact, common in our language (such as a "dark mood," a "warm smile"). I have heard that the composer Scriabin was also one who experienced synesthesia; he saw colors vividly in the sounds of his music and imagined that his listeners would see those same hues. But I do not hear people discuss so commonly that immediate sensation I've encountered in language, words-as-concrete-objects, words as (almost) food. The pure and true palpability of speech as it infuses an idea has taken on a veritable theological dimension for me.

The word made flesh. The inexplicability and accuracy of that one phrase are what keep me a writer, a Christian, and a mother. I want incarnation, I want the word, and I want them simultaneously. And I want that for Wilson too, who appears to experience it effortlessly anyway. Word-as-flesh means that the word is not just concrete and tangible, it also has plasticity and vitality. It *is* and it is *more* than itself in the same instant. I am, I have to admit, embroiled here in the question (the veracity) of immanence and transcendence.

Certainly my Christian commitment informs my understanding, but I do not want to dwell on my theology. I want to mark that as a presence, yet my project in this piece is to address immanence and transcendence as pertinent to motherhood and writing. I hope it's already clear from my discussion above that I perceive parenthood and writing and words and synesthesia as intimately related, as, yes, simultaneous. They have everything to do with each other. To clarify: I want to consider immanence and transcendence, but not as discrete concepts. Rather, I want to explore overlap and saturation.

Unfortunately, though my aim is simultaneity and wholism, I don't know how to get there except by building from parts. Roles and processes—mother, poet, body, mind, word, flesh—may be discretely labeled, but ultimately merge. So I begin in and with my body, my mothering body. And I want, specifically, to cite Iris Marion Young's essay, "Pregnant Embodiment"[2] because it speaks so directly to my own experience of pregnancy and postnatal maternity.

Young starts off in agreement with Merleau-Ponty and other existential phenomenologists who hold that "consciousness and subjectivity [reside] in the body itself," a perspective which Young finds useful because "to situate subjectivity in the lived body jeopardizes dualistic metaphysics altogether."[3] Here, one of Young's implicit aims is to contest the entrenched sexist dualism that would have males possessed of a transcendent rationalism and females limited by biological immanence. Quoting Strauss, Young affirms that

> everything points to the fact that separateness and union originate in the same ground.[4]

However, Young goes on to find a flaw even in anti-dualist philosophy insofar as it retains dualist language in describing the body itself as experienced in two modes: subject and object. Such a position is untenable because it assumes the subject as a static unity.[5] Young prefers the work of such thinkers as Derrida, Lacan, and Kristeva who, instead, describe the unity of the self as "a project sometimes successfully enacted by a moving and often contradictory subjectivity."[6]

The very acute insight of Young's essay is that she demonstrates pregnancy as just such a project. Pregnancy is a process in which body subjectivity is decentered, the self in the mode of not being itself. Although Young's discussion is convincing, my argument is that such decentering is only more prominent in pregnancy. It continues on after pregnancy into the project of mothering. This decentering is also a crucial part of other projects, such as writing.

Or, perhaps, as another author, Roslyn Diprose, writes (using essentially the same hermeneutical framework in "The body biomedical ethics forgets"[7]) the body understood as simultaneously subject and object results in a fruitful ambiguity. For instance, the mother who gives of herself in quite a concrete and bodily way so as to gestate, birth, or nurture her child will often experience a disruption in the texture of subjectivity that occurs when the body's integrity is altered.[8] Is the mother subject or object? Can the mother be said to be alienated from either her subjectivity or objectivity when her efforts focus on so central and mutually influencing a project as her child's growth and well-being? That is, the child is a creative project both to the child him- or herself and to the parent. Thus, the phenomenological ambiguity present here extends beyond discrete individuals. Fruitfully so, because once that ambiguity is recognized and accepted, the supposedly external standards by which difference is labeled and denigrated are called into question. New sorts of relationships, links, overlaps emerge.

Consider, for example, that the child is even less likely than an adult to be put off by the inherent ambiguity of subject and object, engrossed as he or she is in actual process. This morning, I watched Wilson with a red marker. He concentratedly colored his toes and then made thicker connecting whorls on the bridge of his foot, which then continued, naturally enough to his sense, to the grain of the wood on the floor. Inside and outside, self and other, are permitted to remain distant concerns resulting in "expansion of the borders of self rather than a collapse in the structure of the self."[9] Young and Diprose agree that pregnancy (and I contend that parenthood functions this way as well)

> highlights the possibility of altering the structure of the self through rehabituation without the need to think of this in negative terms: in terms of a paralyzing division between self and world, self and other, self and body.[10]

In other words, an awareness of and participation in one's physicality does not prohibit engaged subjective activity.

It may seem that I'm wandering far afield from motherhood's nexus with art-making. Perhaps turning to Diprose's conclusion will help to clarify. She contends with Foucault that the prevailing tendency to view object and subject in dualistic terms will no longer suffice. It is preferable to spurn this conception of selfhood in favor of new forms of subjectivity. An option Diprose (with Foucault) upholds is to create the body as a work of art.[11] Diprose looks to Young's work to reinterpret pregnancy (and, once more, I expand this to include motherhood) as

> an aesthetics of existence [which] is a project for expanding our capacities, working on our bodies to extend the sphere of possibilities of action beyond those that merely feed into the efficiency of our social and economic structure.[12]

Our life projects are continuous, ambiguously defined, and mutually influencing. To sever the process of mothering from the process of writing would be artificial, just as to say that my embodied experience can be differentiated from my poetry would also be a false distinction. Hence, the reciprocal truth that form can only be an extension of content: let us not disregard or underestimate the living subjectivity of form. Nor the wonderfully plastic, excessive, form-altering, and expanding movement inherent in the body of the mother or the body of the poem. As Ann Lauterbach has said of Barbara Guest (who is herself the mother of two adult children):

> the space between the perceiving subject and its objects informs a malleable interactive matrix, unsteady and demanding, like the undercurrents of a lavish river... It is as if the poems were both figural boat and fluid gestural ground, substance and shadow, model and artifact.[13]

Two other statements that Lauterbach makes in reference to Guest resound even more powerfully: "Excess challenges form" and "Writing wrestles with is/is not, trying to reckon with the enticements that thicken into objects."[14]

This is overlap and saturation enacted. Here is a willingness to be influenced by the hard circumstances (be they biological or social or…) that limit us, and yet to refuse them, to soak in them, to salvage limitation for something more interesting and useful. Perhaps for the synesthesiac, where the poignancy of a sound so overwhelms its given modality, the surfeit becomes flavor, dimension, hue. Thickening. Exquisite tension between the is/is not.

For an alternative articulation of synesthesiac poetics, I want to consider an interview of theologian Mary Pellauer (in which, significantly, she insists that all the taped interruptions of her children be included as a proper part of the final publication of the conversation). Here, Pellauer states that she believes "in the creative pulse that makes beautiful warm quilts from scraps of worn-out clothing, poems and song from the words we use everyday."[15] Even the rupture of interruption, the fraying, the mundane repetitions come to make up a salvage that bears freshness, unforeseeable meaning and sustenance. Transcendence bathing in immanence, constraint becomes a new intelligence. I speculate that Jack Spicer was working in the same direction when he claims in "After Lorca":

> But things decay, reason argues. Real things become garbage. The piece of lemon you shellac to the canvas begins to develop a mold, the newspaper tells of incredibly ancient events in forgotten slang, the boy becomes a grandfather. Yes, but the garbage of the real world still reaches out into current world, making *its* object, in turn, visible—lemon calls to lemon, newspaper to newspaper, boy to boy. As things decay they bring their equivalents into being.[16]

Maybe the processes of mothering and writing are always engrossed with juggling paucity and excess, rupture and continuity. Pellauer and Spicer alike demonstrate that relinquishing is necessary in order to make real. In some sense, they clarify that the charge of the parent and poet is to live on the unraveled edges of death and stitch them together as regeneration.

That is to say that the sense that comes unbound from its modality does not altogether forsake sense. Unity broken can be unity found. This is what the mother learns, and it is a frequently painful and occasionally revelatory experience that she cannot avoid conveying to her child.

The coarse seams of the collage, the Poundian dictum that "Points define a periphery," have become invaluable references for me since Wilson has come into my life. The misapprehension that results from fatigue, the constant interruption: insofar as these states of being lead to unlikely but fertile new strategies and ideas, then I willingly accept the gaps for what the diffuse outline may proffer. This has something in common with my experience of the auditory-as-olfactory: implausible, impracticable connections do occur and are generative. Where old forms or processes delimit, I am free to dispense with them. And there's no need to fill in the vacuum where an unquestioned principle had previously resided.

Wilson himself knows this well. As he rambles through the portals of speech, he casually gives factitious accounts of his daily experiences. One day recently, I asked him what had happened while he was at day care. Pausing quite evidently to have a bowel movement, he grunted, "Sam pooped." I doubt that Wilson had been attentive to Sam's bodily functions that day, but his immediate experience equated with the larger experiences of the day. Reportorial accuracy was irrelevant. Possibility makes for truth, and so what if the connections are grunted out of our embodiment? Who cares if the rhyme that finally gets him to drop off to sleep brings together words that have no logical continuity and are, finally, jumbled semi-euphonious syllables?

In conclusion, I turn to paragraphs from Fanny Howe's *The Lives of a Spirit*:

> No one could doubt that this was a model something. Every part of her seemed extra, more than intention could handle, and raised the question: Is the body made to fit the needs of the soul, or vice versa: Since her heart was a seething fountain of blood, people longed to lean their ears to her chest to hear those sinews at work. Her damp skin, soft as a rose petal, was sweet to the cheek. And when she smiled, the world was all confection and air.
>
> They surmised that she had floated from the stars in the navy blue sky. Like rain at sea, and no one to see, the coherence of these events and conjectures was never going to be accounted for. Now nested in sea heather, the baby will, later, learn her tens and alphabets on a pillow in bed. And will sometimes wonder: Little word, who said me? Am I owned or free?[17]

Deftly and succinctly, Howe—who so vitally participates in life as poet and mother— raises the matter of body and soul, of our acute longing, to sense pulse and blood in movement. But there is more than sense and its partnered concomitant intention can handle. I want to join with Howe in the surmise that between subject and object there is a piecemeal coherence that cannot be accounted for. Let such questions as "Who said me? Am I owned or free?" move unfettered, unanswered, and expansive.

Notes

1. I think it is relevant that I wrote this piece as I was caring for a toddler and progressing through my second pregnancy. The very physically engrossing and demanding quality of my current lived experience has influenced what I have had to say here. At a different time of life, I might interpret motherhood and writing in a different way.

2. Iris Marion Young, "Pregnant Embodiment" in *Throwing Like a Girl*. Bloomington and Indianapolis: Indiana University Press, 1990, pp. 160–174.

3. Ibid., p. 161.

4. Ibid., p. 162.

5. Ibid.

6. Ibid.

7. Roslyn Diprose, "The body biomedical ethics forgets" in *Troubled Bodies*, ed. Paul A. Komesaroff. Durham and London: Duke University Press, 1995, pp. 202–221.

8. Ibid., p. 211.

9. Ibid., p. 212.

10. Ibid.

11. Ibid., p. 219.

12. Ibid.

13. Ann Lauterbach, "Unpicturing (Fair) Realism: Notes on Barbara Guest's Poetics of (Defensive) Rapture" in *American Letters & Commentary*, #7, 1995, p. 5.

14. Ibid., p. 4.

15. Mary Pellauer, "Conversation on Grace and Healing: Perspectives from the Movement to End Violence Against Women" in *Lift Every Voice*, ed. Susan Thistlethwaite and Mary Potter Engle. San Francisco: Harper & Row Publishers, 1990, p. 170.

16. Jack Spicer, *The Collected Works of Jack Spicer*. Los Angeles: Black Sparrow Press, 1975, p. 34.

17. Fanny Howe, *The Lives of a Spirit*. Los Angeles: Sun & Moon Press, 1987, p. 10.

◊

Elizabeth Robinson is the author of four collections of poetry, including *House Made of Silver* (Kelsey St. Press, 2000) and *Harrow* (Omnidawn Press, 2001). *Under the Silky Roof* is forthcoming from Burning Deck Press in 2004. She was a winner of the National Poetry Series in 2001 for *Pure Descent*, which will be published by Sun & Moon Press. She lives in Berkeley, California, with her husband, Ken Morris, and is the mother of two sons, Wilson, born in 1995, and Jonah, born in 1997.

The Pinocchian Ideal

FANNY HOWE

In pregnancy a woman is more aware than at any other time in her life of the zone of the unknown. Like a margin of error, it pulls on her imagination and gives her images of as-yet-unknown diseases, aliens, and angels.

As long as her child is inside of her, what he or she is *not* is just as valid as what he or she *is*.

The probabilities are as great as the givens and provide an area of freedom that genetics, karma, and determinism do not.

The mother, feeling like a stranger to herself, recognizes for a short time the existential weirdness of being human in the first place.

Any mother knows that something is made from nothing since she herself (in the Dickinsonian sense) is nothing.

When her body is split to let out a stranger—someone who did not exist before—a part of her nothingness remains entangled in the new flesh she has birthed.

The given infant seems to carry with it a missing potential, a double, the might-have-been, the not-even-imagined.

◊

According to one Gnostic creation myth, a female cloud or mass gave birth as if deaf and blind, unconscious and undirected, to a humanity whose confusion was equal to her own. During the birthing process she had several miscarriages that resulted in a universe fulminating with emotions like disobedience, rage, sorrow, jealousy.

These emotions formed the weathers that we now live and stretch in (thunder, heat, winter, rain), and their pneumatic chaos has cut us off from the actual source of our being, a light that is blackness carried to an extreme point—the Truth.

The Gnostics called it a "ray of darkness."

And because the human received its portion of that darkness inside the womb, each infant, to be a child of the Truth, had to spend time inside the body of a woman. Inside her womb, the flesh-seed encountered a spirit-shape that fused with it and helped it rise like wind under a sheet.

The creature moved against the mother's belly for the first time only when it had been given its dose of spirit.

The Gnostics, unlike the Greeks, did not think of humans as demi-gods but as demi-demons, and the women who produced them were no different.

Elements of negative theology breathe through this creation story: that is to say, who one is *not* is just as disturbing as who one *is*. Twins especially remind us of this weirdness, and like the twin who is said to die during the course of most pregnancies, the continuing feeling that someone is always missing is what gives the birth of a child its spiritual status.

It's a miracle that anyone is here at all, given the original pulsating mass of uncreated waste in the heavens.

After creation stories, it is folk tales that contemplate the gap between the material given and the unrealized probability—sometimes in the form of dreams, fairies, puppets.

◊

The Blue-Haired Fairy in the story of Pinocchio is an alien being who stands in for his mother. She is not his real mother any more than he is Gepetto's real boy.

Nevertheless they pretend to have a mother-son relationship. And in this context she lets her wooden boy be changed into a donkey, beaten, thrown in the ocean, hanged from a tree and chained by the neck, and when he is swallowed, finally, by the whale and is of no more value to the world than a matchstick, he calls *Father! Father!* in the bubbling Disney version of the story, and is saved.

In the original book, Gepetto is a disagreeable old man who takes pleasure from Pinocchio's disasters, so the puppet has to find his own way out of that glossy fish and back into the world of indifferent adults before he can become a real boy.

But he has to perform selfless tasks before his alien mother will say to him: "Brave Pinocchio! Be good in the future and you will be happy." And then Pinocchio becomes a real boy, leaving his puppet form abandoned and looped over a chair. And the fairy evaporates into outer space.

This story of fairy and puppet springs from our obsession with animation. Wood becoming flesh is one of the earliest forms it has taken. If antelopes can grow wooden branches out of their heads, why can't we produce trees and dolls that laugh?

While Pinocchio has to suffer before he can be human and while he also has to learn compassion toward his mean father, he also has to show the fairy whom he calls mother what an idiot he is. When he is a puppet running between people's legs and knocking things down, cutting school, and being rude to policemen, he always gets rebuked and humiliated. Since he is not yet fully alive, he can't die of embarrassment.

He calls on his alien mother for help, but she turns a cold shoulder. She teases and tests him and only pretends to love him. She is a classic not-good-enough mother, one who plays the game of the double-bind with her offspring. He has to be good in order to be loved by her, but she never gives him a clue on how to be good or what goodness means; instead he has to go through literal hell and high water himself to figure it out.

Only then does she say, "I forgive you for all your past misdeeds."

◊

In some ways this fairy mother is not as alien as she might seem. From her point of view Pinocchio is only wood and therefore he can be played with, and she can derive pleasure from watching him screw up without ever having to see him die.

He is her toy, her work.

She is in many ways like mothers who, when the children are small, can stay home and play, hide away from the patriarchs and judges, and let imagination roam free.

She can pretend, with them, that there is nothing really bad out there.

For a fairy mother, a naughty puppet is preferable to a real child who is mortal. It can be twisted, maltreated, uprooted, deformed, and used as a scapegoat.

It can also be sent out the door to be disruptive and adventuresome, to be a rebel.

The condition of motherhood demands that you learn to give birth to someone who won't last, to love someone who will leave, to teach a person who will suffer anyway, to put a life before your own... To have a job that you can never quit.

To be a fairy mother—to be both fairy and mother—you can try to have it all.

This is what a mother-artist does. Her bad puppet is her writing, her music, her painting, her dance, sculpture, film—it is her critique of society.

Unlike her vulnerable flesh-child, her puppet is the work that she can swing from a noose, bang on the ground, stamp on, throw in the water, and send into battle against the outside world.

Her wooden artifact (book, film, painting) shoots from the nothing-air of her imagination.

This puppet is herself heroically projected.

For a mother of children, the artwork is the expression of an unrealized and undefined life. It is a twin and a toy forever, always secondary in value to the animated mortal child.

Her problem comes later when she pushes the poor work out the door and into the marketplace and tries to make it sell.

This confusion between a thing that is made out of nothing and the market economy that prices all materials is perhaps more intense for a mother than for any others. Her awareness of the supernatural is intensified daily by the cries of the natural.

She loves her child and she adores her work.

Her crisis comes at the threshold to a world where there is a terrifying cacophony of machines awaiting her and her children.

◊

FANNY HOWE has published both fiction and poetry. Her most recent novel is *Indivisible* (Semiotexte/ MIT Press, 2000). Her *Selected Poems* were published by University of California Press in 2000 and won the California Book Award from the Commonwealth Club. She has also won two NEA grants, a California Council on the Arts Award, the Writer's Choice Award (for fiction), and a recent Pushcart Award. She has been a Fellow of the Bunting Institute and was Professor of Writing and American Literature at UCSD for many years. She lives in New England and is mother to Annlucien, Danzy, and Maceo Senna, born in 1969, 1970, and 1972.

Acknowledgments

Any anthology is a work of love and involves many forms of support from outside, literary and personal. A number of texts came up in our discussions and provided a rich conceptual ground, and for these we are grateful: Sharon Bryan, *Where We Stand: Women Poets on Literary Tradition*; Nancy Chodorow, *Mothering*; Hélène Cixous and Catherine Clement, *The Newly Born Woman*; Carol Gilligan, *In a Different Voice*; Sandra Gilbert and Susan Gubar; *The Madwoman in the Attic*; Julia Kristeva, *The Powers of Horror* and *Desire in Language*; Luce Irigaray, *An Ethics of Sexual Difference*; Adrienne Rich, *Of Woman Born*; Mary Margaret Sloan, *Moving Borders: Three Decades of Innovative Writing by Women*. This partial list does not include other poetic influences which, in our combined reading, are wide-ranging, drawing on many aesthetic traditions.

Also important to us as we assembled this collection were several conferences. The initiating event, "Artists and Motherhood: Ambivalence, Inspiration, and Creation," took place in June 1992 at Intersection for the Arts in San Francisco. Organized by Kate Moses, the colloquium provided a platform for bringing aspects of private experience in artists' and writers' work into public discourse. We are grateful to Amy Trachtenberg for her work as an artist and her insights into this subject. Finally, two other events gave us a chance to air and develop ideas in wider contexts that have become part of this book: "The Pagemothers Conference: Women Poets, Their Presses, Their Poetics," convened in March 1998 at the University of California, San Diego, by Rae Armantrout and Fanny Howe; and "From Lyric to Language: Innovative Writing by American Women Poets," organized by Claudia Rankine and Allison Cummings at Barnard College in April 1999.

We want to thank Linda Norton, who supported the idea of this project at its inception, and Suzanna Tamminen, Tom Radko, and Lee Gibson, who helped us see it through. We are grateful to Rachel Blau DuPlessis for several close readings of the text, helpful suggestions, which we gladly used, and for her Foreword. Throughout work on this project, friends, family, and other readers gave us valuable advice and encouragement in conversation. Our husbands, Ted Dienstfrey and Bob Hass, provided constant patient support. We also extend our thanks to Charles Altieri and to Aaron, Andrew, Elisheva, and Tobias Dienstfrey; to Barbara Guest, Lyn Hejinian, Helen and Jimmye Hillman, Marie Howe, Denise Lawson, Fran Lerner, Ethan, Jesse, and Louisa Michaels, Jean Nobbe, Nan Norene, Rena Rosenwasser, Sydelle Rubin, Carol Snow, and Cecilia Vicuña. And we gratefully acknowledge the amazing competence of Maureen Forys, Laurie Stewart, Lunaea Weatherstone, and Erin Milnes, who transformed the manuscript into a book, and the cover design skills of Quemadura.

Finally, we wish to note the pleasures of this collaboration. We usually met in Patricia's studio, which is annexed to a garden at the back of her house. The editorial work evoked discussions of poetry, family experience, and a friendship that has spanned over two decades. Seasonal changes in the garden marked the years as we worked on the editing and writing in an antiphonal manner. It was an unusual time for two poets whose sense of writing is as private as ours. The sessions included comings and goings of Reilly the cat, whom we would also like to thank as our snoring amanuensis. All of these presences had some part in the cycles that led to the completed book.

Index